I0529279

More Pockets, Please

Forgotten Dreams

KEN LITTLE

More Pockets, Please

Copyright © 2022 by Ken Little. All rights reserved.

Paperback: 978-1-959224-07-5
eBook: 978-1-959224-08-2
Library of Congress Control Number: 2022919075

No part of this publication may be reproduced, stored in a retrieval system or transmitted in any way by any means, electronic, mechanical, photocopy, recording or otherwise without the prior permission of the author except as provided by USA copyright law.

Ordering Information:

Prime Seven Media
518 Landmann St.
Tomah City, WI 54660
Published in the United States of America

Contents

Introduction

Life was beautiful—formative, inviting, sometimes bittersweet, but always as beautiful as any twenty-one-year-old's life could be. I played with players of exceptional ability, with steadfast strugglers, busy craftsmen, and honest toilers. I played from up the back, where only the mercurial tread, where will-o'-the-wisps watch and wait while the match runs its course in ebbs and flows.

Then, while the pieces dash both here and there, slaves to a moving ball, the mercurial prowl and then, choosing the moment to join the world of mortal men, they pounce and blaze a path across the sky and change the course of the match—a match that is much like life.

A prospect I was, a country rep but now, a hand of Popeye size, swollen by infection, kept me from the playing fields for two long weeks, all because the doctor said, "You could lose your hand if you play with that."

And so I abstained and let it heal, until that time when I could dance once more on fields of dreams, where free spirits ran with youthful vigor, and on untiring legs. After all, it was only an infected finger. And it could cause no further pain ... could it? No, everything would be okay—or so I thought.

But I was wrong; far worse, it was. A silent raider had worked its way deep within until it found a place to hide and grow and multiply—and then, like a will-o'-the wisp, it pounced, and dreams were shattered, a body broken, and youthful vigor gone—for then, for now, but not for evermore.

5

Prologue

Saturday, August 7, 1971

It was just before five that afternoon when Ron brought a doctor to see me. The doctor had just returned to his home next door and after a quick look, he rang for an ambulance to take me straight to Wagga Base Hospital. At that stage, I didn't care what they did with me, because all I wanted was relief from a bladder the size of a pumpkin. I arrived in the emergency room just as their orthopedic surgeon, Dr. Peter Dewey, came on duty—fortuitously for me, as it turned out. He was initially puzzled as to the cause of my paralysis, but while he pondered, I was catheterized and felt instant relief as 1,200 milliliters of urine gushed out of my distended bladder into a bottle. The relief I felt was indescribable, but "sheer bliss" comes close. After some questioning, he asked if I had had any infections lately. I showed him my still angry-looking finger, and his tone quickly changed. "That's it," he said excitedly. He ordered a lumbar puncture—the injection of a dye into my spinal canal—and a trip to the X-ray room.

I was strapped on a machine that tipped me upside down and traced the dye's descent "up" my spinal canal. Halfway, the dye's progress was blocked. I was taken back into the waiting room to hear the prognosis. "You have an epidural abscess," Dr. Dewey said. "It is pressing on your spinal cord and blocking the messages from your brain to your legs." He said it was a very rare condition—a one in a million chance—and only occurred two or three times a year in New South Wales. What he didn't tell me then was how perilous my condition was. I had been paralyzed for up to twenty hours. If the abscess had burst and its poison had entered my brain, there would have been tragic consequences. I needed an emergency laminectomy – where the surgeon removed a portion of the vertebra that covers the spinal canal - just to survive, so what were my chances of ever walking again? He rang my parents in Sydney to tell them he had to operate. He wasn't seeking their permission; he was just informing them what he was about to do. What a shock it must have been for them to get a phone call like that, out of the blue, one lazy Saturday night. To be sure of his diagnosis, he repeated the procedure. A short time later, I was heading off to the operating room. I felt no fear—at that stage I was past feeling anything. Besides, what they gave me made the dark world I was about to enter seem not such a dark place after all.

They were all ready for me when we came into the OR. The lights were bright and the participants masked, so I said, "Should I count back from ten?"

"If you like," someone said.

"Don't start without me," I replied at five. I continued counting down, reached three, and then there was darkness.

Sometime later, I heard furtive whispering as I was being moved from a gurney to a bed in a darkened room … and then nothing.

PART 1

SCHOOL DAYS

CHAPTER 1

Born to Run

The best are the best because they are the best in moments when it really matters. I liked running. When I was a young, I once escaped from our backyard and led my mother a merry chase up Alfred Street. Then, in kindergarten, I discovered that I could not only run, but I could run fast. It happened during a game of Farmer in the Dell. In the game, the chosen "farmer" pranced around a circle of kindie- mates before choosing a "wife," who followed him around the circle before being directed by the class's inane chanting to choose a "child." Then the growing family adopted a cat, then a mouse, and then the biggie: the "cheese." The cheese somehow grew legs and ran away from the farm, so everyone had to run after it. I coveted being the cheese and being chased by everyone, so when the "mouse" came around the circle toward me, I made my intentions known with an impassable navigational hazard—my outstretched hand. I was duly chosen, so I pranced around at the back of the line with the rest of the "family," primed with anticipation and ready for action. When everyone sang, "The cheese runs away," I took off and put so much distance between me and the others that when it was time to "all run after the cheese," I was so far away that the teacher had to call off the game to get me back on to the same piece of real estate as the rest of the class. I came back from the nether regions of the playground, triumphant and exhilarated

11

by the freedom and power that fast running gave, the fame it endowed, and—of no small importance—the adoration of Pam Hyett, the love of my kindie life. The fame of being the first cheese to have escaped a mob of kindies landed lightly on my shoulders as I decided that I could rest on my laurels. A few days later, I put down, in a canter, a rebellion from Jeffrey Dawson against my lofty and universally accepted status as the fastest runner in kindergarten.

Running fast gave me a sense of identity, (I was known as a fast runner) and confidence, because I could run away from any danger when I felt like it. It didn't matter that I wasn't the fastest runner in the school, for in the small world of kindergarten, I was the fastest runner in kindergarten, and that was all that mattered.

The guards at Government House witnessed my blinding speed one day during a family outing to the Botanic Gardens in Sydney. As we approached Government House, they appeared at the gate in uniform. My one regret, in a moment of panic, was that my mother couldn't run fast enough to get away from them. As I charged down the road, I half expected to see my family racing past me in a vain attempt to escape the men in uniform, who, I was convinced, were going to put us in jail when they caught us. I was most worried for my mother. I knew that she couldn't run very fast, and she was the main source of my feelings of security. What would I do, I wondered, if she was put in jail?

Since there were no dragons to run away from, let alone slay, speed was useless in everything but sport—rugby football, to be exact. I developed a reputation as a quick egg during my rugby days, so opposition players often gave me a bit extra when I foolishly entered their territory with the ball tucked under one arm and adventure on my mind. In one match, I raced up field but was hemmed in near the sideline by one determined breakaway. I was built like a greyhound, and he was built like a tank, so as I turned to toss the ball over his head to my support, I was completely defenseless and an easy target for the tank. Even as I passed the ball, I knew what he was thinking. He had come this far, so he might as well get something for his troubles. I ended up getting absolutely smashed into the ground with him on top, his shoulder buried deep into my chest and a seismic shockwave pulsating through my body. When I finally got up, I was in pain. However, pain came with the territory when you played a contact sport. You just had to accept it and get on with the game, or you shouldn't be playing football in the first place. Not all tackles hurt, but as I trotted gingerly back to my position, I was hurting and didn't know the damage that tackle had caused to my back— damage that would come back to bite me a few years later.

1968 Winning the Open 100m final for Narrabeen Boys'
High in the North Shore Zone Championships.

CHAPTER 2

Early Years

I was born at a small private hospital in North Sydney in 1949. After a shaky start in life, when I nearly choked to death and was saved only by the diligence of the hospital matron who nursed me through those first few hairy nights, I went home and spent the first six years of my life on Alfred Street, Narraweena, on Sydney's northern beaches. Back then, Narraweena was "affectionately" known as "Crim Hill," due to the nefarious activities of some of the locals, so my father always stretched the suburban boundaries and substituted next door's Dee Why for Narraweena in our address.

I was the third surviving child of Roy and Beryl Little. I didn't know any of my grandparents. My father worked at the government printing office as a compositor and then a proofreader because the Depression had put paid to his hopes of becoming a journalist. I didn't know much about his forebears except that they came from Ireland and Wales, with a touch of Italian—or maybe it was French— thrown in there somewhere.

The house belonged to my mother's younger sister and her husband but was soon bought by her younger brother, Arthur, when her sister moved down the hill to the real Dee Why.

My mother was the source of my early Christian teaching and my childlike belief of how big and good God is, by what she said and the gentle, loving life she led. She had lost her mother at age six to peritonitis and her heartbroken father to double pneumonia when she was twelve. With her three sisters, brother, and two step-sisters, she had been farmed out to relatives. She was brought up by (and later nursed) her grandmother and then her great-aunt Janet at Haberfield a western-city suburb. Her mother's side of the family came from Galieshiels in Scotland, while her father's side came from Kent.

My father was a good and honest man—a hard worker, who never shirked his responsibilities and felt that he owed his loyalty to those who employed him. He was humble and had no sense of entitlement. It was this attitude that got him into trouble with the Printers Union when he stood up for the employer during a union meeting. His religious input into my life was negligible, as he was a casualty of the Depression, and although he didn't lose his sense of honesty and fair play, he lost his faith in God or, more correctly, in the Catholic Church. He was a nonsmoker and a grudging occasional sipper. He had seen too much during his life with drinking relatives to ever go down that path.

Memories of Narraweena were quite vivid, like going to Manly and back on the bus with the kid next door—quite an adventure for a five- year-old—and feeling naked and ashamed of my bare feet when I saw Pam Hyett wearing shoes at Manly Wharf bus terminus as she waited with her family to catch a bus home. However, worse followed one day when I announced to my trusting kindie mates that Santa Claus wasn't true. Instead of learning something new from my candor, my statement received an angry response from my "mates," who were still secure in life and belief in their happy little illusion.

There were good memories, though, such as making a few pennies by selling old newspapers to the fish-and-chips shop, wearing my galoshes and jumping into every puddle I could find on the way home from school, longing to go to Sunday school with my big brother after seeing a picture of Jesus in our big picture book of the Bible, playing cricket in the backyard with the kids in our street, and being in love with Pam Hyett. She briefly had a rival, though: the girl Sandra, who waved to me during games. However, when I noticed that she had Band-Aids on her heels, I immediately dismissed her from my affections. It was

Pam or nobody. In the end, we moved to another suburb, and it was nobody.

We moved over to Collaroy Plateau, a bush-covered hill about three miles to the north, in 1956. My father had a block of land on the south side of the hill that was left to him by his mother. On it, he had a three-bedroom "fibro house," built with cold floor boards but occupied by people with warm hearts. Outside was a red-dirt road with mostly fibro houses dotting the street, a street that was like a small United Nations—up the road was a Dutch family, across the road were the Hesses from Germany and another family from England, while down the road were Poles, and further down were the Italians, who had a market garden in their front yard. While the different nations' parents squabbled with each other, we, their children, all played happily together.

There were also a number of undeveloped blocks on our street, some covered in virgin bush and one other partly cleared block on which the kids in the street played cricket. One of the kids' fathers played cricket for the Plateau senior team in the district competition. When he remarked that I had a good bowling action, I took it to heart, and a bowler I was determined to be. I was cricket mad and was thrilled when my father bought me a new cricket ball and bat. Unfortunately, my new six-stitcher was lost in the bush on the very first day I used it. It cost my father twenty-six shillings—a not- insignificant sum back then. A new cork ball was only five shillings, but my father was willing to fork out the extra money to buy me the best.

My other love was stamp collecting, and with my brother and sister, Dubbo—a New South Wales country town—became the center of our universe, courtesy of Seven Seas Stamps.

When it rained, our road was a slippery slide down to the bottom of the hill, but on the side of the road, we used to scrape out mud and use it to build dams and create channels for the water to run down the slope. Near the bottom of our road was a stream that led further down into bush and over a waterfall. We collected tadpoles from the stagnant pools, tadpoles that lived a short, meaningless existence in a jar until they either died or grew legs, climbed out, and hopped away, only to die in the sun or be eaten by some backyard predator.

17

A few years later, the street was curbed, guttered, and tarred, so our days of building dams and crawling through underground drains and coming out farther down the road were thankfully over.

I grew up a shy, peaceful boy, lacking in self confidence—feelings I battled against throughout my young life and even into my later life. Sometimes my confidence seesawed between lack of confidence and over-confidence, such as the time when Eric Jollife, a famous Australian cartoonist, demonstrated his artistic ability in front of the whole school. He chose me and drew my profile on the blackboard. I was itching to have a go and when invited to, I drew my usual cowboy firing a gun, such was my confidence in my ability as the best drawer in my class. But other times my confidence came crashing down to earth in a tide of pessimism and defeat that left me feeling worthless and miserable. In my simplistic and naïve way, I trusted people too much. I thought that people always told the truth, so when my abilities were trashed by someone, I believed that person. I remember when I ran for my school in an athletics carnival at Brookvale Oval. As we milled around, waiting for our race, a kid asked what school I came from. I said, almost apologetically, "Collaroy Plateau," which he sneered at. He said Manly West was the best, and I believed him. So when my race came up, I jogged along and came in fourth, because I believed that was all I should have expected. I felt I had no right being on the same field as the "best," which was a reflection of my lack of confidence in my own ability and my often shaky self-esteem.

I grew up loving books, reading all types, whether they were adventure stories, Bible stories, or science books or books about the natural world. I liked stories about knights and adventurers, heroic figures who displayed the highest levels of nobility and always conducted themselves properly, in the days when there was only black and white and no shades of gray.

When I was eight, my father resigned from his position at the government printing office to pursue a long-held ambition of starting a newspaper. He sank all his superannuation, (pension money) into a weekly newspaper called the *City Times*. He was the editor and wrote about life in Sydney in the 1950s. He was not, however, a good businessman and found the paper was delivered to businesses on the weekend, when the Sydney streets were deserted, so he began to lose his advertisers. He also suffered from trusting a well- known journalist, made famous by his adventures in Communist China, and a credit squeeze in the late fifties. Eventually, he lost the paper and almost his house. We struggled on with little money, while my father worked sometimes three jobs to repay all his debts and to keep up with mortgage payments. He even entertained thoughts of uprooting the family and heading off to outback Nyngan to take on the editorship of the local newspaper, but that came to naught when my mother refused to go. Through all this trouble, though, she would say, "Things will get better," but nothing seemed to change, so in my mind, they never did get better. Still, her optimism and confidence kept our home life on an even keel, and although we had little money, there was always enough.

Despite my father's difficulties, for me, those were contented years. Life was simple and the days full. I played with friends from down the road, hiked in the bush, cooked potatoes wrapped in wet clay in the hot coals of a campfire, and started playing rugby as a nine-year-old with the Plateau's under-twelves "B" team. The kid across the road was the captain and had taught me interesting words, such as "zig" and his favorite, "baby's goo," so I was more than willing to put my body on the line for him and the less-than-mighty B's.

And so we turned up each week and learned to lose graciously, trampled under the mighty feet of eleven-year-old giants from Seaforth Pirates, Balgowlah Heights, and St. Matthew's. St. Matthew's had tall, bony kids who were hard to tackle and treated us with such disdain, I didn't feel they acted very saintly. As a fast runner, I would often chase the ball carriers up to our try line without feeling any great compulsion to actually try to tackle them. My self- confidence was not particularly high in the face of the Goliaths we faced—I was David without a sling, but each week, I turned up with my mates to take part in our weekly beatings. A few years later, my mate Paul and I would muse that the air up on our 400-foot-high Plateau was probably rarefied and stunted our growth. One time I did tackle a kid from the Saints, when he ran into my head with his stomach. He lay flat on his back, gasping,

19

wheezing, and crying, while the coach used the tried-and-true method of pumping his legs up and down. I thought I was a murderer, while my team thought I was great. "He'll be scared of you after that," someone said encouragingly, which made me feel better.

Not content with weekly beatings in rugby, I joined the Collaroy Plateau cricket club to learn the rudiments of the game. Then, later that year, I played with the under-twelve B side and continued the weekly beatings from Manly West and the Balgowlah giants of my world.

The other place where I could get together with other kids was the local Baptist church, where I continued my relationship with God in the Sunday school. I attended religiously and found no problem in accepting the teachings about Jesus that gentle, humble Christians used to impart into our lives. With sport, church, and a successful period at school, I had the best upbringing a boy could have. They were innocent days, growing up on the northern beaches in the fifties. Doors were left unlocked, money was left out for the milkman and the baker, and "give him a fair go" was the cry in the school playground when a bully picked on a little kid.

My belief in God deepened when, at nine, I went to the Billy Graham crusade at the Sydney Cricket Ground one rainy night with a large number from our church. Many were convicted by Billy Graham's words, including Ron Baker, our rough, hard-drinking bus driver who was converted that night and later became a well-known Australian evangelist. Although it was raining, I wanted to go out to the front with the others when Billy Graham made his altar call, but my mother wouldn't let me, as I used to catch colds easily, and it was wet. So on that night, I stayed in my seat, but my heart went out in the rain and joined the thousands in the front, committing their lives to Jesus. It was my choice to believe, but I know I was touched by the spirit, and from that time on, the truths of God were fixed in my heart. My steps to belief were not entirely a response to my mother, although her words and life had a significant impact on me. Nor was it just blind faith. It was because when I observed my small world, all I could see were good things. I was content, I was loved, I had friends, I was always fed, and I was free to play sports that filled me with such joy that surely the God of my world just had to be a good fellow.

It was also a significant time emotionally, when I fell in love with Miss Taylor, a speech therapist of some sort. Apparently, I had developed a stutter in fourth class, so I was shunted off to Medusa Street School at the top of the Spit to be investigated by her. I felt ashamed at having this perceived "weakness" and joked with my mother that I would have to learn how to parrot "How now brown cow" to mask my feelings of humiliation. However, Miss Taylor was not the stern old stick I had expected. We didn't go through vowels and rhymes and exercises; instead, we talked, and she asked me questions and got me to do things, like kick a cupboard door. She was more of a child psychologist than a technician, as my brief affliction seemed to have its roots there; she was blonde, tanned, smiled and laughed a lot, and was, according to my young eyes, beautiful. In the end I never needed to see her again, as my stutter seemed to cure itself. I did find out that she was as taken with me as I was with her, and she confided to my mother that she had never met anyone with such high moral values. I had no idea what that meant or how she came to that conclusion and can only muse that our conversation revealed a lot more about "me" than any nine-year-old could ever understand.

One of the highlights of this time in my life was going to the 2GB Macquarie Radio Auditorium on Macquarie Street, Sydney, and appearing on *The Pied Piper Show*—a radio show based around opinions of children, with Keith Smith the interviewer. That night was our night, as it featured kids from Collaroy Plateau school. At the end, there was a segment called "Riddle Round-Up," where we all asked him our favorite riddle and, for our troubles, received a one- pound book voucher. The book I bought with it was called *Venture into the Interior*, and it continued my interest in the natural world as well as good books, all thanks to my favorite riddle: "Why is a duck always worried?" (*Because it's always got a bill in front of it, of course.*)

Afterwards, we joined the audience to watch the radio play, *Life with Dexter*. I left after it finished with mixed feelings—happy I had seen my favorite radio show but disappointed the stage looked nothing like what I had pictured the "family home" at 4 Gumnut Street, Ashfield, would look like.

During the holidays, I often met the baker at the front gate to save him a trip up the stairs to our front door. He remarked to my mother rather carelessly one day that I was so helpful, he'd like to take me around with him in his van next holidays. Offhand comments are for casual moments but not for a ten-year-old with the memory of an elephant and who feasted on every word uttered and treated it with the utmost seriousness. So on the first Friday of the next holidays, when he arrived with our daily bread, eager little me was waiting at the front door, just raring to go. This led to a hurried discussion with my mother so that in the end, a deal was struck, an agreement reached, and a pound was to be earned. Early Monday morning, he arrived at the front door, and when he saw I was ready and willing, he just shrugged and said, "Let's go, then."

We drove down to the Dee Why Bakery off Pittwater Road to pick up our first load. Jack drove into a large factory-size bakery and parked next to shelves and shelves of freshly baked bread. He opened up the back of his panel van to reveal empty shelves, just waiting to be stacked with the sweet-smelling loaves. As we stacked the back, he explained to me the different types of bread—white, brown, milk loaf, fruit loaf, kibbled wheat, whole meal, sliced and wrapped, half a loaf, a full loaf, and a few others I've since forgotten. I was so keen to do a good job that I remembered their names in a very short time. But what gave me the biggest thrill was that he had brought me my very own basket, a smaller version of his. His was large and unwieldy; mine was small and compact and fit snugly next to his in the back of the van. Each stop we made, I would dart around to the back and, after verbal instructions, fill my basket before scurrying off to "my" customers, who, more often than not, were waiting at the front door, because in those days of door-to-door service, it wasn't only bread the baker brought with him. There was always a cheery greeting and a comment for the day. My favorite customers were the old war veterans living in the cottages at the War Veterans Home on Collaroy Plateau. They were gracious people with friendly smiles and kind words and always left me feeling appreciated when I delivered their bread. I had my own moneybag, as some customers paid for their bread when it was delivered. I loved the sounds of the shaken bag— of copper pennies crashing against each other, of the tinkling of threepenny and sixpenny "bits," the little silver sparklers we called "trays" and "zacs," and the more robust sounds of shillings (*deenars*) and the two-shilling pieces, *florins* (although I rarely had them) crunching together. After a few deliveries, Jack would stop to divvy up who had paid and who would pay at the end of the week. He trusted my memory, so I tried hard to get it right. If I didn't, he was a patient mentor. Sometimes, I stayed in the vehicle if Jack had a quick delivery to make and didn't need my help. He only had two rules: make sure the bread in your basket is always covered, and don't carry a loaf in your bare hands—two rules he broke only often. When we started, he told me to call him Jack, but I didn't. I thought it would be disrespectful, so I called him Mr. Goggins—my rule I broke only occasionally.

I did have one small misadventure that I decided to keep to myself. It happened when I was taking a shortcut over a high fence between two houses, rather than go the long way around. (On this particular avenue, houses were set well back from the road and had long driveways.) I dropped my basket as I came over the fence and sent fresh loaves of bread tumbling out all over the grass. I hurriedly put the bread back into my basket and continued on my way. Only the ants and I knew my little secret.

I never forgot to bring my own lunch after Jack kindly shared his sandwiches with me on our first day together. In his arsenal was a thermos flask full of hot chocolate, which we shared at lunchtime. Then, part of the way through the afternoon, he'd stop for a break by the side of the road and sometimes smoke a rollie while writing things down in his book, as we finished off the last of the hot chocolate. It was intriguing to watch how he worked the tobacco into a long but compact strand in his cupped hand before stretching it with his fingers into the folded paper, which he rolled around before licking it, sticking it together, biting off loose strands, and poking any excess tobacco into the cigarette with his match. Jack intrigued me; he was a lot what my father wasn't. In another life, he could have been a happy pirate and I his cabin boy.

Friday was our biggest day, and double orders for the weekend meant a second trip back to the bakery to replenish our supply of bread. It was also payday. I received six shillings, which, when added to two four-shilling days and two lighter three-shilling days, made an even pound for the week. With that, I was able to buy Christmas presents for my mum and dad and a plastic hairbrush and mirror and a two-shilling sharpening stone for our next-door neighbors, who let us watch television at their place after school.

I worked for the next two years during school holidays with our new baker, until it was time to go to high school. By then, the excitement had worn off, although my final pay of one pound ten shillings replenished my money box until Christmas. My other after-school job was occasional paperboy, but it was less lucrative, only earning enough to buy a lolly or two.

No job though, ever interrupted my interest in sport. I had a huge passion for cricket and went with my father to the Sydney Cricket Ground to watch a well-attended Sheffield Shield match against Queensland. However, the highlight was to watch the West Indies team of 1960–61 play against New South Wales. I idolized Norm O'Neill and watched him score 114 before being stumped late in the day, but what fascinated me the most was watching Wesley Hall, then the fastest bowler in the world, loping in from near the boundary in the longest run-up I had ever seen. Over the next few years, I would occasionally go in to watch test cricket with my father, sitting either on the hill or, once, in the Sheridan Stand as the new Australian favorite, Doug Walters, battled against England in a beaten Australian side. I also came in to watch St. George beat Western Suburbs in a Grand-Final, with Paul and another mate Geoff, sitting right in front of the spot where Johnny King scored the match-winning try. It was an epic match, where heroes were made, and a statue was struck, which became the symbol of rugby-league supremacy when the captains embraced after full time. Other matches I went to with my father were at Brookvale Oval, to watch a succession of Manly sides having mixed success. In one match, I watched my idol, Reg Gasnier, carve up Manly as St. George had a solid win. He was my other sporting favorite who I wanted to play like when I grew up. We drove to the matches and were able to park across the road at the service station owned by one of my father's friends. Those were good times with my father, which neither my brother nor my sister cared for or shared with him.

We did, however, go to the Easter Show as a family when we were young, and we always came home with five shillings' worth of sample bags. They, too, were great times, as my father took us on excursions into town by bus to the two museums, up to the lookout on the southern pylon of the Bridge, to the City of Sydney Library, the Art Gallery, the Botanic Gardens ... again, Hyde Park War Memorial, the Herald printing factory, the observatory, and a one- time walk across the harbor bridge, which seemed to go on and on forever. All great adventures for a young boy. My father, for all his shortcomings and lack of money, tried to give us the best experiences young children could have, and he awakened in me a love for the outdoors. The northern beaches, dotted with fibro houses and beach shacks, became another place to explore. After a few shorter excursions with him—the penultimate being the 'Hole in the Wall' at Avalon—I felt great excitement when we finally made it all the way to Palm Beach at the end of the peninsula and up to the top of Barrenjoey Lighthouse.

Still, I loved running. It gave me a sense of freedom and purpose, so every time I went shopping for my mother, running back home— with two shillings' worth of best neck chops and sausage mince—was always part of the journey. One time, after visiting my mate Paul, I was running down the red soil of Blandford Street when I tripped on loose stones and fell onto a protruding rock, which caused a deep gouge in my left hip. I lay there, unable to move, until a lady helped me up and took me to her place. I was too embarrassed to let her see my injury, so I thanked her for her help and tearfully limped home. My mother patched me up, as always, but that experience still didn't stop me from running as my preferred mode of transport— when the bruising had subsided.

25

By the time I hit sixth class, I was doing well at sport and in my schoolwork, as well as being the only person who paid attention during Scripture classes. (I was a prefect then.) I came third in 6A, and received a mounted cricket ball after taking eight wickets for two runs (a monstrously flattering assessment of my bowling ability), and a 'double hat trick' against Newport Primary School. For those of us who played cricket, a hat trick (three wickets in three consecutive balls) had a mystical quality about it. It felt much like Christmas Day, when cicadas and Christmas beetles ruled, and real Christmas trees dominated rooms from the corner while spreading their mesmerizing aroma across the room. However, amongst players there was always debate as to what a double hat trick was—six wickets in six balls; or four wickets in four balls, where wickets two, three, and four constitute the second hat trick. Both views were equally compelling, depending on who you were listening to. Included in my double was the son of Keith Miller, a famous Australian cricketer, who turned up to watch his son play cricket and get out first ball. Taking the catch to give me a hat trick was future Australian rugby coach Rod Macqueen, who had squatted menacingly under the batsman's nose. I bowled, the batsmen blocked, and we all went up. Our teacher looked up from the scorebook he was filling in and, seeing the suspicion of a catch, gave him out, much to our collective joy. The next batsmen had his stumps rattled, and if my aim had been straighter, it would have been five in five balls. Then we would have stood around talking about it as possibly being a triple hat trick. I didn't ask Rod any searching questions about the catch, accepting that it had been taken fairly, but I remember feeling a bit hollow when the catch's authenticity was questioned later. A nagging feeling—"did I deserve it?"—hung around, as my sense of fair play was challenged somewhat by the catch and the possibility of receiving an undeserved honor. Afterwards, I was invited to bowl to Keith Miller and cleaned him up too, with a straight ball he somehow missed. He later told my teacher he was trying to put me into the bush on the other side of the road as some sort of get-square for his son's humiliation at the hands of my deadly straight ball. After I'd cleaned him up, he let everyone else who picked up a ball clean him up too, so now everyone could boast.

My sterling efforts made the *Sun* newspaper in a weekly article called "Spotlight on School Sport." I was famous for weeks after that and was able to milk it a bit longer after we won the competition.

Our school first grade rugby league team had less success as it struggled to compete with the better teams. I was the captain and scored eleven tries during the season in a team that always gave its best despite losing more matches than it won.

At the end of the year, I won the biggy: the school's General Proficiency Prize, which everyone—except me—had expected me to win. It was a book about the history of the world and made a welcome addition to my meager library. I eagerly looked forward to reading it. I would have to say I was popular and had expressions of interest from a few girls, which sadly, I ignored. I was also a school prefect and carried out my duties with considered diligence, except on one occasion when a dobber said to me in the playground while running past, "Tommy's weeing on the dunny wall."

I reacted instantly to Tommy's evil deed and quickly made my way to the toilet and caught Tommy in the very act.

"Did you wee on the dunny wall?" I demanded. "Yes," he said unabashedly.

"Why?" I said, taken aback by his good-natured confession.

He didn't look a bit embarrassed as he grinned at me. "Jacky and me were seeing who could piss out the window."

I couldn't keep a straight face and dissolved into giggles. After cautioning him not to do it again, I let him off, and we both left the toilet, sniggering all the way back to our classrooms. I didn't have the heart to tell him it was Jacky who had dobbed him in.

At the end of the year, I left for high school with a feeling of incompleteness. Maybe it was because I was sick and missed the last days of school and the sixth-class graduation "walk out" of the school. I didn't even get to say good-bye to my teachers, so maybe, in my mind, I never really got to leave school with everyone else.

Still, I remember my primary school days fondly as happy times, when cricket ruled and rugby matches on Saturday mornings were not always character-building floggings from the giants of Balgowlah

Heights and Seaforth Pirates, as they once were, but were occasional victories. I had joined the Dee Why Lions when I was ten, and I kept turning up each week to play in the under-twelve B's and resume getting flogged. But the next year, I turned eleven and played in the under-twelves again. I was a reserve, and I remember watching my team getting thumped by Balgowlah Heights at Inman's Reserve. What impressed me was the Dee Why center, whom the kids called Beaver, after the television character, toeing the ball downfield and running a long way to score a try, while the rest of the team stood back and watched, after deciding that they would just "leave it to Beaver." When Beaver didn't take up future invitations to play, I found myself replacing him and playing inside center.

If we were near the bottom of the competition table, Narrabeen Tigers were even nearer. I won my fame at Dee Why by scoring nine tries in two matches against them, including five at North Narrabeen Polo Grounds, where I spent as much time sidestepping horse dung and dog droppings as I did Narrabeen players, only to be shocked afterwards when I was made captain. I didn't mind a pat on the back, but I felt uncomfortable when given any authority. Even at that young age, I had no ambitions other than doing my best and playing my part on the team. I loved seeing the smiles on my teammates' faces when I scored a try. But authority and making decisions was for other people, so I spent the rest of the season trying to give the position away. One of our coaches tried to shout me a meat pie during a rugby carnival at Manly Oval one day. I refused, thinking that he shouldn't buy me one if the rest of my team wasn't getting one too. I didn't expect any special treatment and recoiled when I was singled out for it. In those days, you didn't "big note" yourself, or you'd be called a poser, and criticism for posers back then was harsh.

Unfortunately, my team thought that what I did to Narrabeen, I could do to the top sides as well, so when we got an occasional penalty, Beaver or Chicka would tap the ball, give it to me, and say something inspirational like, "Run!" Most of the time, it was from our half; rarely did we venture much closer into the other team's territory. Then the team watched as I dodged and jinked my way upfield and scored a runaway try. I soon became known for my dodging and jinking, and the good teams knew what to expect, so when we got our penalty against Balgowlah Heights, I found myself looking at a wall of fat kids who were expecting me to try to run through them. I reasoned that being much smaller than they were, it would be quite silly to try, so I took off running diagonally across field toward the smaller kids in the backs. I soon realized I had found a better way of planting the ball down next to the posts, and that was by using my speed to get away from the fat kids and then using my sidestep to sneak inside the rest. Some called it being smart; I saw it as survival. However, the one try I scored in that match didn't negate the five that Big Andy scored against us. He played outside center and would be my nemesis for years to come as he trampled his way over or around anyone who got in his way. He was big, fast, had muscular thighs, and outweighed me by at least forty pounds. Even when we surrounded him, he would burst through and rumble upfield, trailing bodies and swatting tacklers away like flies, as we desperately tried to hang on to his legs. I suffered many bruises from our dreaded but twice-yearly encounters. Clearly, my mother didn't care about my heroic efforts in football. Her only concern was that I didn't get hurt.

In my last year of cricket in the under-twelves, we had a strong team and finished third, despite comfortably beating Manly West, the eventual premiers. My mate Paul was the district's premier batsman, while Allan "Skinny" Frazer was the top all-rounder. I opened the bowling and took nearly eighty wickets, coming third in the district, with the ridiculously low bowling average of 2.90, while a hat trick and other notable feats with the ball gave me two mounted cricket balls and selection in Manly's under-twelve rep side as opening bowler. We played two matches against Sutherland, both serious affairs, where I felt excited by the prospect of playing the best of the best from another district. We lost the first match at Keirle Park and then went down to Sutherland and won the second. I bowled my heart out in the first match and picked up four wickets, for twenty-one runs, receiving a confidence-boosting accolade from the opposition's manager that I was the fastest under-twelves bowler he had ever seen.

Selection for the cricket team matched my selection for Manly's under-twelves rugby team a few months earlier. In that selection, thankfully, Big Andy was on my side. Two years later, we did it all again in the Manly under-fourteens rep side. In one match, I managed to scoot in for a try against Randwick after being set up nicely by none other than Big Andy, playing inside me.

1952 My brother Geoffrey and sister Jane. I'm three years old.
Front yard at Narraweena.

1953 Ken and his mum. Front yard at Narraweena

1958 Down at Collaroy Beach.

1961 Captain of my primary school football team. I'm in the centre
holding the football. 6'12 means a weight limit of 6 stone
12 pounds (98 pounds).

CHAPTER 3

High School at Narrabeen Boys

Although I was looking forward to high school with a fair degree of optimism, the reality of it was an entirely different matter. Soon after I started, my brother left school in fourth year to join the police force. Then, my self-confidence was further eroded by the sheer size of the place, the number of kids in the school, the number of classes in first form, and the number of kids in my class (which ended up as forty- two). As well, there were different teachers for every subject, so the close relationship I'd had with my one primary school teacher was a thing of the past, something I had to get used to. And I didn't adjust to it very well either. Not only was I competing against the bright kids in 1A, but I also had to prove myself all over again to be selected for the school's cricket and football teams. I felt quite affronted when kids who had just made up the numbers in our primary school team were picked ahead of me in the sixth-grade rugby team. I had to wait until they were discarded before I resumed playing in a team of midgets that suffered ritual beatings by other schools in our strong North Shore zone, schools such as Balgowlah High, where Big Andy reigned supreme. One time, while standing under the goal posts after another try had been scored against us, Peter Montgomery, one of our players, said authoritatively that if we charged the goal kicker, waving our arms in a circular motion, the ball would follow that direction and miss the goalposts. We tried it once and quickly discarded Monty's theory after we guided a wayward kick, which looked like it was heading for Mullet Creek, back over the black dot of the crossbar. Peter soon discarded his own theory as well, and years later went on to become school captain, an Olympic water polo player, a top trump in the Australian and International Olympic Committee, and a stunningly successful businessman. I went on to become opening bowler for our sixth-grade cricket side, which, after winning the first match, lost the habit until the end of the season, when we fluked another win. Monty didn't play cricket and so had no theories to share with us in regard to bat and ball. He did have theories, so I was told, about water polo, though.

By the end of first form, I had successfully underachieved my way into the next year's 2B. With that notable accomplishment under my belt, I escaped to Toukley on the Central Coast for a couple of weeks during the Christmas holidays. As in previous years, we stayed in my aunt's primitive fibro "cottage," which had two rooms, no electricity, a rainwater tank, and a truly smelly toilet way out the back. We spent most days down at Canton Beach, paddling around Tuggerah Lakes on skiffs. At night, we'd net schools of prawns, which had a suicidal attraction to the kerosene lanterns we carried into the water with us. I found the Stone Age facilities of the cottage absolutely fabulous and always looked forward to our holidays there.

At my school, second form was the time when galloping hormones exploded all over the bedrooms of thirteen-year-old boys. It was like we all went to bed one night and then woke up the next morning, suddenly consumed by sex. Comments and innuendos in class were all about sex; in fact, most of the conversation was about sex. It was all pretty crude and immature stuff, but it did arouse my interest in the girls school that was tantalizingly close on the other side of the school hall. So with hormones awakening, I found myself in confusing times. Being a Christian, I felt I should be disgusted by the "dirty" talk, but it was all so new and strangely hypnotic. The male teachers were no help, as they seemed to "understand" and only mildly chastised the participants in this type of conversation. That disappointed me, because I had expected—or more realistically, hoped—the teachers would put a lid on it all (conveniently removing my own personal responsibility) by applying a legalistic rule for the suppression of all hormonal urges. When they didn't, I felt let down. To me, they appeared to be complicit in that type of behavior.

Those were confusing times but gradually, my resolve increased, and I was able to step back from the accepted, to the disdain of my mates, who didn't share the spiritual conflict I was going through. Once they realized I was over it all, I became the butt of their taunts and jokes. They started calling me "the reverend" and made up a lewd story about a local girl wanting to meet me down in the bush for a sexual encounter. That really turned me off, and she was embarrassed when she found out what they had said about her. Apparently, she had seen me on the bus and liked me—but in an innocent way. However, their taunts, although hurtful, were always muted, because they had to keep me onside, as we played football and cricket together. To be honest, it wasn't easy; it was a constant battle, as I was never totally disgusted by what was said or shown, but I always felt it tacky and cheap, as I believed there was a higher way of looking at sex. I had been brought up in an atmosphere of moderation, modesty, and respect, especially for women, so after the initial hormonally driven burst, it all started to seem a bit grubby and demeaning to me. Despite conflicting thoughts about it, I felt I needed a disciplined mind not to become part of it. Maybe Miss Taylor knew more about me than I realized.

I was fortunate to have a healthy obsession with sport. Unlike my contemporaries, I disliked rock music and the ostentatious lifestyles they lived. The Beatles and the Rolling Stones were just coming into prominence, and the latters' strutting, preening ways on stage were as foreign to me as my Christian faith was real to me. Still, I suffered from my peers' taunts because I was different. I had different values, and I went to church rather than parties, where Spin the Bottle was tame compared to what some of them really got up to. Sex and the pursuit of it was a big deal for my peers, but over the years, it only made me more determined to wait until I met the right one—the girl I wanted to marry. Besides, what would my mum think of me?

Surfing was a popular pastime among the boys, as was the beach lifestyle. I was self-conscious, as I had fair skin up until then, so I started going to the beach during the summer holidays and developed my skills in body surfing, as well as a suntan. Zinc cream applied to the nose and for some lips was the only protection we boys used against the sun's rays, while the girls allowed the boys to touch their bodies by applying absolutely useless "suntan lotion" (SPF 5), which washed off after their first excursion into the surf. Other brown-skinned beauties cooked themselves with coconut oil— and by their thirties, they had skin that looked like wrinkled prunes. As silly as it seems today, sun-bleached hair and a tan were important status symbols for the northern-beaches youth, while surfboard riders, or "boardies," as they were called, carried extra status. While my "friends" plied and honed their surfing skills on weekends, joined surf clubs, and embraced their lifestyle of parties, dances, beer, and sex, my weekends were different, as I followed my love of cricket. I graced the cricket grounds of Sydney, went to church, and stayed home on Saturday nights to watch television with my family and drink cups of tea. It was a life I was comfortable with, although the talk at school of drinking, sex, and parties led me to see how easy it would be to be seduced by that lifestyle. I didn't feel any inclination to be part of it and found the uncomplicated life in church youth programs more to my liking—although always lurking in the back of my mind was the sneaking suspicion that I was missing out on something, even if it was only looking at forbidden fruit.

In my senior years at high school, three of us started a Friday night Cinema Club in the school hall. Geoff Pickworth, the instigator, hired 16mm films and started a membership drive from the boys and girls schools' students. We also had a tuck shop, or snack shop, operating, selling mostly cinema food—chocolates, ice creams, and chips. Most nights were well attended, with numbers anywhere from fifty to two hundred, depending on which film we were showing. I enjoyed being part of it and playing my role. Being a school prefect, I patrolled the darkened hall and stubbed out cigarettes with my fingers—an act that was painfully stupid. However, we continued playing the game of "hide the cigarette" over the two years we ran the club, although the telltale glow was almost impossible to hide before the 'super conch' prefect, usually me, caught up with you. Still, it fit in with my view of order and rules. We hadn't discovered that the little rebellious act was a precursor to lung cancer, which we all rail against today.

Sport continued to play a big part in my life at high school. I played inside center for our school rugby side, but we inherited the Collaroy Plateau disease and suffered for two years with heavy defeats from the giants of every other high school in the North Shore zone. Then in my third year at high school we had our one and only victory when our now fourth grade team beat North Sydney Tech, to the absolute shock of Tech and joy of the school watching the match from Billy Goat Hill, a landfill over a large effluent tank. They had watched us battle on for nearly three years, and despite all those losses, the team never gave up and kept at it until that one memorable afternoon, when we somehow destroyed, demolished, and thrashed Tech, 8–3. I had one of those magical days, where gaps appeared every time I touched the ball, so all I had to do was run through them. Unfortunately for me, our team planning for the rest of the season revolved around getting the ball to me, as I seemed to have discovered ways of finding gaps that had eluded us for the past two and a half years. Still, we trained hard and approached every match with confidence. We finished the season on a high after a stunning draw against a much more favored team in the last match of the season. We felt like kings.

At this time a significant moment occurred for me one night. My brother had recently moved out and left behind an old cheapo tape recorder with a dodgy spool and a primitive handheld microphone, which I often used for private recording sessions. I was having a karaoke moment one night when the spool jumped off the box and deposited its contents all over the room. On the floor, on the bed, and under the bed were meters of tape, twisted and knotted into an almighty mess. When I looked at it, I was tempted to dive in and tear it to shreds in a fit of controlled rage, but I didn't. My rage was momentary. Calmness descended, and I decided to unravel the twisted mass before me. It took me nearly two hours before every length was unraveled and wound back onto the spool. Although the tape was a bit damaged and creased in places, it was still usable— but more important, it was back in its correct place.

So what did I make of all that?

I felt I had learned a good lesson that night, which was it was all right to be strong-willed about some things. If it was important enough, I could control my impatience and my tendency to act in haste and give up if the task was too intricate or was taking too long to complete. If I applied myself to the job at hand, I could see it through until it was completed, not in a rough-and-ready way but as well as I could do it. To me, it was an important discovery, because it gave me confidence in my ability to do something well, if I felt it was important enough. On the other hand, if I didn't feel it was important, I wouldn't get so caught up with it. I would be more detached—like an observer or a spectator—not indifferent but not driven to the point of treating it as a contest I had to win. Letting unimportant things slide and not letting them occupy too much time is something I had to learn later.

When I was fifteen, a mission group from Missouri came to our church. Then, it was old-time evangelism, as a move of God swept through the church. It was then I felt convicted to publicly declare my faith in Jesus Christ by being baptized. I didn't like the emotionalism of religion, but I knew it was right for me. I knew I was a sinner and was grateful that Jesus had died on the cross for me, so my chosen way of life wasn't one of parties, drinking, and sex. My attitude hardened against forms of cheap talk and loose morals when I found an equally pious mate from Avalon. The fact he was the school-aged athletics champion didn't do any harm either and kept the knockers at bay. At school, I was a part of the "in group" only through sport. I found that friendships didn't extend beyond the sporting fields, as I had little interest in their lifestyles. I even had lukewarm interest in Saturday night youth activities at church; I was happy to stay home on Friday and Saturday nights after a full week of school, three football training sessions, two matches, and two or three junior matches that I refereed. In the cricket season, there were two matches a week in the hot sun and two afternoons of cricket practice. No wonder my nights were for relaxing and not partying.

I had a brief reacquaintance with Wendy, the girl next door at Narraweena, and although we hit it off well, I was too shy to even try to kiss her. My view back then was that unless I really liked a girl, I wasn't going to flirt and lead her on. I thought that if I got to the stage of actually kissing her, then I was pretty well committed to marrying her. I was also baffled by the signals she gave me, especially the following year when she came to watch a cricket match I was playing in at an oval just up the road from her place. She came with a girlfriend and introduced me to her, saying, "This is the one I was telling you about." She then made some inference to my "mad" (crazy) behavior. I think she was being complimentary, but I wasn't sure how I should respond or why she even came to watch a cricket match.

My involvement in sport during those years extended beyond that of being just a player. During our mid-teens Paul and I coached a boys' cricket team for two years, when they were under-elevens and then under-twelves. It was a team full of talented youngsters and finished up near the top, both years. We would coach them up on Plateau Park after school. By 6:00, I'd had enough and went home, but Paul stayed on with three or four of the better players to practise for another half an hour. I couldn't understand why; but Paul had a hidden secret which I didn't find out about until seven years later.

My second desire as a teenager was to become a qualified referee. I was quietly pleased when I passed my theory exam on the forty- three laws of rugby union. On the next match day, I passed my practical exam and could wear the green-and-white Warringah Junior Referees Association badge on my white jersey. I looked spiffy in it with my white shorts, long navy blue socks with white topping, black polished boots with thick white tape, and of course, my whistle. There was some rivalry among the younger refs as to who had the best whistle and could blow the loudest trill. A "Thunderer" was generally accepted as the best whistle and could also make the loudest trill. My whistle was given to me by our PE teacher and was better suited for a postman. Still, when blown hard enough, it did the job. My most interesting experience was refereeing an under-sevens grand final. The kids were great; it was the parents who were the problem. Refereeing under-fifteens was easy compared to six-year- olds and a cynical under-nines' captain who decided I was against his team and back-chatted me throughout the match, despite its being a trial match. I suppose from those two activities, my true calling shone through. I didn't like being the center of attention and or being expected to perform wondrous deeds, but I did enjoy coaching, teaching, and mentoring youngsters, as well as having a benevolent control over the direction of their efforts, so they could be the ones to perform wondrous deeds. My calling was to be either a teacher or a slave master. After the under-nines match, I would have gladly settled for slave master.

As teenagers, my mates and I were very active, playing a variety of sports during the school holidays. We played squash, mostly at the Avalon and Mona Vale courts, almost to the point of exhaustion. If it was a Saturday morning and I was free from any refereeing commitments, we would play for an hour and then double up and head off to play football in the afternoon. Such was our endless supply of energy. Golf, though, was a real passion. We were spoiled by the many golf courses that dotted the northern beaches. We looked forward to an early morning start on the day's course of choice, as well as a brain-freezing chocolate malted milkshake— sometimes two—at the closest milk bar afterwards. The Palm Beach course was too short, flat, and easy but very scenic. Mona Vale was a good test on our young talents, while Long Reef had difficulty, length, and a tremendous view, which I could admire when I wasn't hunting around in the adjacent fairway or peering over the cliff, looking for my ball. My slice worked brilliantly on those occasions, until I perfected a hook and visited the onside fairways instead. Other courses were popular with us—Warringah was long, flat, and unthreatening, while Bayview was scenic and a touch easier, except for one hole where you hit blind into a valley and hoped you'd find your ball when you made your way down to the fairway. An embarrassing moment occurred at Bayview when, within sight of the clubhouse, my aged 3 wood disintegrated in my hands and the head went further down the fairway than the ball did.

I wasn't very good at golf—inconsistent at best. I had a cricket swing, a slice, and an occasional booming drive, but I rarely had time to practice, so I saw little improvement over my teenage years when I played, and I never improved on my best score of eighty-four at Bayview.

Some took it seriously, though. The keen ones earned money by caddying down at Long Reef, so I caddied once. After lugging a huge set of clubs around, I decided the money wasn't worth it. Besides, some of my mates told dark tales of the temper tantrums some older golfers threw, then being sent out to fox a thrown club when they had cooled down. Thankfully, the golfer I caddied for that day was a good-natured gentleman, despite his regular fluffed strokes and visits to the bunkers.

Up on the top of Long Reef headland was a great place to stand and look up and down the coast. Sometimes I watched the South Steyne ferry bashing its way up the coast on a Sunday afternoon excursion to Broken Bay. I planned to bring a girl up there one day (or night) in the future for a romantic tryst, if I ever had one.

When I was in fifth form, we had a strong first-grade rugby side. Two teams were outstanding, and we were pretty well on par with the rest. Highlights were beating North Sydney High twice and giving premiership favorites Manly High, who had three future Australian reps playing for them, a real run for their money. I scored twice against both schools with my try against Manly, one the most satisfying I have ever scored. I was set up by our fullback Steve, who put me into a gap with a reverse pass and sent me galloping merrily down field. That the try line was sixty meters away was inconsequential, as scoring was not an insurmountable problem, although the fullback tried to make it one. Rather, when I took off, I put on my sprinter's cap, knowing there was a good chance I'd reach the try line well before the defense got anywhere near me.

That year, I was apparently on the fringe of Combined High Schools selection but one of the selectors told me that I wasn't selected because they thought I was too young. I thought at sixteen I was old enough, especially as Big Andy was only a few months older than I was, and he was selected in the CHS Firsts as outside center.

The following year, with almost the same team but a year older and a year bigger, we were joint premiers, beat every team at least once, and had two players selected in the CHS side. I wasn't one of them; apparently, I lost out to a fifteen-year-old "boy wonder." So much for my faith in selectors choosing players on merit, especially as I'd had a good year that year, once I brushed past Big Andy to score the match-winning try against Balgowlah High. Even so, I was never particularly confident marking Andy, and I half expected him to jump on me at any moment as I raced past him.

We were also runners-up to Christian Brothers Lewisham in the state open-weight rugby league knock-out competition. In one match, I was able to score the match-winning try that got us into the final and then ran in a fifty-meter try in the final, planting the ball down between the uprights in front of the old Sheridan Stand at the Sydney Cricket Ground. We played a rugby-style game of running and passing and not the barging type of game that most of the league school teams played. Having two players who played first- grade rugby league a few years later showed the quality of the players we had in our ranks. Again, I enjoyed playing my role on the team and contributing with a try here and there.

Cricket was my other major sport. I opened the bowling for my school teams right through the years (except for one year, strangely, when I found myself opening bat for our second-grade side when I was fourteen). I had good anticipation and skills at ball games, so my fielding, throwing, and catching was a strong point of my game. If we struggled over the years in rugby because of our small size, we had no such trouble in cricket. We were strong in batting. My mate Paul was outstanding, scoring a number of big fifties and hundreds on the way. Our bowling was solid, and we came first in first grade, beating the giants who had donkey-licked us for all those years in the rugby.

One day I came home late from school after football practice. On the bus was Pam Matthews, one of my "loves" from primary school. I hadn't seen her since sixth class and was stunned by how pretty she looked, all dressed up in her work clothes. She smiled at me and said she had left school after fourth form. I mumbled something incomprehensible and then got off at my stop—and mooned about her all the way home. I was too shy to try to make contact with her.

In my final year, I surprised myself at the zone athletics carnival by winning the sprint double, along the way beating not-so-big-anymore Andy quite comfortably. This meant I would be our zone's number-one runner at the state carnival at the Sydney Cricket Ground. I never considered myself a sprinter—more a football player who could run fast. I didn't give myself much chance until Phil Diamond, our PE teacher, convinced me I could not only make the final of the 200 but run a place. In fact, he even offered to train me during the school holidays on the GrassTex track at the National Fitness Camp. My mate Jim offered to train with me, so I agreed and trained solidly for two weeks, building up my strength for the 400 and speed for the 100. In between those distances was the 200 meters. Apart from continuous 60-meter sprints, the hardest part of my training was the exhausting, energy-sapping pattern of walk 200, run 200, walk 200, run 200, which I did for eight laps at top pace without a break. Each day was the same—walk, run, walk, run, walk, run for eight laps, and then sprint, walk, sprint, walk another eight times. It was hard work, but I enjoyed every minute of it. I had to push myself past and well beyond the point that, in other circumstances, I might have said, "That'll do me."

I realized that results didn't happen by chance; they came from hard work, so if I was going to compete against the best in the state, I had to train to be the best I could.

At the state carnival, I won my heat of the 200 from the outside lane. I was a good bend runner but found the outside lane daunting, as the final bend before the finish line tended to deposit you into the ladies stand, so close was it to the fence. Still, I made two finals, the 100 and the 200, and if I hadn't just loped along in the heat of the 400 after the state champion passed me, I would have come second and made the 400-meter final as well. As it was, I finished strongly, came third, and just missed the final in the fastest heat of the day. In hindsight, if I had trusted my fitness and ability more, I could have come second in the final, but I hardly ever ran the 400 and didn't know the right tactics,

43

apart from a big finish, when everyone else was stuffed and just hanging in there.

I didn't get a quick enough start and came sixth in the 100 meter when I should have done better. I was put off by the brash gamesmanship of one of the favorites who told everyone at the starting line that he was going to win the race. Happily, he didn't; he came second. I was off the pace at the gun and was just getting into my stride when we hit the finish line. I learned a lesson from that— the best don't think too much; they just go for it and run like the clappers.

I had a chance for redemption in the 200-meter final. I knew I was a strong finisher, but did I have the speed to catch the two favorites? No, I didn't. However, third place was beckoning as I surged around the final bend, while avoiding entry into the ladies stand. I glanced inside and saw I was running almost neck-and-neck with another runner, who seemed just as shocked as I was when he saw me. About three meters ahead were the two favorites. I pushed hard for the finish line, as coming third is far better than coming fourth, especially when the afternoon *Sun* newspaper had the first three place-getters in the stop-press section on the back page.

I learned another lesson from that race: it's how you finish the race that counts; it's not how you start it. Failure comes when resolve falters, even if for just a brief moment. I faltered at the finish line by not pushing just that little bit harder, which was the difference between giving 99 percent and 100 percent, so I came fourth and didn't get my name in the paper—a disappointment that lasted all of two days but was still not forgotten years later.

At the end of year ten, I joined the school choir. After exams, we had school activities to fill in four weeks of post-exams inertia, so when a cricket teammate answered the impassioned plea from the music teacher for new choir members for a Christmas musicale, and he asked me to join with him, I said, "Why not?"

It was apparently quite a coup for Don Neville, our music teacher, to have a football player in the choir, so when I turned up, he was very pleased. So pleased, in fact, that he made me stage manager. Then, he giggled his head off when my goonish sense of humor took over during a rehearsal, and I carried music stands onstage three at a time, with one clenched firmly between my teeth. From that time on, Don told me later, he knew I would fit nicely into the madness that was the school choir, a madness I soon found I was content to be a part of.

The reasons I joined the choir were not because I was a music tragic but because I had four weeks of post-exam afternoons to kill, and I wanted to do something that was different, interesting, wouldn't be a complete waste of time, and with "different" people. Second, there was the girl factor—meeting girls from the adjoining girls school, which was forbidden unless you were in the choir. I found the fellows so different from the brash macho types I usually hung out with. They were more aesthetic, totally unsporty, and genuinely loved music. I felt comfortable being part of that particularly interesting subculture of school life, despite my less-than-impressive music credentials.

I also found that I could move between both groups without having a major allegiance to either. Even if my football mates thought I was a bit unusual, they never said so, as I had already proven myself on the football field.

For the musicale, we were joined by the girls choir. Although we weren't going to perform anything too complex, it was sufficient to show me what it was like to be in a serious choir among serious musicians.

The next year, I was back in the choir, ready to continue my fascination with Beethoven and his pals.

Our choir was part of the Combined High Schools Choir that rehearsed and then performed matinee shows at the Sydney Town Hall. My eyes were opened at the rehearsals as to how keen everyone was about music. Furthermore, the quality of the principals allowed me to be a part of a music scene I never would have known about if I had closed my mind to anything other than sport. Another benefit was that I got to check out the delicious girls from Fort Street and North Sydney Girls High. One of the Fort Street girls spoke to me, but I was too naive to say much back to her. Then, on our way home after one rehearsal, Jim and I followed a group from North Sydney Girls, with our eyes firmly fixed on one of the girls, as we were heading back to Wynyard to catch our bus home. Our noble sides shone through when one of

45

the group wandered back to us and asked us to stop following them, as the girl in question had a boyfriend at the university. It seemed a reasonable request, as we apparently weren't the first to be smitten with her. After that, I went back to chatting up the girl from Fort Street, which naturally got me nowhere.

Later that year, we joined with the girls school for another musicale. It was then when I first noticed a pretty young girl bustling off to the bus after rehearsals. I liked the rear view of her and her busy walk, so I began a covert operation through Merrilyn, one of her classmates and my friend from church, to find out more about her. Nicola was sixteen, bright, talented, and one of the choir's leading sopranos. At the musicale, I spoke to her backstage. After getting her phone number and address, I accompanied her outside to where her parents were waiting. Apparently, my politeness impressed her mother, but very early on, Nicola said that she didn't want a steady boyfriend; she just wanted to be friends. I got on well with her parents and two older sisters, as did my brother, and for six months, we were looked on by other choir members as an "item." I was introduced to her world of music and had cultural experiences that I never would have had in my narrow and somewhat unsophisticated upbringing. She was mildly interested in my sporting activities, and I tried hard to be interested in hers. I walked miles along Dee Why Beach to see her, in a relationship that extended only as far as hand- holding and an occasional kiss.

In the end, cricket and opera didn't mix, and after six months, we broke up by mutual consent from our claytons' relationship. I don't know how she felt, but I was devastated—such was the softness of my heart for her. She was my first girlfriend, and the way she made my stomach churn for months afterwards whenever I saw her showed me how vulnerable I was to sweet girls with their own agendas. Still, it was hard to forget her, especially as I only had to look out my bedroom window across the valley and see her house sitting large up there on Dee Why Point.

Despite my heartache over Nicola, I stayed in the choir and enjoyed the social and musical activities that were organized. Close bonds developed between some couples, which ultimately led to marriage. I got on well with a number of the girls, some of whom hinted their availability. One, a German girl, was both pretty and sophisticated—more advanced in relationships than I was—and although a friendship of sorts started, nothing developed. I hadn't really considered getting involved with anyone again, so I completely missed any signals from her, or I was too timid to act upon them. With the outings, parties, and music events, as well as my other life as a sportsman, I had enough on my plate and didn't consider investing the time or emotional energy needed to build up another relationship.

At the end of fifth form, I looked to supplement my meager pocket money by getting a job at the Collaroy Plateau Post Office, delivering Christmas mail. It wasn't because of my initiative but because my sister had declined to saddle up again for the laudatory task of trudging around the Plateau delivering Christmas cheer to the Christmas-minded Plateau-ites. So the position was available if I wanted it—and I did.

The post office was situated in a small shopping center on Aubreen Street and was housed in a poky little brick building, one part of a duplex, with the other part being a pharmacy. It was narrow, with a dark dungeon-like area in the backroom behind the counter where all the sorting was done. I arrived before seven and was ushered into the back room with the other casuals. In the back room, bags of Christmas mail were brought in and dumped on a long table, where we eager-beaver casuals waited while the postmistress, as she was called, divided the mail into the various streets we were doing. Each pile of mail was put into a long wooden frame, with the streets separated by movable wooden stocks. The individual streets were then sorted into house numbers, for ease of delivery. For example, you would start with houses one and three and then cross the road and do two, four, and six. Then you would come back across the road to do numbers five to nine, before trooping back across the road to do eight, ten, and twelve. This was how it was done. It was the most efficient way of progressing down a street without having to backtrack, unless an errant letter was found out of place.

Letters were sorted in that order and were then bundled together using thick rubber bands, before being put in order into the bag, making sure that the first in would be the last out, and of course the last in would be the first out. You would then crisscross the road, pulling letters out of the bundle you were carrying, until you had finished delivering the letters from that bundle and then would dip into your bag and take out the next bundle. Easy. When you had emptied your bag, you would come back to the post office and fill up for your second load of the day. It had the feeling of déjà vu about it but without the sweet-smelling aroma of freshly baked bread.

At the first house, as I pulled out the first two letters from my bundle, the rubber band acted as a catapult and shot the rest of the bundle all over Blandford Street. As I fossicked around, picking up envelopes, the post mistress, who had followed me, stormed over and snatched the letters and bag from me and sent me packing. I went home upset, and when I told my father, he didn't think it was fair. He went up to the post office to talk to the postmaster. The long and the short of it was that I was given a second chance and had a teary reconciliation with the postmistress—mostly hers—before lunch. She said my heroic dad had said she had treated me unfairly and I deserved a second chance. That was in keeping with my father's character—he was an honest and fair man who thought everyone should be given a fair go. He once intervened when a group of bullies set upon my brother as he was on his way to tennis. He said it wasn't fair to gang up on one person, so he made them fight my brother one at a time. He did not tell them he was my brother's father. After fighting each of them, my brother wasn't bullied again. It horrified my mother when he told her, but he stood by his decision to make my brother stand up for himself in the face of bullying. It was that sort of attitude that got me reinstated. From then on, I got on famously with the postmistress and had a very enjoyable two weeks delivering the Christmas mail, with nary a mishap with rubber bands again. I also felt grateful that my father had stood up for me, not for the sake of advantage but just for the sake of fairness

—a perspective I took with me into life. All I ever expected in life was fairness, not undeserved favor, so if I wasn't good enough, then that was all right by me. On this occasion, I was good enough and came away with a fortune of $48 for two weeks work.

48

I had a weird relationship with my sister. She was popular with the boys because of her personality, long blonde hair, and impressive figure. A constant stream of fellows began to turn up on our doorstep to see her. Most of them, I thought, were shallow drop-kicks. Still, she was flattered by them and welcomed the attention of fellows who I felt always arrived in quantity and rarely in quality. That lack of quality became obvious when she declined their overtures. Jane had a consuming passion for study—osteopathy to be exact—and no one, especially not those academic pygmies, was going to thwart her by proffering their opinions that girls should be doting, unambitious, and compliant.

Still, she was a sister with benefits. Despite my shyness with girls and obsession with sport, she became my number-one promoter after responding positively to a satirical poem I wrote, lampooning the fellows who used to turn up on our doorstep, clamoring to see her. She was sufficiently amused by my little effort that she decided to take me around on the back of her bike to meet nice Christian girls at the WEC (World Evangelical Crusade) meetings she attended. I was all for that. She was into those sort of high-powered Christian meetings and used to go religiously to Christian youth camps such as Teen Ranch—camps that held absolutely no interest to me. However, she led a somewhat high-energy, high-risk life, riding horses and motor bikes, and she suffered the consequences. She ended up in coma for nearly two weeks after being thrown from a horse and had a broken collar bone after coming off a motor bike. She took a long time to recover and had to give up her medical technology course. Then, however, she studied osteopathy for two years while doing a teacher-training course at the ASOPA College.

What with her many boyfriends, photography, scuba diving, seemingly never-ending spiritual journeys, world travel, and an adventuress lifestyle, she led a most interesting life. The effect on me was negligible. I wasn't interested in her interests, but I did admire her pluck, her determination, and her passion for all the things she did, especially in the area of natural medicines, of which she had an almost encyclopedic knowledge.

My Christian life, though, differed from hers. I wasn't touched as emotionally as she was. My beliefs were determined by a quiet assurance

49

and determination to continue through life in relationship with Christ. I had thought deeply about the things I had learned during my early years at Collaroy Plateau Baptist Church and had been thoroughly persuaded it was the truth. It seemed to me, it was just so obvious. Goodness, justness, rightness, perfection—qualities that people respected and aspired to in their lives were all attributes of God and spoke of who He was. My sins and my faults were many, and that He would actually think enough of me that He would pay the ultimate price to restore a relationship with me and show me the way to eternal life just seemed so obvious. Knowing Him as I did meant living a life for Him, in "fear and trembling," which wasn't an emotional response to fear but a conviction borne out of a relationship with Him. My childhood memories of Jesus were that He was always smiling, and we had a relationship that comforted and assured me rather than affected me emotionally. When I was disappointed in myself, it was because I didn't live up to His standards, whether in faith, my behavior, or even when playing sport.

One of my mates, Robert (Robbie, for the purposes of this muse), was having family troubles and ideological differences with his businessman father and was forever moving from place to place. He needed someone to help him load up his car, a black Austin A40 he called Bertha (and after it was wrecked in an accident, its replacement, Bertha II) with his wardrobe, books, clothes, and sundry other knickknacks, including his precious twelve-string guitar. He was also in need of periodical raves, as we called them (discussions about anything, where he got to let off steam), to keep some sort of mental equilibrium in life. He would turn up on my doorstep in Berthas I and II on weeknights and expect me to drop everything to come out and have a one- to two-hour rave with him. The fact I always did showed that if nothing else, I was flexible.

"Pay a visit to flexible Ken for a rave, and Ken will oblige, no matter what he's doing."

I always did, too I was that easygoing and obliging. Robbie had joined the church football team I was playing for, as well as flirting with Christianity. I think it was because he was more interested in flirting with one of the girls at our church, so he came to some of our youth meetings. He took on a softer, happier, and less belligerent demeanor, unlike the angry ant I had gotten to know over the last few years. He was boarding with Ray, a player in our church football team, and his wife and children at this time. Ray was later a Wycliffe Bible translator, so Robbie was getting good Christian guidance at a time when he needed the right support, while studying for the HSC. (Higher School Certificate.)

Robbie was attracted to stable, married Christian couples with young families during this period of his life, possibly because he saw a happy, balanced side of family life that he felt he had missed. One story he used to relate to us with absolute relish concerned one of our senior players, Jim, who was also a maths teacher at our school. Robbie had just finished having dinner with the family when the youngest child apparently spilled his drink all over himself and all over the table. As they rushed to mop it up, the oldest girl, all of seven years old, said to Jim, "Daddy, I didn't spill my drinks when I was Timmy's age, did I."

"No, petal, you didn't," Robbie mimicked Jim saying. "You used to just wee and poo and sick all over everything."

We heard that story many times from Robbie, and each time it got better in the telling.

At another time when Paul and I went to a party with Robbie, we were somehow prevailed upon to give a Christian perspective to a girl who was having moral issues about whether she should or shouldn't "do it." Before we could share a Christian homily on sex, Robbie took over and gave her an ear-bashing on the side of not "doing it," which went on and on—well beyond the moral attention span of a flighty young girl. She agreed that she should be a good girl. Some weeks later, Robbie was crestfallen when he told us about her lapse to the dark side and that she was a serial offender of somewhat loose morals.

I mention this because at that stage, Robbie had embraced the Christian life and Christian worldview and was a much nicer person.

At the end of the year, it was job time—how to earn some money for Christmas. One of the members of our church offered Paul and me casual jobs laying telephone cables at Coasters Retreat for his company. He also arranged for us to be picked up at Collaroy by an impulsive

51

young fellow we called "mad Millsy" and his mate Craig, in an unsafe FJ Holden. Millsy drove us to Palm Beach, where we joined the rest of the team at a wharf on Barrenjoey Road. Then we hopped on board a launch and took an idyllic cruise across Pittwater to Coasters Retreat, enriched on the way by the pungent smell of petrol fumes.

Millsy drove at one speed—breakneck. After each day, he would drive home as fast as he could because, he said, he had to get back before the police were out, as he had bald tires. It didn't matter to him that his erratic driving almost killed us one afternoon, when he raced down Warriewood Hill, happily overtaking a line of cars and just getting back into our lane before the gap between us and the oncoming traffic closed—for good. He didn't take too kindly to my criticism of his driving, though; he turned around and slapped me on the face. I was furious and sat there fuming. I always believed in respecting people and basically thought his slap was a complete sign of disrespect. Even his mate Craig was embarrassed. Later, Millsy found out that he'd gone to school with my sister at Narraweena and from then on, he was my best mate and toned down his driving. Still, after the slapping incident, I lost all respect for him and tried to avoid him. He and Craig were different types than those I grew up with, likeable but pretty rough around the edges, without any Christian values. Craig liked to drink and gamble, and when I asked him what happened when his money ran out, his immediate reply was, "Get more bucks." I realized then that he saw money as something to spend, whereas I saw money as something to save. It didn't occur to me that my moneybox mentality wasn't universally appreciated.

On our first day, I made the mistake of taking my father's advice and asking the foreman how to use a shovel. If my father thought it would endear me to him, he was mistaken. The foreman looked at me as though I had just crawled out of a swamp, and he spent the next two weeks watching and waiting for an opportunity to sack me. I didn't have the nous to work the system either. I was a slow plodder, working with pick and shovel at a steady pace. Millsy, on the other hand, played the system. He was usually sitting around on an extended smoke break as I plodded on, but when the foreman came into sight, he was up and at it like there was no tomorrow. So what did the foreman see? Me going *plod, plod, plod,* and Millsy going *whack, bang, smash shovel.*

One Monday morning when we were supposed to be picked up at Collaroy, Millsy didn't turn up. When Paul and I found our way down to Palm Beach, the foreman just glared at us and told us we weren't picked up because we were sacked.

"But you can't do that," I said, thinking how unfair it was. "Yes, I can," he said. "You're only casual labor."

We were shocked by how heartless he was. The fact that Paul and I were fired after two weeks didn't matter. Two weeks laboring was just about our limit anyway. It was the way he treated us that showed me that not all employers were benevolent and cared much for their employees. We were just a commodity in the endless supply of casual labor they could find. Still, I had never seen so much money, as two weeks work netted us $112 each. Christmas presents for my family were going to be upmarket that year.

Although I received no plaudits for my shoveling, I did have a moment of glory when I picked up a snake with my bare hands and removed it from a lady's outdoor shed, while the other hairy-chested laborers cowered in the background. Although I wasn't afraid of snakes, I thought that the sluggish reptile curled up in her shed was a diamond python and quite harmless. It didn't put up much of a fuss when I deposited it back into the bush.

After Christmas, I heeded my sister and went up to Beach Mission at Brunswick Heads Caravan Park. There, we stayed in a large communal tent, and there I met some nice Christian girls. Megan came from Empire Vale, near Ballina, and was a year younger than me. Her male cousin, a big gentle fellow, was my sister's comic friend. Megan was gorgeous, witty, and bright. She provided the music every morning as we trooped around the camping ground, rounding up kids for the morning program. We got on well but I was like a big kid there, more intent on having a good time than being an ultra-serious Christian. Not that most of the team weren't of the same mind, but they were mostly older than I was, beach mission veterans, and balanced both sides with more panache than I ever could manage. Still, I enjoyed my time there and appreciated being part of the children's work. Back then, parents happily sent their children to our tent and readily accepted the Christian input into their children's lives.

After a few days, I found my feet and threw myself into the games with the children. If I'd been less innocent, I would have pursued things with Megan. Instead, I shyly settled for writing to her (and Grace and Judy) after beach mission was over. However, innocence was a boon as I came to the attention of eight-year-old Carly on her annual holidays. She attached herself to me at the first meeting, as little girls do, so that I ended up being her unofficial minder during the mission. On the final night, she led me into the meeting under the tent flap and plonked herself down on my lap. Uncle Ken was at his noble best, although I thought it was a pity it wasn't Megan.

Regretfully, I didn't go back the following year, because I had my mind on cricket fields and surfing when the time came. Only later did I find out that a few of the girls were disappointed I wasn't there. If only I'd known—such was my innocence.

Being in sixth form gave us responsibilities and privileges that we had never had before. As well, we had our own prefects room, where we could hide away during breaks and play 500 or Euchre or Pontoon. As senior prefect the previous year, I made up the prefects' duty roster. I always had requests for school hall duties, because that meant patrolling the area between the boys and girls schools, ostensibly to catch runners heading off for an early surf. In reality, it was a plum duty, where you could check out the girls and occasionally spring school army cadets hanging around for too long at the QM store (Quarter Masters Store.) In sixth form, the Avalon set voted in one of their own as senior prefect, so our headmaster created a position for me as the school's liaison officer. That gave me greater freedom to go over to the girls school carrying notes and messages to their headmistress, as well as participating in the "biggy." The biggy meant going along to Government House with the girls school captain and vice captain to meet the state governor, Victoria Cross winner Sir Roden Cutler. It was such an honor that I wondered if Miss Taylor had been corresponding with our headmaster. A photo appeared in the Sydney newspaper of the girls captain and me, sitting next to the fountain, chatting with the governor. *At least I don't look a complete idiot in the photo this time*, I thought.

My two senior years were great years, with trips to the Snowy Mountains and camping out in the New England ranges on a geology excursion. We handled responsibilities and privileges well. But in the end, I had no idea what I wanted to do, and with a less than startling HSC result, I didn't bother about applying for university. Instead I applied for a job in the public service as a valuer. I didn't know much about what a valuer did other than value property but was attracted to the $4,000 a year salary, an amount I didn't earn until three years later in my first year of teaching. As the position entailed study at university I was offered a position instead in the police department of the public service – a position I duly accepted. Each morning I'd go around to the bus terminal, join the old warriors on the bus, find a seat up the back, hide there until it got to Wynyard, and then trudge down Grosvenor and up Bridge Street to police headquarters in Philip Street. On the way, I stopped at a park on Loftus Street so I didn't arrive too early. It was a pleasant way to kill time, made all the more interesting by the pretty girl sitting on a nearby bench, whom I checked out each day.

I stayed at police headquarters doing clerical work for about two months, all the while hearing from Paul about the great time he was having at Balmain Teachers College. I soon found life in the public service or the prospect of joining the police force, like my brother, was unappealing, nor did I like the work-avoidance strategies and the mentality of a number of the fellows with whom I worked. With my mind fixed on becoming a schoolteacher, I resigned and went back to school to do the HSC again. It was back to rugby (cricket having finished for the summer), back to my security blanket, back to being captain of the school First XV, back to athletics and naturally, back to the school choir.

That year, I won the 100 and 200 at the zone carnival, improving my 200 meter time by nearly a second over the previous year. With more training, I reasoned, I could get down into the twenty-ones, which would give me a good chance of winning at the state carnival. So what did I do? I withdrew from the zone team to concentrate on my HSC—a decision I have regretted ever since but which seemed right at the time. I wasn't a great scholar, and taking on two level-one subjects led me to push sporting endeavor to the background. In hindsight, it wasn't the right thing to do and didn't help me do any better—I could have gone to teachers college on the previous year's results—but it was my battle with self-confidence that was hanging over me. In the end, I passed my first levels and came first in three subjects, but not because I gave up athletics.

On Saturdays, I played rugby for the church side again. I'd had a good first year with them, coming in as an unknown and scoring a bucketload of tries. Now a year older, and with Paul playing in the centers with me, we carved up all the teams until the grand final, which, although we were favorites, we proceeded to lose. Apart from scoring a lot of tries and kicking a lot of goals, I remember that season for the tackle that almost put me out of football for good and which had serious repercussions for me further down the track. Even after I passed the ball, I knew he was still going to hit me, but there was no way I could prepare myself for it. I wasn't very impressed with the lateness of the tackle, but rugby wasn't a game for wimps, so I just had to grit my teeth and get on with it.

A new cricket season started, and Paul soon found himself selected in Manly's first-grade side, while I struggled to get past thirds. I always thought I was good enough, but self-doubt kept on cropping up when my progress through the grades seemed to stall. Still, I had a new season in front of me to get wickets and prove that I deserved to be in the higher grades. Then circumstances changed all that.

1968 Winning the Open 100m final for Narrabeen Boys'
High in the North Shore Zone Championships.

1967 Seaforth Baptist Church football team. I am
third from the right standing. I was 17.

1968 I'm just about to have a shot for goal
for the church rugby team.

1967 Narrabeen Boys' High School Open Weight
Rugby League Team. We were runners-up in the State
championships. I am far right middle row.

1968 Standing with my brother and sister in the
same positions as on the cover photo.

PART 2

WAGGA YEARS

CHAPTER 4

First Year at Wagga Teachers College

All I knew about Wagga was what the map told me—it was six inches southwest of Sydney. But that didn't matter, because I was going to university in Sydney to become a high school teacher. Then it did matter when I received a teachers college scholarship—to go to Wagga instead, so if I went to university in Sydney, I'd have to pay for my first year's tuition fees. After telling God He'd got it wrong, I humbly accepted my fate and headed down to Wagga Wagga, with my city life put on hold.

Only my parents saw me off from Central Station on that warm February evening in '69. The party that was just breaking up as the train pulled out from Central wasn't for me; it was for someone else. *Someone's popular*, I thought as I looked back at the streamers and bunting left on the platform and at the crowd of girls waving to someone or some people. I marveled at how popular some people were. Then I settled in for an uncomfortable night, sitting up in second class while others continued to party on, minus the girls left behind. We would all be equals when the train disgorged us at Wagga Station at 4:30 a.m., leaving us to find our own way to the college. Fortunately, the local taxi drivers were lined up, waiting. Over the next half hour, they transported a trainload of students to the college, just as the sun was coming up.

I was not impressed with my first look at Wagga. It was hot, dusty, and a long way from home. It was early Monday morning as we of the train milled around the administration area, waiting patiently for our nine o'clock enrollment. If a flying saucer had happened by on its way to Sydney, I would have been on it, but instead, I found myself in Kambu dormitory, room fourteen, all alone, waiting for my designated roommate to arrive. I sat there, contemplating unpacking, when a lanky red-haired fellow bowled in from up the hall and introduced himself as Ross. Then he started complaining about his roommate. "You know what my roomie was doing? Studying. I can't hack that." Then he looked around and said, "Where's your roommate?"

"Don't know," I replied. "He isn't here yet."

Big Red was suddenly interested. "I don't think I can hack my roommate. Why don't I move in with you?" he said, more as a statement than a question. We found the warden, and he agreed to a room change after we convinced him we were now best mates. I took the bed farthest from the door, and Ross took the bed closest to the wardrobe. I took the side of the wardrobe closest to the door, and Ross arrayed his splendid set of clothes in the side closest to him. We soon found the floor could act as a second wardrobe—that is, until morning room inspections. Then our clothes were transferred to the floor inside the wardrobe. We used a common laundry to wash our clothes, usually once a week. I used to wonder why my shirts were always twisted and knotted after drying them on the clothesline until I discovered some dried theirs on coat hangers and then they were relatively smooth. We didn't think of ironing our shirts—never, ever—except on special occasions. Some fellows were lazy—or just lucky—and had theirs washed and ironed by their girlfriends. I vowed I'd never let a girl near my underpants, no matter how much I liked her.

Later, Ross and I talked about the trip down, and I told him about my parents seeing me off and the crowd of girls on the platform seeing someone else off. He said with a grin, "That was me they came to see off. They're friends from school."

If you had a good roommate, you were blessed. Your roommate first had to live with you and accommodate your peculiarities and whims, as you had to accommodate his. If the relationship survived those early days, then your roomie became your confidant; your soul mate; your trusted sidekick; your understanding, empathizing, clothes-lending, ever-loyal, always-protective … mate. So on that basis, Ross should never have been my roommate … but on the other hand, he was the best roommate I could ever have had. Ross was six three, three inches taller than I was, a year my junior but more worldly than I was, probably because he grew up in Greenacre, went to a co-ed school, and had a social life that I had always shunned. In fact, we couldn't have been more opposite. He didn't have a religious bone in his body, and his views on girls were more carnal, unlike the almost ethereal reverence I held for the very ground they walked on. He drank and partied but thankfully didn't smoke. Ross loved sport and played both soccer and cricket. Throughout his high school years, he played cricket against some of the Bankstown boys I had recently played against with Manly. Two of their bowlers weren't bad players back then, and some years later were both selected to open the bowling for Australia.

As for Ross, I found him loud, brash, and over-confident, ready to meet girls and determined to play the field—everything I disliked in fellows. We got on famously.

After a week of orientation on our own (second-year students would return to college a week later), I caught the train back to Sydney, as I had cricket commitments to complete with Manly. I felt comfortable leaving Ross on his own because as roomies go, after one week, we were comfortable with each other, just like an old married couple. By the time I got back to college on Monday morning, Ross had already hooked up with Pauline, a girl he met while I was away from him for two whole days, and he proceeded to go out with her for the next five years. So much for playing the field. Ross and I soon formed a friendship with Ron from next door, who at that stage was on his own. Ron was an easygoing fellow from a farm in Deniliquin, and his being a whiz with cars won him over to Ross. Ross and I bought a pushbike for nine dollars, and after doubling each other for a while, we lashed out and spent twelve dollars on a second bike. We now rode in style, down to town or down to the beach (a strip of sand on the Murrumbidgee River) for a swim. We needed to. It might have been early autumn, but it was still hot.

At one time, the Murrumbidgee was up, so Ross decided to see how far he could swim against the fast-running current.

"Ready? Go!" I said as I stood in waist-deep water, watching him dive under and swim as hard as he could for the next twenty or so seconds. He pushed forward and powered his way through the water. Then, spent, he stopped, stood up, and looked around to see how far he had gone. He looked back to where I should have been standing but was nonplussed to see I was still standing right next to him. Despite his mighty effort, he had gone absolutely nowhere.

We used our bikes up until Easter. Then, when Ross's relationship with Pauline heated up, the bikes became neglected symbols of our early days at college. Ross sold one bike, while the other quietly rusted away on its own, unloved and unused. Despite its passing, we reckoned we'd gotten more than twenty-one dollars' worth out of them when they were most needed. It wasn't the case now, because now we had friends with benefits—cars.

I met Bob Neich, a twenty-three-year old age mature age student from Canberra, a few weeks later. He had been recovering from recent surgery so his arrival at college was delayed until after Easter. Bob had left his job in the public service to follow his younger brother to teachers college, moving into the room next to ours with Ron. Bob was worldly compared to me. He was organized and businesslike but friendly, and he became my lifelong mate. We got on well, although in those early days, Bob talked himself up when it came to girls and talked himself down when it came to exams. Bob had planned his social life at college around playing the field, whereas the thought of taking a girl out and then casting her off hadn't occurred to me and left me feeling uncomfortable. Bob's other asset was that he owned a car, so we were able to go to the drive-in on a disastrous double-date, where he realized how very ordinary my girl skills were. Bob's girl was fine and friendly, whereas mine was very strange. Not surprisingly, I didn't go out with her again;

66

in fact, nobody did, which I felt was more a problem with her than with me.

I was a bit cautious about showing interest in a girl, because I was quite sure that if she found out I was interested in her, she wouldn't be interested in me. That thought typified my often bizarre battles with negative feelings of self-worth, so much so that I expected rejection, possibly the legacy of my relationship with Nicola. So I didn't let on that I was interested, even if I found myself attracted to someone. However, to keep a certain balance in my life, I went to Wagga Baptist Church, which was situated next to the railway station. Sunday became a lazy day at college, so I went at night, where there was a younger feel to it.

Meantime, Bob's playing the field ended abruptly when he met Jenelle from second year and became part of her group of friends—Helen, Johanna, and Ada. I became an honorary member of the group due to my relationship with Bob. I enjoyed their company and became more relaxed around girls, especially as there wasn't the thorny issue of romance on the table. Things were so relaxed between us that Jo would rush up to me and stand alongside me while we compared our feet size. It was quite silly, but it was our little joke, although I could never work out whether she liked me or was just being friendly.

It wasn't until the beginning of second term that I bit the bullet and formed a steady relationship with Delvene, a dark-haired girl from Canberra with a doll-like face, whom I had noticed in the first week of term. Bob had done some preliminary scouting for me, so I was able to see her when Ross and I stayed at Bob's place on our way back to college. She came back with Bob and me to college after Ross had headed off earlier to meet up with Pauline in Albury.

Emboldened by her positive signals, I took her for a walk a couple of nights later and then —courageously, I thought—I kissed her. But in actual fact, she kissed me and in way I'd never been kissed before. Frankly, I didn't really like it. It was aggressive and forceful, whereas to me, a kiss was an end in itself—soft, gentle, romantic, and not just the preliminaries to something else. However, by the end of the first week, I was attached and had someone to cuddle and keep me warm during winter. It was the first "real" girlfriend, without conditions, that I'd had and the first girl who really seemed to like me. She told me she'd had an affair with a married man while at school, but that didn't worry me, as I had no intention of trying it on with her. I believed that she'd been an innocent schoolgirl, preyed upon by an older man, and that she was chastened by the experience, so as to never want it to happen again. And with good old noble Ken in tow, it never would.

But the longer we went together, the more uncomfortable I began to feel. I was a bit naïve for not seeing that to some girls, there was a natural progression in a relationship, from hand-holding to more intimate contact. I was content to take my time and not push the boundaries with her, but I was surprised to find out that was not how she wanted it. When she got word back to me that I was "a bit slow," I decided it was time to act. I took the easy way out and engineered a break-up. The question in my mind was, "Could I marry this girl?" My answer was no, so I didn't think there was any point in continuing our relationship. Besides, I didn't think she would be particularly upset and would quickly get over it, as she was a pretty girl and had a number of suitors before we started going out together.

Afterward, I felt a sense of relief that it was over, although I was happy for Ross and Pauline and Bob and Jenelle in their relationships.

I thought some of the fellows overdid the social side of being away from home for the first time. The drinking culture took over too many lives, and after our half yearly exams, a number were given warnings to either smarten up or lose their scholarships. The fairly strict discipline of college life was difficult for some after their less-than- strict final year of high school, so they chose to leave, along with a number who realized they weren't cut out to be teachers. I didn't find college life and college rules the problem that some did. I actually preferred it that way, but at first, I did find it amusing to be called "mister" (the girls were called "miss") by our lecturers. Early, I realized that the academic staff actually wanted us to pass our courses and become teachers, but they wanted less of the frivolous, larrikin behavior in which a small number indulged. As it was done back then, one of the senior lecturers had a quiet word with me about Ross's wayward ways. I assured him that Ross was keen to do well and would be good value as a teacher. And true to the roomie code of protection, I had a quiet word with Ross. It shook Ross up a bit when he realized how close he was to being turfed out. It was also all Ross needed—a wake-up call. He learned his lesson, knuckled down, got on with it, and did well.

A couple of the fellows went out to the trots at the showground and the races down at the racecourse. I had absolutely no interest in any form of horse racing and especially gambling, the Melbourne Cup being the one exception. I remember when I was about ten, I was listening to an athletics meeting on the radio. The commentary of a hundred-meter race was short, loud, and frantic. My father came storming into the bedroom and demanded to know why I was listening to a horse race. It took my insistence for him to realize it wasn't a horse race. I don't know whether that had any influence on me, but I did grow up without any interest in horse racing. Gambling too was something other people did and was pretty much one step from oblivion for those who made it their pastime. The concession I made for "the race that stops a nation" won me six shillings on Even Stevens in a class sweep in the 1962 Melbourne Cup but left me with mixed feelings as to the propriety of a good little Baptist gambling.

We had to choose an elective course for our two years there, with the most popular option being dramatic art. It seemed pretty soft but not very challenging, so I chose creative writing, with English lecturer Jack Thompson. His enthusiasm for all things literary was infectious, and the group had an exciting year studying a variety of twentieth- century authors and their writing styles, as well as writing our own masterpieces. I also found myself president of the Revue Club. At the first meeting, there were five of us, three of the four girls being from my creative writing group. Our club patron, math lecturer Arthur Trewin, said we needed to elect a club president, so the four girls looked at me. I didn't know anything about revues, other than they needed to be fast-paced and topical, but I was a quick learner, and by co-opting an energetic group into the club, we were able to put on a highly successful revue. Used to high school apathy, I stuck "teasers" up around the college to publicize the revue and hopefully to attract a bit of interest from the student body, although my expectations weren't high.

69

On the night of the revue, I stepped out on to the stage to kick things off with my "Sprayfresh Ad." As I gazed out over the auditorium, I was pleasantly surprised to see grinning staff members sitting in front and a hall packed with enthusiastic students who had all come to be entertained. Although I appeared in a number of skits, I was much happier being behind the scenes, watching others perform who were much more adroit and talented than I was. Without much encouragement, Bob had come on board early and used his contacts and organizational skills to co-opt a number of talented and sometimes unlikely participants into the show, such as two second- year girls in golden bikinis. Bob also kept things moving behind the scenes, while our backstage team rose to the occasion and kept it a tight, fast-moving production. Topical skits proved to be a real hit, especially one where Ross brought the house down just by riding across the stage with a cheesy grin on our one surviving bike, dressed like one of our lecturers.

In the end, it was a production with no egos, where everyone put in to make the revue a success. Even last-minute helpers did their best to make a positive contribution to the night. Afterward, we were commended by the college principal for putting on a revue that had both humor and good taste. It was always my intention to entertain without being smutty. To be commended for that was a credit to all the people who had contributed to the night.

It was in rugby, however, where I had most of my success, although it didn't start too well in a trial match against Griffith. We were playing well and looked like scoring, when one of their backs took an intercept on his line and headed off upfield. With about eighty yards to go, I put my head down and chased after him as hard as I could. About twenty yards farther on, I looked up and was shocked to see I had already caught up to him. I was about to run into him, so instead I launched myself at him and crashed into his back, face first. I could hear an "ooh!" from the spectators as he went down like a sack of potatoes, with me on top. He had to leave the field, while I ended up with a sore face and a damaged blood vessel inside my mouth—a minor injury that became a problem only the following year.

Our college A team won the competition easily, beating college B in the final. We played in the Colts competition because of the less-than-charitable treatment to our college teams by Army the previous year. Apparently, it was a bit of a bloodbath, with a number of college players hospitalized, so our coach's dire warnings convinced us to play in the Colts competition. We took a lot of criticism from some agricultural college students who were at our college dance because they knew we wouldn't be playing their best teams. I lamely defended the decision, saying I came down to become a teacher, not a football player, but it became apparent that we had made the wrong decision, as we were far too good for the opposition from Yanco Ags, Wagga Ags Colts, and the RAAF (Royal Australian Air Force) recruits. I played center that year and had the first of two successful years, culminating in winning a college blue (in my case a trophy) for rugby and selection for Riverina District and the New South Wales Country team.

Despite playing in the Colts competition that year, I was selected to play for Riverina against the Warringah Club from Sydney. I was playing against some of my old mates from school, but they wouldn't let us have any of the ball, so we spent all afternoon tackling everything in green-and-white that moved. On one occasion, I chased my opposition center downfield and tackled him into touch, causing spectators to scatter and landing almost in the lap of Delvene, not long after we started going out together.

"Good move, roomie," sniggered Ross, standing nearby.

As was my normal practice, I saved most of my allowance of $18.20 a fortnight, because there was little need to spend it. I rarely went to Turvey Tavern, the college drinking hole, so I became a popular person to borrow from when the other fellows inevitably ran out of money before payday. They always paid me back first on payday, because they knew they would need me for drinking money when they ran out again. After nights of feasting, my old favorites would sidle up to me for a loan when they couldn't support their alcohol diet any longer and their withdrawal symptoms had become too acute to wait until the next payday.

71

Going out with college girls was inexpensive, though, because you always went dutch. The girls were very understanding, insisting that they pay their way. Despite having little money, there was a touching sense of honor among students when money was concerned. A T- bone steak dinner only cost $2.50, so I had enough saved to occasionally splurge, once buying a two-dollar pair of shoes, a nice pair of dark brown corduroy trousers for eight dollars, and two flannelette shirts, which set me back another two dollars each.

As I had at school, I was able to mix easily with the hard-drinking footy types—because I excelled at football—and the mild-mannered, sober Christians, because I was one of them and went to church with them. And being easygoing, without a dominating personality, I was able to comfortably blend in with everyone else.

Down at the far end of our dorm was a likeable fellow from Bega named Ken Kermode, who would have been my roommate if he hadn't turned up a day late. When he arrived the next day, he drove up on an impressive 500cc bike, so we, not surprisingly, called him Wheels. Wheels was friendly, had a ready smile, and punctuated his conversations with laughter. We thought he was a top bloke. Later, Wheels came back from the winter break in a Holden Ute, which seemed to be held together with chicken wire and kept running by his expertise with a screwdriver. Back then, that was all you needed. A tweak of the carburetor here, a wipe of the distributor cap there, and Bob's your uncle, you were off, as long as you hadn't forgotten to put in twenty cents worth of petrol from the servo up the road. That twenty cents' worth was enough to get down to town and back, or to Forest Hill, when I needed to go to the airport one afternoon. I was one of the select few to whom Ken would lend the Ute (his roomie, Animal, was quite rightly another,) and of course, I never forgot to put in twenty cents of super. Since I was driving Wheels's Ute around the place quite regularly, it set me thinking that it would be sensible to get my driver's license some day—a small matter that didn't seem to bother the two Kens.

What did bother Wheels one night, though, was when we were downtown at the Way Inn, and I introduced him to three nurses I knew. Unfortunately, as I was telling them his full name, I missed his frantic gesturing but caught their stifled grins. How was I to know his name was the same as a certain hospital apparatus?

We had our meals in the dining room, and I found the food plentiful and sustaining, despite what others had said. My love of food, especially chops, led us fellows to the tables of girls who didn't eat as much as we did and had plenty left over. We would eat whatever the girls couldn't and then call for seconds. I had the dubious reputation of being a big eater among the catering staff, who started calling me Lamb Chops. One lunchtime, I ate fourteen chops and still had room for more, while Bob, who foolishly tried to match me, had clocked off after ten. The reason I ate a lot was to put on weight for football. If I was going anywhere in football, I reasoned, I needed a bit of bulk to complement my speed.

During that year, the student body waited, like the rest of the world, to witness the first landing on the moon. Our history lecturer, however, told us he expected to see us at every lecture, so on the day of the moon landing, I sat in his history lecture with two other students— while the rest of the college students were in the dormitories' common rooms, watching history being made on television. *Ridiculous*, I thought afterward, realizing I had just missed witnessing one of the highlights of the twentieth century.

That winter, I had my first taste of snow—not counting the night a few snowflakes fell on the college—when the SRC's Social Committee organized a day trip to Falls Creek, some 125 miles away in the Victorian snowfields. The coach took ages to get there, and when we finally arrived at the top of the mountain, it was snowing— hard. My memories of that day are of cold hands, burned sausages, my jacket melting on the barbecue, and my incompetence on skis. I struggled to stay upright, even on the nursery slope, as I came down forward, backward and, when I tried to work my way back up the slope, sideways, which I thought was amazing, if not impossible. I retreated from the slopes after that cold, miserable and completely over my first trip to the snow.

When football finished for the year, I looked locally to find a cricket club to play for. Jack, my creative writing lecturer, played for Lake Albert, so he asked me to try out for the team. I ended up opening

73

the bowling for Lake with Jack. In the first match of the season, I took five wickets. On Monday, in the sports section of the *Daily Advertiser*, I saw a photo of a dour-looking opening bowler, trying not to look self-conscious. I enjoyed my time with the team, especially matches played down by Lake Albert. Everyone played their part, and I was made to feel part of the team, so much so that I even went to the pub with them once or twice after matches. In fact, the whole sporting tradition of Wagga reminded me of my early years, growing up on the northern beaches, where playing sport was a way of life.

We had a number of talented musicians in our college Christian Fellowship Group. Soon, the churches of Wagga got together and rented an old Salvation Army hall on Baylis Street and set up a youth drop-in center. They called it the Way Inn. I spent a lot of Friday and Saturday nights there, listening to good singing (much of it from our college group), testimonies, and messages, and drinking hot chocolate and eating melted cheese on toast. It became a popular place for the locals, including some unruly types who, unfortunately, only came in to cause trouble. What they brought with them was an attitude I found hard to understand.

One night I was asked to help when a group of trouble makers tried to force their way in. They were kept out and I had to stand on the footpath and use bluff and bluster to deter them from trying to come back in. They eventually left but I found the situation quite intimidating which said a lot about my attitude and history with violence.

I wasn't a fighter, nor could I pretend to be one. The idea of punching anyone was anathema to me. However, violence has a way of finding even the most innocent. I was used to getting knocked around by bigger kids on the rugby field—the higher the standard I played, the harder the knocks were. While growing up, I used to spar with the boy across the road with boxing gloves. The sparring continued into my teens, but I gave it up completely at college, after I hurt a couple of fellows in sparring sessions. Even with boxing gloves, it became a pointless exercise, so we stopped doing it altogether.

While growing up, however, fights were never far away. Some kids solved their problems by punching other kids. One day, the boy down the road took out his frustrations on me by punching me in the head. I didn't respond and proved an easy target. I didn't have a violent bone in my body and tended to believe others didn't either. In primary school, I was bullied by some of my mates, so I solved that problem one day by taking on one of the bullies after school, while he was on his own. It stopped after that, because we were basically all mates, and it was just a passing phase. Standing up for myself no doubt helped as well.

In high school, though, some of the older boys would punch younger kids for no reason other than being looked at. I escaped a belting one day by ignoring a bully when he tried to have a go at me on the way to assembly. Some would have stopped and had a go, but I left all my aggression on the football field, and it would have taken a lot to provoke a response from me. I hated the randomness of violence—someone who was angry or had a bad day. Violence could explode for no rhyme or reason, usually on the most unfortunate.

Two instances I remember, though, show how easy it is to be caught up in a violent confrontation.

Like most schools, we had boys who hated authority figures, whether those figures were teachers or prefects. I took my role as a prefect seriously and became disliked by a certain section of boys. One afternoon, when I was waiting to catch a bus home, two fellows approached me. One, who no longer went to the school, swore at me, while the other just looked on and grinned. He continued to swear at me and dared me to fight him. My response was to ignore him as I waited for the bus. I did not look at him either, as that would have been taken as a challenge, and I wasn't an angry ant who could explode and tear into someone—and I needed to do so, if I had any chance of beating him. I was shaken when I got on the bus, still ignoring the abuse behind me and wondering whether I was too smart to fight or just afraid to. The next day, I found out what one of his mates thought when he asked me, "Why didn't you fight him?" I felt that the measure of a person was in what he did in life and not how he used his fists, but that obviously was not the prevailing attitude among certain types. Anger didn't come easy to me, and I did not have to battle to suppress it, as my Christian faith was one of a peaceful disposition.

The other instance happened at college. I was at the Wagga show on my own when one of our girls told me that a couple of college fellows had been picked on by townies and needed help. I raced down to where people were milling around and where there'd obviously been a fight. Bill was holding his jaw, and Henry was supporting him, while some ag college students who had intervened were off to one side. I found myself standing between Bill and Henry and the four townies, who towered over me and were standing menacingly close. I was concerned as to what might happen next and pondered whether I should hit the biggest one and try to break his nose, or stand there and hope some of our college fellows would turn up and even up the numbers. It seemed like ages but was probably only seconds until two uniformed policemen arrived, and the heat was taken out of the situation, and the four townies quickly disappeared.

The incident highlighted my attitude to violence. I wasn't a violent person, although I played a sport that could be violent. As long as there were rules and I knew what to expect, I could cope and use an appropriate amount of aggression, but if it was a random act with no sense to it, and there was no control over it, I found that situation quite unsettling. I liked order and to me, violence was an affront to order. It took a lot to provoke me, and while I could leave all my aggression on the football field, random acts like I had just witnessed were disturbing. Just as disturbing was whatever was going behind the uncaring, callous looks in the perpetrators' eyes.

At the end of the year, a busload of us went up to Narrandera School for our first prac (practice teaching session.) My first meeting with the principal was not very auspicious. He asked our supervising lecturer if I combed my hair with my fingers. That was duly passed on to me as a mild rebuke. Although it was true, in a last moment of spit-and- polish before getting off the bus, I thought it was a pretty ordinary comment for him to make about someone on his first prac who he didn't know. No doubt it was related to dress standards in the school.

I was placed in an affable teacher's fifth class, along with an affable fellow from my dormitory, Geoff Goodfellow, a Narrandera local. Being young, athletic, and full of energy brought a positive response from the children, who were just as excited at having their usual dose of student teachers as we were of having our first face-to-face contact with them as "teachers." Our previous contact with children had been through our weekly trips to Turvey Park (and once to Lake Albert) Demonstration Schools, where we would sit around the back, watching teachers teach and manage their classes. Afterward, we would discuss the particular lesson with the teacher and our lecturer, while writing down anything that seemed important.

I was confident about my teaching ability, despite having some remedial work on my enunciation. When we acted as lifesavers at the school swimming carnival on Lake Talbot, I received hero status among the giggling girls for diving in and helping a struggling young swimmer back to the pool edge. It was easy to be flattered by their attention, but there was always a danger that things could go too far, especially as we were all scantily clad in our swimming costumes. On one occasion, I had to quickly move a fifth-class girl when she suddenly plonked herself down on my lap. Her actions were innocent but certainly not appropriate.

Despite that, the swimming carnival was one of the highlights of our four weeks at Narrandera School, but overall, the whole experience—even the hour's trip in the coach, where we'd drop off and pick up student teachers at Collingullie and Kywong Schools—was enjoyable.

Now with exams finished and first prac over, it was time for our end-of-the-year ball, and I was going with a girl I was hoping to get to know a lot better than I already did.

Early in the year, I had noticed Julie on a college bus tour of Wagga. All I knew about her was that she was from Wagga, and she had a beautiful smile. She was a Christian too, so by the end of the year, I had gotten to know her a bit, and we had gone out a few times. She told me about a fellow she had known through high school and that he didn't like her going out with me. She said she told him it was her choice, which sounded to me like she was trying to break up with him. We used to talk about church matters—her particular concern being the animosity between people in her church, when church should have been a place where people were united by their love of Jesus.

I had a good feeling about Julie—she was a girl with strong Christian beliefs who I respected and wanted to get to know better. I met her parents and invited her to the end-of-year college ball. On the Friday night, I picked her up from her home and we walked back to the hall where the ball was being held. As the evening wore on, it was obvious she had something on her mind. We walked back to her place afterward and talked, despite it being early Saturday morning. She told me her friend was upset that she was going out with me and that he had gone off the rails. She didn't say she had strong feelings for him, so her concern seemed to be more about his welfare than about matters of the heart. We parted on a good note and later that day, I was on a train with the other students, heading back to Sydney for the Christmas holidays.

We wrote to each other during the break, and everything seemed fine. Her tone was bright and friendly when she wrote about the things she was doing on a family holiday to Melbourne. After that letter, I looked forward to seeing her again when college resumed.

The week before Christmas, Bob and Jenelle were married in Canberra, and I was Bob's best man. I trotted out my one and only suit, which I had worn the previous week to the ball. Jenelle had finished college and would be teaching in town until the birth of their first child, my goddaughter, Kerrie, while Bob continued at the college but quite naturally not as my roomie neighbor. They rented a flat out the back of a house between town and college, close enough to both and for my regular visits.

Back home for the summer, I reacquainted myself with the beach and, belatedly, Manly Cricket Club. After one lower-grade match, I was surprised to find myself selected to play for Manly's Poidevin Grey Shield side as the opening bowler. It was a competition for grade players under twenty-one and held over the Christmas period while the grade cricket was in recess. You could find yourself playing against state or even international cricketers on one hand or humble lower-grade players on the other, such was the range of abilities found in the grade cricket ranks. I always felt like an outsider at Manly because I wasn't a party person, preferring to go home after matches rather than going back to the club to socialize with officials and other players. I knew I had only been selected because the first- choice opening bowler, a precocious talent, was in the West Indies with the Australian schoolboys side, so I had to make the most of my opportunity.

In our first match, we played against Northern Districts. I batted last but still contributed a quick twenty, which included hitting the opening bowler back over the sight board for six, when he was brought on to knock over a tail ender. In the next match, I tripled my tally of sixes by hitting two out of Manly Oval. The one on the bowling green next door was pretty unspectacular, while the other was low and flat, over the fence and hit the concrete wall that ran around the north side of the ground on the full. Not so successful was my bowling, as a pattern was set early. If I didn't pick up wickets in the first few overs, then that's all I was given for the rest of the match. I found this difficult to understand, as captains had looked to me as their main bowler, and their encouragement and support brought out the best in me. I thrived on responsibility, but it didn't happen with Manly. The captain, a fellow I'd played against over the years, was unsupportive, ready to discard if he didn't get immediate results, and without a clue as to how best use me. One of the frustrations I had was in knowing I was up to that level, even though I wasn't a naturally hard-nosed competitor.

However, the right approach by captain (or coach) could get the best out of me, as happened the following year, when I was selected to play rugby for New South Wales (NSW) Country. If I felt it was worth it. I knew I could match it with the best, and playing rugby for Country was definitely worth it. Still, I did get an opportunity from the selectors, which I didn't make the most of, much like that 200-meter race a few years before, and for that, there was no one to blame but me.

Toward the end of the holidays, I passed my driver's test and finally got my license. Now I could drive legally. I used it when I came back for my brother's wedding a few months later and drove his Volkswagen from the church in Sydney up to Emily's family home at

Beecroft for the reception. Emily's father was a university professor, so my father was quite taken with Geoffrey's social elevation, despite the fact that the professor thought Geoffrey was "just a policeman."

A few weeks after the school year commenced, I had a two-week home prac at my old school on Collaroy Plateau. It was an obligatory infants prac, so I was assigned to second class with a group of young children who were excited by the prospect of having a male teacher, even though it was brief. It was the same room I remembered being in when I was in second class, and very little had changed. The teacher was a very competent and most engaging young lady. She was supportive and made my time there both enjoyable and productive, as I picked up a number of clues from her that I used in my own teaching career. I had a good relationship with everyone, and we were all sad when my two weeks were up. During the year, I had a nice card from her and the children and was able to visit them during my next holidays.

CHAPTER 5

Second Year at Wagga Teachers College

I commenced my second year at college with a crew cut. It wasn't by design, nor was it a fashion statement—no, I had to get one from the barber to even up the holes I left in my hair when I cut it with a "hair magician." First day back, I tried to sneak into the dining room for lunch but had just made it past the door when it seemed the whole student body noticed my crew cut. Red-faced, I waltzed past grinning lecturers at the official table and found a seat, to a background of laughter. The following days saw lots of head patting, feigned impalement on the spiky ends, and profound impatience from me as I waited for my hair to grow out.

I was looking forward to seeing Julie again, so second day back, I bowled up to her and spirited her away from her girlfriends, who gave me stern looks. I assumed everything was fine between us after the letters and her flippant remark about my hair, but when we were alone, her reticence led me to ask if anything was wrong. She said she had come to an understanding with her boyfriend and had agreed not to go out with me again. I felt sick in the stomach, and my first inclination was to demand an explanation and then try to talk her around, but instead, I said nothing. Their relationship had a history I didn't understand, nor did I know what had been said between them after she had come back from Melbourne. I could see that she was upset and to question her, though understandable, would have prolonged her pain. And achieved what? It would have hurt a girl I really liked in possibly a vain attempt to change her mind about a relationship where I was the interloper. I had no time for the brash types who cut in on other fellows' girlfriends. I thought they were selfish and showed no concern for the feelings of the boyfriend and no respect for the girl. Now, when confronted with a not dissimilar situation, I felt it was wrong to try to talk her around. She had made her decision, so all I could do was respect it, walk away, and have another little heartbreak. But life would go on. A door had just closed on anything between us, as we could never be just "friends."

That's how I saw affairs of the heart—when it was over, it was over, so move on and stop getting in the way. And that's how it was. After that day, I saw Julie around the college, but I never spoke to her again. And over the next few weeks, the pain softened, and life went on.

With that little drama over, I returned to the cricket field on the following Saturday with Lake Albert. During the time I'd been away, Lake's best batsman had been transferred away, and Jack had relocated to Bathurst Teachers College, and they had not done well. The captain was pleased to have me back and let me know how important I was to the team. We had one chance of making the finals and that was by winning the next match at Gissing Oval. It was close, but in the end, it all came down to the last three wickets of the match. If we could take them, we'd win and make the finals. Lose or draw, and we didn't. With three wickets to get, the captain brought me back on for one last attempt to win the match. I soon had two wickets in two balls, but my hat-trick ball was met by a dead bat. One ball flew through slips for four, and the last two were blocked. Match drawn, because I couldn't pick up that last wicket that would have won us the match. I was disappointed and felt I'd let the team down, but our captain reminded me that they had lost matches while I was back in Sydney, which they should have won and which would have made all the last-minute heroics unnecessary. I appreciated his words and looked forward to helping the team make up for the disappointing result when the new season started in October.

I was soon back into college life, lectures, ball games on the "jerks'" court, dances in the gym, football trials, and a pretty consistent social life. Despite all this, however, there were times when I felt very lonely. I would often go for long walks on my own, wondering why I felt that way. For the two years I was there, mushy sentimental songs would reverberate up and down the hallway of the dorm, nurturing the romantic loner in me, who flitted between the world of macho footballers and gentle Christians but didn't feel totally at home in either. The fact is, I didn't like the drinking, party culture, nor was I totally at peace with the wimpy side of Christianity. My faith in God was real, but the actual flavor I was comfortable with elusive.

Our college Christian fellowship group had its numbers increased by first-year arrivals. One weekend, we had a retreat down near Tumut, and I found myself admiring two Sydney girls, Marie and her friend Sarah. Marie was a statuesque blonde—pretty and vivacious. Sarah was dark-haired and quiet, with lovely, smoky eyes. I was attracted to Sarah and after some time, it became apparent they were both attracted to me. Marie was the stronger personality of the two, but when I was near Sarah, I could feel something bubbling along between us. One night, a group of us was sitting at a table at the Way Inn when Lenny, a fellow college student, started making asides about a situation where two girls liked the same fellow. As I was sitting next to both Marie and Sarah, it was obvious to all who he was referring to. I ignored what he said and said nothing. I enjoyed both girls' company, but I hadn't thought our relationships any more than friendly.

I continued my creative writing course with a new lecturer, as Jack gave way to Jock. Jack had taken up a position in Bathurst and was lost to our group, the cricket team, and to me, personally, as a mentor and a friend. I really missed him, and although Jock was an able replacement, Jack had brought a special passion to the course we all missed, especially in our studies of Ernest Hemingway's literature.

With cricket over, out came our rugby boots and our rightful place in the senior competition. We had a strong college team and could easily have been premiers, if not for a set of circumstances. I played fullback for the firsts and had good moments on the field, scoring tries and kicking goals, including one out of a gluepot in the center of the cricket ground, which won us the match against Wagga City. My form was good enough to earn selection in the Riverina team for country week, an annual competition for country regions, held at the TG Milner Field in Eastwood. A week before country week, I hurt my left shoulder in a match against Waratahs. We had an easy win and although my shoulder was bruised and quite sore, I wasn't going to let it stop me from playing at country week. We only had three matches played over three days to show off our talents to the country selectors, so it was important to make the most of every opportunity that came our way.

Our first game was almost my last. Early in the match, the opposition team's center slipped past our center and ran toward me, with his winger outside him in support. It was a simple case of draw me and send the winger away for a try. We both knew what was on, so I waited until the center was sure he had drawn me, and I was sure he was going to pass the ball. At the last moment, I changed direction and dived sideways, and grabbed hold of the winger with my left hand, just as he was about to scoot away for a try. I remember hearing an "ooh!" from the spectators as we both crashed to the ground. Unfortunately, in the process of bringing him down, I wrenched my sore shoulder and had to leave the field and, as I thought, the tournament. A doctor examined it and told me it wasn't dislocated and that I should be able to play again in two or three weeks.

After the final match of the day, I was deposited at Eastwood Station to find my own way home to Collaroy Plateau, where I had opted to stay, rather than with the team at the motel. There, I would tell my father he wouldn't need to drive me over to watch our last two matches, because I wouldn't be playing. Fortunately, we knew a chiropractor with whom my sister had worked. After a hurried phone call, he treated me the next day and then surprised me by saying that my shoulder would be sore for a few days, but it wouldn't stop me from playing on Sunday, if I really wanted to. Playing with pain never bothered me, so I rang the motel where the Riverina team was staying and told our manager I was fit to play. He told me that as we'd lost again on Saturday, we'd be playing the first match of the day out of the picture and, as I thought, out of the sight of the selectors.

Just before I left the chiropractor, he asked me if I had suffered any hard blows to my back. I remembered that tackle the year before I went to college, as he went on to say that some of the vertebrae in the center of my back had been depressed, so if I was to have any back trouble in the future, it would be in that area. I had forgotten his words the next day as I arrived at the ground in time for our eleven o'clock start. As luck would have it, no winger had shown anything special, so when I got my one chance, the only time I got hold of the ball all week, I tucked it under my left arm, took off upfield, and ran forty yards, almost to their try line. I didn't score but apparently when the country selectors were selecting the country teams, they remembered that one run—and thankfully, not that injury—and selected me in the Country Seconds side.

A few weeks later, when I came back to Sydney with the country team, I didn't go home but stayed with the team at the old Manly Hotel, overlooking Manly Beach. We had a young side, trained under our coach on Tuesday, and thrashed Combined Sydney Second Division at Manly Oval on an overcast Wednesday—the very ground where I had smacked two sixes for Manly just a few months earlier. I was surprised to see my old schoolmate Rod Macqueen turn out for the opposition but not surprised at his wholehearted play in a well- beaten side. My father was hovering around, as usual, and happened to be at the right spot to take a photo of me scooting over for a try in the corner.

We trained together with the firsts (who had just played Victoria in their warm-up match) for the next two days, before playing against Sydney at North Sydney Oval on Saturday. Sydney had a number of state and former test players on their side, but we had youth, passion, and future Wallabies on ours. We also had Daryl Harberecht, a popular and inspiring coach, who a few years later coached the Australian Wallabies.

We were up for it that day and beat a complacent Sydney team quite comfortably. I had a hand in our first try and was satisfied with my general play (especially my full-blooded tackle on their bulky representative winger). I felt I had measured up to that standard of football and that it had brought out the best in me. I was encouraged by Daryl's comments after the match, when he said I hadn't made any mistakes, so the selectors wouldn't forget me.

As we were leaving the field at the completion of our match, I saw one of the boy wonders who had kept me out of the CHS team a few years before, on the sideline as a reserve for Sydney. I allowed myself a satisfied smile as I walked past him. The only downer to the afternoon came when our first team couldn't continue the good work of the seconds and our under-eighteens and were well beaten by Sydney Firsts, who featured a number of Australian players in their ranks, as well as a few who I'd played against in high school three years earlier.

A somewhat amusing sidelight to the week was played out when I asked the college principal for the week off (after committing in writing not to get behind in my college work) to carry out my country "duties" —that is, train on Tuesday, play Wednesday, prepare for the next match on Thursday and Friday, and then play against Sydney on Saturday. *Quite simple*, I thought but not according to our college principal. He gave me guarded permission, but in the letter, he delivered a little homily about how he had been somewhere, doing something one day, came back to Wagga for two days to shuffle papers around his desk, and then went back to somewhere to resume doing something another day. Then, he added in his letter, "Do you see the point I'm making?" I did. He was obviously alluding to the fact I should have considered coming back to college for Thursday and Friday before finding my way back to Sydney to play on Saturday and not presume to automatically have been granted leave to stay in Sydney for the two days between matches. I thought his point was ridiculous. I wasn't the first college student to be selected to play for country, so I assumed he shared the same homily with them as well. Besides, there was no point in even considering coming back, as I was required to train with the team on Thursday and Friday. When I showed his letter to my college rugby coach, he just rolled his eyes.

The drinking culture at college was an unfortunate product of fun-loving boys living close together, many away from home for the first time and with little world experience to fall back on. I would occasionally go up to Turvey Tavern, the traditional college drinking hole, for a drink—

usually a lemon squash—and a game or two of pool, and then go back to college. But quite a few of the fellows had almost taken up residence there and stayed and drank until closing time. It was quite common for drunken students to come back from Turvey Tavern, singing at the top of their voices and stirring up the wardens and most certainly Cecil, the night watchman. My early observation—that after the initial freedom of first year, everyone would knuckle down and drink in moderation— proved false. They drank solidly for two years, and some extended their two-year course into three years.

Two alcohol-fuelled instances come to mind. The first was at our SRC president's bucks party, downtown at the Federal. The fellows went with the intention of drinking all night and blow the consequences. There were only two who stayed sober. I was one, and Bob was the other. I had the task of being a good roomie and helping a highly inebriated roommate back to college and the safety of our room. It took more than two hours to get back and included many comfort stops on the way. Obviously, Ross and most of the fellows there were completely wiped out on Sunday. Bob, like me, drank lemonade and then had to ferry carloads of drunken students back to college. Next morning, as a "reward" for his efforts, he had to clean all the dried vomit off the side of his car.

The second instance was my only incursion into the drinking culture, one Friday night at Romano's. At college, I was seen as a "wowser"—a non-drinking, church-going, football-playing wowser. So it was somewhat of a surprise for the fellows to see me at Romano's after football one Saturday night, ready to sink a few with them. I had half a dozen middies that night, which for me was quite a lot, so when I was happily tipsy and felt I'd had enough, I walked back to the college with Ross. I felt fine on the way, invigorated by the cold night air, but by the time we were near the college, the world had become a very strange place. I had just about made the front door of the dorm when I made a sudden detour to the college rose garden instead, where I was violently sick. Then it was into the shower, where I was sick again and again, and although it didn't purge my soul, it certainly purged my stomach of everything I'd eaten that evening. During my shower moment, I was heard to mutter over and over, "I'm never going to do this again." Not my proudest moment.

Next morning, my head throbbed and my stomach protested, but I did what I thought I should and went down to the football ground for a Riverina squad training session. However, my fellow drinkers didn't, as they were back in their dorms with hangovers and still in bed. I wasn't too sure what God thought of it all, although "serves you right" would have been appropriate.

Life went on in the outside world and mostly passed us by. I used to get a Sydney newspaper from Smithy's tuckshop each day and vaguely remember reading about the Apollo 13 mission, when the astronauts were almost lost in space. Nothing outside the confines of our small world at Wagga seemed all that important, while the Vietnam War was relegated in importance as to whether your marble dropped and you were conscripted, rather than body counts and the anti-war activism going on in Sydney and around the country. Ron's mother came to visit him at college and made her opposition to the war known to us, as well as her involvement in the anti-war Save Our Sons movement.

We, though, were a conservative lot. Our wildest political statement was a protest march down Baylis Street in response to some less- than-reliable information from a representative of the teachers federation about the government supposedly meddling with our pay. For the locals, it was all a bit of fun, as we marching, chanting, banner-waving college students had our moment of significance before slinking back to college with nothing achieved and to the locals' collective yawns.

Afterward, I regretted participating in the march, not because we were duped (which we found out later we were) or that a gung-ho "let's have a party anyway" attitude prevailed, but because I let myself be led by others, when my instincts told me not to go. I was reminded of that later when Lesley, one of the girls in our Christian fellowship group, commented that the only ones who didn't march were the Christians. At the time, I had felt that if someone with a suspect political agenda came down from Sydney and spun you a tale, believing him was not a particularly smart thing to do. But in spite of that, I still followed the crowd and joined the party, completely ignoring my conviction that as future teachers, we shouldn't get caught up in issues that were politically driven. Once credibility is lost, it's hard to regain. The march of no justification didn't do anything for our credibility or for our social standing as trainee teachers. Instead, it showed we took our own self-interest far too seriously.

Mid-year took me to Temora for our winter prac. I was assigned to fourth class with another student and again had a great time with the children. Their teacher was the school principal and, unfortunately, had his son in the class—unfortunately, because the teacher/principal favored his son too much, always getting him to answer questions and encouraging a certain superior air in him. His son even tried to correct me one time when I was teaching the class so I had to quietly explain to him why he, the student, was wrong, and I, the student teacher, was right. Apart from that, I enjoyed my time in what was another well-run country school. Each day, I looked forward to getting on the bus outside the Dame Mary Gilmore gates on College Avenue for the one-hour trip to Temora. My briefcase was bulging with my observation book, lesson preparation book, writing equipment, and—important—lunch packed for us by the ladies in the college kitchen. No lamb chops, just fat, healthy sandwiches.

While there, we introduced the kids to a ball game we played at college called "jerks." They took to it as country kids do and showed their appreciation by playing it at every break while we were there. I thoroughly enjoyed being part of their lives and felt my teaching skills and confidence growing with each lesson I taught. And all the while, I was learning the importance of taking my time, and preparing well, and not wasting any opportunity to become a better teacher.

It was quite amazing that Ross and I got on so well—as I've mentioned, we were such opposites. We both, however, were pretty easygoing types and there was a blokey sort of chemistry between us. Although we had some epic wrestles, we rarely had disagreements. Together, we could act like dorks, such as the times we lay in our beds until five minutes before our first lecture, grinning at each other. Then one of us would say, "Now!" Then we'd dive out of our beds, throw on some clothes in a minute flat, grab our lecture notes, and race off to our first lecture, slowing on the way to run silly lines through the fog and arriving just in time to be acceptably late. We were just big kids, but we looked out for each other, sympathized with each other for at least five minutes after any heartbreak, and did distinction science together, which led to our meeting with Celeste, my girlfriend for much of the second half of the year.

It all happened quite by accident, I think. I had noticed her waiting to be picked up by her bus as we headed off in ours for prac teaching at Temora. (She later told me that's when she noticed me.) Our science lecturer had told us a girl named Celeste was doing distinction science as well, so she would be working with us. We met her at the airport at Forest Hill one cold day, where Ross and I were waiting to do our thing. Our "thing" consisted of sending up a weather balloon to record changes in temperature at different heights and then writing them down and making a big deal about the results. Not particularly hard. When Celeste joined us, we were both taken by her good humor, her enthusiasm, and her friendly attitude. We thoroughly enjoyed working with her.

After taking measurements, we adjourned back to college, only to have to take more measurements on the college football ground the following week, on a freezing-cold day. The only warm thing about the day was Celeste's good humor and her hands, which she rubbed furiously against ours and endeared herself to us by warming them up. Ross and I both agreed she was a good sport as well as being good sort.

I wasn't going out with anyone when Marie asked me to take her to the college Winter Ball, so I did. We had an enjoyable night, and Marie was good company. Later at the ball, they held the Miss Teachers College competition, so we got up, paraded up and down, and then went back to our table. I was a bit surprised when she was crowned Miss Teachers College, so we got up again, paraded up and down again, and then went back to our table. I found it all a bit amusing, but when it came to beauty and brains, Marie certainly stood out from the rest.

The situation, however, became a bit tense between Marie and Sarah when I took off with Sarah one night after church. Having our hands in the sink together, as we washed and dried the dishes after a young peoples' function, was a bit too tempting, so we sneaked out and went down the train line and into the tunnel for a kiss and a cuddle. "We shouldn't be doing this," Sarah kept saying as we continued doing this. Marie was furious when I walked Sarah back to their flat afterward. When I later asked Sarah how Marie was, I was left with the impression that I was coming between two good friends. What had been an innocent—albeit brief—romantic interlude with Sarah had suddenly become more complicated and was threatening to have a negative impact on relationships within the college Christian fellowship group—not a good situation. So I did the only thing I could think of and I backed away from both of them.

I continued my interest in music by joining the cast for our college production of *Trial by Jury*. It surprised the director, Noel Harper, our music lecturer, when he saw me at rehearsals and realized I was serious about music. Even Ross was interested—my flawed membership in the CHS choir had seriously impressed Ross, but he was not Noel's favorite student. Still, when he saw Ross's unique acting ability in the revue, he asked me to get Ross for the jury—as long as he didn't try to sing. That left everyone happy, although Noel was still a bit doubtful after the experience of seeing the college choir disgrace itself in the Civic Theatre earlier that year. Most took the musicale seriously, but a number of the lads in the bass section turned up drunk. They stood out in the back row, and then kept disappearing off the back of the stage as their intoxicated state became too much for them to handle. I heard about it later because thankfully, I wasn't there that night—I was away playing football somewhere else, as usual.

I went to the first few rehearsals with other cast members of the chorus and was assured by Noel that the principals had all been selected. He spoke glowingly of the girl who would be Angelina, so I was looking forward to hearing her sing. *She'll have to be good to match Nicola*, I thought.

The whole cast turned up for a rehearsal, and I was surprised to see that Celeste was cast as Angelina. When she sang, I could see why. She had a pure, though not overly strong, soprano voice and a good feel for comedy. We renewed our friendship, and after rehearsals, I walked her back to the house where she was staying on College Road. We rabbited on like old friends each night, and I soon found myself enjoying her company once again. I hadn't thought of our being anything but friends until one night, when I said good night, she gave me a punch on the arm. That seemed to be an invitation for something more than a handshake, so I thought a good-night kiss was in order. After that night, there were a lot of good-night kisses as we began a fairly private relationship. And that's how I liked it—a no- pressure secret girlfriend.

She invited me down to Albury one weekend to meet her parents and be squired around by her longtime "boyfriend." I don't know what she told him about me, but he acted like he owned her, and I was just a college friend. I wondered if he thought all we did was study together. It was all a bit bizarre but I thought, *Just be cool about it. After all, we are in Albury.*

Despite being a lovely Christian girl, Marie just didn't spin my wheels like Sarah did. Call it lack of chemistry, but with her looks and personality, she should have had no end of suitors, so why she liked me, I had no idea. I heard she was upset that I was going out with Celeste now, so her confidant and go-between, my English lecturer and fellow godparent to Kerrie, asked me to be her escort for the Miss South West pageant. Apparently, her other suitors didn't cut the mustard. When I agreed to take Marie, Celeste became a bit upset, so I had to visit her in my hired suit before picking up Marie, just to placate her. I found affairs of the heart just a bit confusing.

Marie stood out from all the other girls, and like our college representative from the previous year, she was crowned Miss South West. And why shouldn't she be? She was smart, pretty, and had a sparkling personality. And I was her escort again. A photo in the *Advertiser* of our victory parade showed a confident, photo-friendly beauty, with a grinning, dorky-looking escort. I always knew I took a pretty ordinary photo—if it was natural, I was fine, but if I had to pose, then it was dreadful. This one was dreadful, although not as bad as the blushing self-conscious dolts who staggered past the camera before us. What it didn't show, though, was a panicky girl clutching my arm, moments before the photo, as I whispered words of encouragement into her ear.

She was a bundle of nerves before that, but when the cameras were on her, she metamorphosed into Miss Confident and took a fine photo.

As Miss South West, Marie's next task was to go up to Sydney to represent the district in the Miss New South Wales pageant. She asked me to be her escort but thankfully, that proved unnecessary. I wasn't disappointed to find out that all the regional winners would be provided with escorts for the occasion, so I wouldn't be required.

The actual occasion turned out to be a bit of an anticlimax for Marie. She told me later that the contestants were all but ignored by the officials, as most of the attention was heaped on the favorite, whose subsequent crowning as Miss New South Wales surprised no one. I was still romancing Celeste at that stage, so my relationship with Marie (and Sarah) continued to cool like a fire going out after it had burned up all its fuel.

The week before *Trial*, we played against Cootamundra. I had been moved to outside center to mark Peter, my country teammate. We had played our parts in our victory over Sydney a few weeks earlier, but now we were on opposite sides, so I wasn't expecting any love from Peter. I was, though, looking forward to making amends for the previous match, when I dropped five easy high balls at full back, and they scored four tries from them. It happened before halftime and pretty well put us out of the match. The fact we were playing the match on little sleep after the college winter ball was a factor but did not excuse my shoddy display. We won the second half, though, and although I was able to gallop seventy yards through their team to score our only try, it didn't make up for damage done in the first half. This match was going to be my redemption, but it didn't turn out that way.

It was early in the match, and we were just inside their half. I remember turning to watch the ball being floated slowly toward me by our inside center. The ball was still on its way when I was hit in the face and went down like a sack of potatoes. Unfortunately, my body twisted, and my leg stayed rigid when my sprigs got stuck in the ground. I was soon up again, but when I tried to run, I couldn't, as I had a badly damaged ankle. Clearly, I had to leave the field, and our coach came on and replaced me. He was livid at what had happened to me and spent the rest of the match smashing into anyone wearing a Cootamundra jersey.

After the match, we went back to the club, but I wouldn't speak to my mate, and by the time we got back to Wagga Hospital, my ankle was badly swollen, and I couldn't put any weight on it. The X-ray showed no breaks, but the ligaments were torn away from the bone. The treatment was basic: a tight elastic bandage and crutches and nothing else. That pretty well finished my representative career, as the ligaments were so badly damaged, I was never again able to run like I used to run.

Six weeks later, I was selected to play for Country against New Zealand Services in Wagga, despite my less-than-robust ankle. It was a memorable match for me, but not in a way I cared to remember. I gave my opposing winger two tries—one when he fell on the ball I mis-kicked from behind our try line, and the other when I ran through a gap in the New Zealander's defense and headed downfield for a glorious, outstanding, unbelievable runaway try. Unfortunately, one of our forwards was lagging behind the play, so when I ran past him, he called out to me to pass him the ball—and stupidly, I did. My pass sailed over his head and lobbed straight into the arms of my opposing winger. With all our players running one way, all he had to do was catch the ball and run the other way and score his second— and what I thought a most undeserved—try. At least the ground had been softened by rain, so I didn't cause any further damage to my ankle. Then, after the match at the reception, I had a conversation with a country official, which was of some importance to me, as it concerned my first appointment after graduating from college.

My ankle was still tender when I played for College in the preliminary final some weeks later. I was unable to stretch out, when another seventy-yard try would have won us the match. The ankle felt weak and loose, and I felt like I was running on one leg. When I tried to accelerate, there was no strength in it, so the chance was missed, and the match was lost to a weaker ag college team.

During the week after my injury, doors were opened for me and equipment was carried, as the girls (not the fellows) rose to the occasion, while I hobbled around the college on crutches. Their many kindnesses were touching, but Noel looked mortified when I turned up to our opening night of *Trial by Jury* on crutches. However, the night went well, despite our judge forgetting a complete verse— he remembered it on the second night. The review in the *Advertiser* was positive, albeit from a college lecturer, and a lively jury provided some comic relief. My crutches came in handy as we devised an amusing little routine (in our eyes, anyway) to compensate for my injury. It got a few laughs, but through both nights, Celeste acted her socks off and, like her namesake instrument, sang like an angel.

After the final show, a few of us decided to go downtown to celebrate. Unfortunately, Celeste's Albury buddy had come up for the show. As we were waiting to get into Bob's car, he hung around and wouldn't go away. I didn't think our celebration was any of his business, so I told him, "I'm taking Celeste out, so see you later," or words to that effect. I naively expected him to do the right thing, but he didn't. Instead, he piled into the front seat next to her, leaving me to get into the back with the others. For the rest of the night I fumed as we sat in the Mari, drinking cups of tea and eating raisin toast. It didn't occur to me that I was acting like a sook. Instead, I felt aggrieved that he had committed the unforgivable sin of not respecting my rights to Celeste in Wagga. I fully believed she had explained the situation to him and that he would keep out of the way, but instead, he hung around like the pest he was—although since he had outsmarted me, I was the one who was probably the pest. The next day, I complained to Bob, expecting his rock-solid support, but all he said was, "What did you expect? Celeste doesn't know where she stands with you." That revelation stunned me somewhat and brought our secret relationship to an end. What had happened that night was apparently my fault, as was my somewhat naive miscalculation that our relationship could exist entirely within my comfort zone. Now, it had been brought out into the open, and there was no way of avoiding it.

The confluence of Celeste's previous life in Albury, mine in Sydney, and ours at Wagga left me with a decision that I didn't want to make—did I feel strongly enough about her to take our relationship to the next level and see where it led? The complication was that the other fellow thought he was her boyfriend. As for me, I didn't have a muse back home and didn't believe in running two motors at the same time anyway. In the back of my mind was my usual question: "What do I feel about her, and could I spend the rest of my life with her?" On top of that, I didn't realize how deep his feelings for her were, as Celeste hadn't said much about him or expressed any great regard for him. But the events on that night brought it all to a head and made it impossible to go back to where we were, because our secret relationship was a secret no more. So it was with some reluctance that I told Celeste I was willing to give it a go, knowing that her feelings for me were stronger than mine were for her. Maybe I could change.

In the end, she went back to Albury to tell him, and he was upset, she was upset, they both cried bucketsful, and I felt like a heel. I didn't think it was really Celeste's fault, as I was pretty new to the "three's a crowd" thing, but I did wonder, *Why all the drama?*

I knew if I was going to see another fellow's heart broken, it had to be for a pretty good reason and not just because of a fling that could flame out after a few weeks when I got my usual cold feet. I had to put all thoughts of where this could lead behind me and just see what unfolded. It meant Celeste could move on as well and gave him a chance to do the same. As for me, I found it scary, as I'd have to let someone into my life. I wouldn't be alone, but I was still a loner who tended to keep things, especially feelings, to himself.

During the spring break, instead of spending her time back in Albury, Celeste came up to Sydney, ostensibly to see her brother but in reality to see me and join me for my twenty-first. My brother and his wife took us to the Gap Tavern for dinner and we both had an enjoyable evening. (It cost forty dollars, so unlike Wagga, where similar meals would have cost five.)

As Celeste had use of a car, we spent the next few days together at home and down at Long Reef, enjoying the view from the headland and wandering up and down the beach. It was such a relaxing time—no pressure and just the two of us. I watched as Celeste splashed around in the Long Reef surf with that same abandon and excitement she had shown Ross and me on that cold day at Wagga.

What I soon realized about Celeste was that our relationship wasn't just a fling for her; it was more serious than that. She had strong feelings for me, she cared for me, had faith in me, and thought I was a good person. She was idealistic about "us," quoting a well-known line from *Love Story* to make her point, as well as singing lines from "A Man without Love" or "When I Fall in Love" as her way of expressing her feelings for me. She waited for words of affection from me, but they never came, and all I ever called her was Celeste, retreating from using pet names that would have caused me to lie. I knew she had touched me deeper than any girl I'd known, and although I wanted a relationship with someone, as the weeks passed, I felt at twenty-one that it wasn't now—and Celeste wasn't the one. As much as I liked her, I didn't love her, but I did respect her and would never use her or do anything to hurt her.

Over time, Celeste perceived my doubts. When we talked about it— something I never instigated, because I was uncomfortable, to say the least, with having to open up in areas I didn't really understand— I would say, "I do like you," and she would give me an unconvinced look and say, "You do, but you don't." The L word was never mentioned, but it seems it was always on her mind. Celeste would say to me, "You know how I feel about you," and leave it at that, but I found I couldn't respond in kind. It's not a word I was ever going to use lightly, nor was I in love. Maybe I just liked having her around and appreciated her qualities, without having to make a public display of it. Our relationship had reached the point where it could go either way, and I wasn't sure if I wanted—or was even ready for—it to go any further. So we broke up, and Celeste was in no way to blame. I was all the better for knowing her. Even after we broke up, she felt she needed to reassure me that she still cared for me.

The day before returning to Sydney, I found a letter from Celeste on the letters' noticeboard. I rarely looked at the noticeboard even though it was next to the dining room, so when I read it, I went straight over to her place and found her sunning herself in the backyard. We went inside, hugged, and said good-bye. There were tears from her and regrets from me, as well as distracted thoughts about what I was going to miss out on.

Her final words were both gracious and generous. She said something to the effect that she was grateful to be part of my life—a comment I didn't think I deserved. She was a girl of quality, but I wasn't the one for her. She wasn't beautiful, but there was a beauty about her. When she smiled at me, it was genuine and her eyes shone, and behind them, I could see kindness and love. Love, however, can't be forced. Although I respected her and had a deep affection for her, it wasn't enough. I asked her where she was going next year, and she said, "Broken Hill." She didn't want to be around if she knew I was still going to be in Wagga.

During second year at college, I went out with quite a number of girls, including three on our Sadie Hawkins weekend, when the girls got to ask the boys out. (It was based on Sadie Hawkins Day from the *Li'l Abner* comic strip.) Football and my involvement in another successful revue had given me a fairly high profile at college. I got on well with the girls in our creative writing group, as we often critiqued each other's work. We were a tight group, supportive of each other and each other's work, so all those positive responses boosted my confidence in relating to girls.

The Sadie Hawkins weekend brought an amusing little incident with Cecil, the night watchman and his trusty torch— (flashlight.) Cecil was known to come up to couples who were doing what couples do and shine his torch on them, or he'd sneak past the girls dorm and shine his torch through the window while claiming he had heard something suspicious.

On this occasion, I had just brought a girl back from our night out together and was about to drop her off on the Milky Way, as per college rules. Then I thought, *No way. I'm taking her up to her dorm.*

I walked her up to the front door of her dorm, gave her a good-night kiss, and was on my way back down, when Ross, who was canoodling on the Milky Way with Pauline, called out, "It's Cec! Run, roomie."

I said to myself, *So what?* And I kept walking. Soon, there were footsteps rushing up behind me as Cec caught up to me. Completely puffed out, he managed to blurt out, "I heard your mate tell you to run. It's a good thing you didn't," He was breathing hard, and after a dramatic pause, he said, "If you had, I'd a' put the torch on to you."

I tried hard to look serious, although sniggering away in my mind was, *No, no, Cecil. Anything but the torch.*

I also went out with a couple of nurses. One nice young nurse was a church girl who I asked out while visiting a college mate in hospital. I heard later she was disappointed with me and on reflection, I could understand why. I could have kicked myself when I thought about my over-the-top behavior that night (my self-confidence pendulum had swung too far the other way), and I later regretted that when I saw her again one night at the Way Inn, I didn't speak to her and apologize. I hadn't shown her enough respect, nor had I considered what her expectations about the night might have been.

The other nurse was Miranda, a night-duty sister I met during my short stay in the male medical ward of Wagga Base Hospital.

I was there as the result of another football injury. After the match against Cootamundra, I had an obvious ankle injury, but what was less obvious was that the hit to my face had caused further damage to a hematoma inside my mouth, caused by my face-first tackle the previous year. Then, a couple of months later, it became infected.

I had just been down to Albury with Celeste for the weekend to visit her parents, somewhat inconvenienced by the now enlarged hematoma. By the time we got back to college on Sunday night, my face was swollen, and when I woke up on Monday morning, I could feel it was *really* swollen. When Ross saw it, he looked horrified and then ducked next door to grab Ron. They drove me straight down to hospital, where I spent three days in male medical with an IV in my arm. Apparently, when I was admitted my face looked a real mess— very swollen and lopsided. I didn't feel so good either.

I was in an open ward with beds pushed back against the walls. I was the youngest there by about forty years, the next youngest being an unspritely sixty-year-old. One of the older fellows, who obviously had a brain injury, was in there getting treatment for some sort of infection. The nurses called him Poppy and had to lead him around the ward.

One nurse told me he had been a very successful businessman until he had a serious car accident a few years ago. And just like that, his old life was snuffed out, and now he was a shell of the person he once was. My emotions were so guarded that all I felt was that I was looking at one of life's tragic moments. I was just twenty-one and with so much ahead of me, I found it hard to empathize with someone in that condition—or understand how much he had lost.

After three days, the antibiotics had done their job, The swelling had gone down, and I was feeling much better, so late Wednesday night, while everyone was asleep, I thought I'd pay a visit to the night-duty sister at the nurses desk—Miranda, a dark-haired beauty. She was friendly, and after a short time, I went back to bed feeling better. I was bemused, though, by her comment that now that my face had gone down, she could see how good-looking I was. I didn't think the bar was set particularly high in male medical, but her comment did show me that sometimes it wasn't just the male patients who did all the checking out.

For some obscure reason, my parents drove down to Wagga to see me, expecting to find me still laid up in hospital but instead finding me back at college. They visited me there and then, seeing I was all right, they drove straight back to Sydney. I didn't fully appreciate their visit, because I didn't think being in hospital was such a big deal. Then again, I wasn't a parent.

A few weeks later, after I'd broken up with Celeste, one of the girls I knew from our fellowship group asked me if I would be willing to take one of the nurses to the hospital's Christmas ball, as she didn't have a partner. It was a strange request, so I said we should meet each other first. The nurse turned out to be Miranda, and after our initial meeting, we went out for dinner. We had dinner downtown, and the evening went well. But later, on the way back to her place, things went pear-shaped, and we had a most peculiar falling out. I had been on my best behavior—there wasn't even a hint of hand holding, so I couldn't understand what had suddenly gotten into her, unless it was her way of flirting. She said something like, "I know what you want," and "All you fellows are the same."

I had no idea what she was talking about and started to wonder if she had received a bad report about me from the other nurse I had taken out. By the time we got to her place, I headed back to college, completely nonplussed, and she headed straight through her front door. After that, there wasn't any further contact between us. I wondered if I had misread what she was saying. Girls were still too confusing for me.

After I broke up with Celeste, Robyn asked me to help her with English. Robyn was a quality girl I'd liked since first year but not in a romantic way. We became closer and better friends over the next few weeks, but although we went out once, nothing ever came of it. We were able to remain good friends and often flirted verbally with each other, but there was never any tension or pressure to take it further. By the end of the year, she started going out with an ag college student, so she was, in my eyes, forbidden territory.

College life was most enjoyable. My sometimes-hectic social life led one of the Christian lecturers (my moon-landing nemesis) to remark to my parents during their flying visit, that although he knew I was a Christian, I didn't always act like one. I wasn't sure how he expected I should act, as being a Goody Two-shoes was too repressive for me and not altogether comfortable, although I knew I wouldn't be venturing too far over to the "dark side" either. An interesting sidelight to all this occurred when my mother swapped stories with the lecturer's wife Margaret, and discovered she had been Margaret's Sunday school teacher back at Petersham Baptist Church in the 1930s.

Still, I enjoyed going down to the Baptist church for the Sunday night service, which was more youth-oriented. Although I was never going to compromise my Christian beliefs and always felt happier being in church than going to the pub, I still struggled getting the right balance in relating to Christian girls. After my experience with Christine at the beginning of the year, I was more cautious about involvement than I realized, which might have had something to do with my cavalier attitude to the nice young nurse I took out that night. Reasons are not an excuse, though. I should have been kinder and more understanding of her point of view, rather than just seeing it as a one-time night out, as was the norm for college students. At least I didn't try to take advantage of her, as some fellows would have— small credit to me as it was.

On Sunday nights, films were shown for the student body at irregular intervals in the college auditorium. On this particular night, which just happened to coincide with a period when Ross and Pauline were fighting, I had just returned from church to find all dormitory lights on and all male students standing around in the hallway, mumbling to each other and looking sheepish. I had never seen such a bunch of nervous Nellies, as the fellows looked genuinely on edge.

"What's happened, Wheels?" I asked, stopping at a group standing outside his room. He muttered something about a film they saw. By the time I reached my room, I saw Ross and a few others talking furtively in the hallway with that same sheepish look. When Ross saw me, he grabbed my arm and said half seriously, "I gotta go to the toilet, and you're coming with me."

After we returned from Ross's trip to the toilet, I heard what had happened. They had shown the film *Wait Until Dark* in the darkened auditorium, and everyone was so affected by it that they all hung around the hallway in numbers, rather than going back to their rooms. Ross told me that at the scariest moment, when the killer leaped across the screen, with a knife lit up by the light of an open refrigerator, the girls in the auditorium absolutely shrieked. Ross said he looked up to see someone rushing up the aisle straight at him. "I had my right cocked and was just about to throw a punch when Pauline dived on to me," he said.

So it seemed a scary film had its compensations. Dispute solved, fight over, romance restored, and embarrassed students finally went to bed. No doubt in the girls dorms, lights were on, and hallways were filled by nervous Nellies possibly wishing there were some brave boys who could spend the night with them.

One of my recreational activities over the two years there was rabbit shooting. I had bought Jamie's .22 for twenty dollars after he ran out of drinking money and needed a quick infusion of cash. Ross and I and a few of the city fellows from our dorm would drive out to a property to surprise the little critters as they came out of their warrens for breakfast. I was a reasonable shot, one time bagging five but often bagging none. We would usually stay out from sunup until about ten, sometimes arriving at a furthest point and then splitting up and working our way back to the car from different directions. I liked being on my own and enjoyed the solitude of the Wagga countryside. I felt content wandering up and down the hill paddocks on my way back to the car, while stopping to take the odd random shot. Things got a bit more sophisticated in second year, when Ross and I went spotlighting with Bob, shooting from his car as we careened around friendly paddocks.

Brianna was a local girl in first year and was from Julie's circle of friends. Over the year, I had gotten to know her through our college fellowship group. I liked talking to her (my abortive wooing of Julie was quite forgotten by now) and found her bright, witty, and very engaging. Whenever I bumped into her, we would chat, and she once told me about her man in Sydney. Toward the end of the year, I asked her how "her man" was, and she told me they had broken up, and she didn't have a boyfriend anymore. I didn't have anyone to take to the graduation ball, so I felt safe in asking sweet, wholesome Brianna to go with me. I had no serious intentions about her, other than enjoying her company and being friends, which in hindsight probably wasn't fair on Brianna. I was a bit surprised by how quickly our relationship developed and how readily her parents had accepted me, even letting me use one of their cars. I wasn't thinking about where it might be leading; all I was thinking about was the end of the year and someone nice to take to the college ball. Beyond that was the unknown, as was the school where I might be sent next year. To me, we were in college, learning about life, and I certainly didn't see myself as marriage material or even serious-boyfriend material at this time of my life.

With our time at college almost over, Ross and I were thinking about our final prac. We had informal discussions with lecturers as to where we would like to go. I was asked if I minded doing my final prac at a one-teacher school, if the opportunity should arise. I was happy to go anywhere and try anything—life was an adventure then, and anything new was part of that adventure. We had learned about teaching in small schools in our course, so I wasn't at all put off by the prospect of going to one for my final prac.

A few days later, Ross came into our room with his big toothy grin and said, "Guess what? We're both at Harefield."

With that stunning news and our prac sorted out, our next task was to pass our exams and graduate.

Our final exams were conducted in the Kyeamba Smith Hall, across the road in the Wagga Showground. Because Ross and I were conscientious in the way we approached our coursework—reviewed material frequently; completed work on Friday, rather than late Sunday night; and finished assignments on time—we weren't studying "new" material when the exams came around. The courses weren't difficult if you worked, but they were easy to fail if you didn't. We ended up with credits, while the brainy girls who could have been brain surgeons or scientists got the distinctions. Even so, I only passed music with what I had crammed into my head five minutes before the exam began.

Harefield was a one-teacher school situated off the highway down a dirt road, eighteen miles north of Wagga. It was a bit out of the way, except for the Sydney-to-Melbourne train line, which ran straight past the school. Each day, the coach would head up the Olympic Way toward Cootamundra, turn right down a dirt road, and drop us at the corner outside the school before continuing up another dusty road to Junee, then on to Coota, and eventually finish up at Harden- Murrumburrah. The teacher in charge was Ashley Thompson—or Asho, as we called him—a top bloke in his third year out. He remembered me from football when our college team played against City. His recollections of the match were that I palmed him off and ran around him and scored a try. Sometime later, he broke his ankle in the match, from which he was still recovering, so he was delighted we were both on the same side this time.

The four weeks we spent there were the most enjoyable of all the pracs I had at college. Ross and I had a ball—the kids were great country kids; trains passed by; two sisters rode to school on their horses; we rode around the quadrangle on bicycles; and Ross and I honed our teaching skills on multiple classes in the one schoolroom. It was only a short drive from Wagga by car, so we could live in Wagga, close to everything, and drive out to school each day. It ticked all the right boxes for me—if Ashley ever decided to move on.

The following Friday was the last day at college, except for a group who chose to come back and do third year (after the principal stunned everyone, especially the lecturers, by announcing they would be providing a third year next year). We wondered what more they could fit into another year. Although ours was only a two-year course, lectures went from Monday to Friday, nine o'clock to four (sometimes five), and crammed into it was the equivalent of what is now done in a full four-year degree course.

It was also the day of our end-of-year ball at the Kyeamba Smith hall, where tears were shed, photos taken, and a few got emotional and told others, whom they hadn't spoken to since the first day of college, what a great person they were.

After the ball, I walked Brianna back to her place. On the way, we stopped off at a park and lay on the grass, counting stars and having a kiss and a cuddle. Then we headed off, arriving at her place just as the sun was coming up. I had a great night with Brianna. I liked her a lot and enjoyed her company, but my feelings weren't strong enough for her to consider taking the relationship any further at that stage— but I had a lot of respect for her and would never have taken advantage of her. When I left her, there were no promises about next year, other than I expected to be back in Wagga and then we'd see what might happen. The problem with that was that Brianna was a special type of girl—one I was mad to let go, but I did, because I just didn't feel that she was "the one." If I was in love, then it wouldn't have been a problem, but my feelings and emotions were so guarded that I had difficulty committing to anyone. *Next year is next year*, I thought, but as for now, I was booked on the train to return to Sydney with the other college students, later that afternoon.

As I was expecting to be back in Wagga the next year, I played cricket with the Plateau A Grade side instead of rejoining Manly. Besides, my cricket season was going to be cut short, as Ron and Ross and I were heading north to Queensland for three weeks. I only had time to squeeze in two matches in December and finished with a ridiculously high batting average and equally ridiculously low bowling average. It ended on a worrying note, though, when I rolled my ankle when I was bowling. I felt a sharp pain as the ligament seemed to roll across the bone. It was only momentary, but it didn't fill me with much confidence about the coming football season.

CHAPTER 6

To Queensland

Before college finished, Ron and Ross had organized a trip to Queensland, with me coming along as ballast. To pay for it, we each put in sixty dollars, which was used for supplies and petrol. We were using Ron's Hillman, so Ron stayed at my place until it was time to meet up with Ross at Hornsby Station. After loading Ross's gear into the back, we headed north up the Pacific Highway as the rain tumbled down. As for much of the trip, I occupied the backseat and enjoyed the scenery, while Ron and Ross fussed around in the front.

We made Port Macquarie at the end of the first day and pitched our tent away from the township on the beach. Ron had bought all the tinned food we would eat and cooked it over a spirit burner. My contribution was financial, as well as being a willing hand to put up and take down the tent. Ross's contribution was a stick that he picked up from the surrounding bush. "It's going to protect us on our trip"—this was his explanation for tying it to the luggage racks on the roof of the car. After being chased away from the beach by a council ranger the next morning, we continued north to the Gold Coast, where we visited my uncle and aunt at Burleigh Heads and stayed the night in their caravan. With promises of a more lengthy stay on the way back, we continued on to Brisbane and the northern suburb of Aspley, where Ron's uncle, aunt and three young cousins lived. They had a large, comfortable house, with a swimming pool and a rumpus room, where we slept. The oldest cousin, Roslyn, was about seventeen or eighteen and was a real heart-breaker. Being the holiday period, her boyfriend was around most of the time, and because Ross thought he was a good bloke, she was off limits to both of us.

We enjoyed the few days we spent there, swimming, eating, and playing cards. We were fully rested when we continued our trip north. Our next stopover was at Bundaberg, where we again pitched our tent and then drove up to Rockhampton the next day. We had an unnerving experience when we stopped at a pub on the way. Being hot and thirsty, we each ordered a lemon squash. That immediately attracted the attention of the locals slurping on their FOUREX beer. It was entirely incomprehensible to them that three grown men didn't drink beer, so after quickly downing our squashes, we were out of there, leaving their dark mutterings and threatening stares behind. But apart from that time, we were never in a hurry. Ron had convinced us that the optimum speed for the Hillman was forty-five miles an hour, so we poked along contentedly at forty-five, listening to music and looking at the scenery until we reached our destinations.

My three memories of Rockhampton were of crossing the Tropic of Capricorn, sweet-and-sour pork for dinner, and stuffing ourselves on pineapples, which were cheap. Our goal was to go as far north as time would allow, but as Queensland was huge and our progress slow, Mackay or maybe Airlie Beach loomed as possibly our most northerly stop. Cairns, over seven hundred miles further on, the perennial destination for boys on the loose, might have to wait for another day.

It was a hot and humid day when we caught the launch over to Brampton Island as day-trippers, knowing we had to come back at the end of the day—unless something happened and we missed the ferry. We spent the day looking around, swimming in the resort's ocean swimming pool, and chatting to three girls who were holidaying there. They were very friendly, and when they said they'd look out for us at the dance that night, we didn't have the heart to tell them we were only day-trippers.

When it was time to catch the launch back to Mackay, instead of making our way to the wharf, Ron and I headed off in the opposite direction. We wandered around looking for Ross and a place to sleep for the night, while giving every impression we were guests. We left our gear in a shelter and eventually found Ross, emerging from a toilet block, looking very sheepish.

"Where have you been?" he asked.

"Just walking around," I said. "Where were you?" "I've been hiding in the toilet for more than an hour."

"Why?" said Ron. "We've just been acting like we're meant to be here."

As darkness fell, our thoughts turned partly to meeting up with the girls but mostly to our stomachs. The plan worked perfectly, as we feasted well at the smorgasbord and danced our way into the evening with the girls. I was dancing with the impressive Tanya, who was generous with her smiles and had a great pair of legs. After the dance, the six of us paired off and went our separate ways, off into the night. Tanya and I found a quiet spot down on the beach where we settled down to talk. Then the situation became a bit tense. She seemed uneasy, being away from her friends, and gave me the impression she had a boyfriend back home and was having second thoughts about being out with me. I had no idea what was going on in her head, nor did I particularly care, because I had no great expectations of something happening while we were out there. Rather, I found her interesting, just as I found most girls I had been out with, and I was quite happy to just sit and talk. After a while, it all became a bit silly, so I walked her back to her room and then headed off to the shelter, where our gear was stashed. Ron and Ross eventually arrived back, seemingly more successful than I had been, but little more was said of our evening's adventure.

The next day we continued acting like guests, exploring the island and swimming in the ocean. The water was very salty and buoyant, so swimming offshore to a floating platform was easy, even for me, whose greatest swimming exploit was in not drowning. Later that afternoon, we joined the day-trippers and guests returning to Mackay on the launch. I bumped into Tanya on the boat, and she gave me what looked like a slightly embarrassed, even apologetic, smile.

It was confusing and reminded me of a situation that occurred a few years before when I stayed at a school friend's place during the Christmas holidays. Keith was a youth leader at his church, so I went to a few meetings with him. He warned me that being new, I'd be popular with the girls. I didn't think much of it initially, until one of the girls took a liking to me. She had a fellow with her but ignored him and talked to me. Later, she asked me to go outside with her, where she confided in me the she was trying to break off with him. We talked about it—or more to the point, she talked and I listened—but as I'd only met her five minutes before, I didn't want to be dragged into something I didn't think it was any of my business. There was obviously something going on between them, because he stormed off when she stayed outside with me for far too long. Afterward, she asked if I was going to the pictures with the group next weekend, and I said I was. She seemed pleased and said that if I wasn't going, she wouldn't have gone either. I did go the following week but only because it was my last day at Keith's place. She turned up holding hands with her boyfriend, their relationship seemingly reconciled. When she saw me, she gave me that same embarrassed look that Tanya had. I was glad to see them together, though, because I was never interested in her in a romantic way, less so now, and was quite happy to be out of the picture and out of their little intrigue.

Both situations showed me a few things. First, whenever I went out with a girl, my intention was to give her a good time, and if I managed that, I was generally satisfied. Second, I didn't enter into deeper relationships easily, nor did I take brief ones seriously. Furthermore, I found girls could be flirty, flighty, and frivolous, as well as honest, angst-ridden, and deeply loyal. No wonder they confused me, which was probably a factor in why I had trouble committing to a relationship with any great conviction. It also reinforced my views that you can't trust your emotions. I guarded mine—too well at times—often giving the impression I didn't care, which wasn't the case. I'm sure being a Christian and having self control was a factor in all that.

Back on dry land and with the rain setting in, we decided not to go any further, giving Airlie Beach and the other Barrier Reef islands a miss. Instead, we headed back south to Brisbane and the Gold Coast, stopping on the way to view some caves near Miriam Vale and then stopping over at Aspley for a few days. It was a welcome stopover, as it gave us time to relax, wash clothes, play cards, and drool over Ron's cousin again.

We hit the Gold Coast a few days later and stayed at Burleigh Heads in my uncle's caravan. That left us free to spend time at Surfers Paradise and roam the nightspots. We weren't big drinkers or risk-takers or party animals, so there was little chance of our getting into any trouble out there.

After cruising around for a while, we went into a beer garden and ran into some VFL (Victorian Football League) players from Melbourne. Ross knew one of them, a well-known Collingwood player, from the time he was going out with one of the teachers we knew in Wagga. They were having such a good time, we took ourselves off to another place. In a mostly empty beer garden, we saw three girls sitting at a table on their own. That was encouragement enough for Ross, and we soon joined them. I sat next to Susie, the best looker, while the others didn't seem to mind being chatted up by total strangers. Then again, we weren't the worst-looking fellows they had probably seen. Ross did most of the talking, and I did most of the listening but did enough to find out my girl was a nurse, and they were all down from Brisbane. They had rented a house, so we all headed back to it to get to know each other a little better.

We ended up staying the night. I don't know what went on in the other bedrooms, but I know nothing went on in ours—apart from a kiss and a cuddle. In fact, we both wanted it that way, without having to say so. In the morning, she thanked me for not trying it on with her, so I wasn't surprised when she told me she had a boyfriend— but I was surprised when she said she wanted to see me again.

I came back on my own over the next few days, because Ron and Ross weren't interested in the other girls and were a bit surprised I wanted to see Susie again. We spent time with my aunt and uncle and young cousins, but I also made time to drive up to the house and go for a walk along the beach with Susie, while Ross and Ron found other things to do. It was hard explaining to the other two girls why I kept turning up on my own.

At the end of our week's stay at Burleigh Heads, we headed back to Sydney. Before we left, I drove back to the house to say good-bye to Susie. Then the girls headed north to Brisbane, and we headed south to Sydney. We were in a hurry now and full of anticipation, because waiting for Ross and me were our appointments to our first schools. On the way down, we were stopped at the "tick gate" near Grafton, where an inspector tried to confiscate Ross's stick, which was still riding shotgun on top of the roof racks. He changed his mind when he saw there were three of us, and it wasn't worth the effort.

"So how did the stick protect us?" we asked Ross later.

"Well, we didn't have an accident, did we?" Ross replied indignantly.

Home again, I could look back over the years and say I had just come out of a time in my life that was sometimes exciting, often confusing, occasionally exhilarating, but always interesting. And I had come through the years mostly unscathed—physically, emotionally, and especially spiritually. Now it was time to get on with the next phase of my life and hopefully to grow up some more. I was confident in who I was—a teacher, a sportsman, a fast runner, and a Christian whose life of responsibility and independence was about to open up even more. I felt confident in my ability to go out and conquer "a" world—not "the" world but a somewhat smaller version of it called "my world." Above all, I was a free man, unattached and a slave to no one.

CHAPTER 7

Via Grong Grong

My first appointment left me with mixed feelings. I was glad to be back in the Riverina but had expected to be in Wagga, based on a conversation I'd had three months earlier. It was with a country rugby official after the match against New Zealand Services, who I surmised held some sort of position in the education department when he said to me, "So where do you want to teach next year?"

"In Wagga," I replied. "Leave it to me," he said.

So I did, and that's why I ended up at Cowabbie West, sixty-five miles northwest of Wagga, in the middle of nowhere. My official appointment told me it was not a "real" place: it was "via" a real place, Grong Grong, a place of no significance to anyone other than the locals, traffic heading through to Adelaide, and cartographers. So I'd gone from Wagga Wagga to Grong Grong. "Great, great," I muttered.

When we got back from Queensland, Ross headed back to Greenacre to find he had been appointed to the one-teacher school at Murrumbateman, between Yass and Canberra, while Ron stayed at my place. He had chosen to do third year at college, so he had time to kill. Second day back, I went out with my father and bought a four-hundred-dollar car, a Skoda—a ridiculous choice, but a slick salesman saw me coming and talked me into it. Ron did what he could to it,

113

and it even made the Central Coast and back on a test drive. With the engine in the back, it was very light in the front and felt like it was ready to take off at the slightest hint of a breeze.

A few days later, I headed down to my school in my Skoda, following Ron in his tried-and-much-traveled Hillman. Ross had already gone down to check out his school and found a place to stay in Yass. But most important, had palled up with Mick, the mechanic (whose name was actually Ian, but Mick sounds better), first servo on the way in. Just past Goulburn, at the junction of the Federal and Hume Highways, we followed the Hume in its westward sweep toward Yass. Well, Ron did, but I didn't. Instead, I found myself parked on the side of the road, going nowhere and watching a white speck disappearing off into the distance. Fortunately, Ron came back and towed me to Yass, where we met up with Ross and—more important—Mick the mechanic, first servo on the way in. So I stayed the night in the back of the garage and then left my useless, broken-down car with Ron and Ross to ponder over, while I took Ron's useful car to Cowabbie West and, thankfully, arrived at Goulburn Park, Don Evans' farm, my first-term's domicile, only a day late. My lateness didn't seem to worry the locals, who were just thankful I'd made it. However, it did worry Frank Russell, my district inspector, who had driven over from Temora on the first day of school to meet me. It took me just a little longer to win him over to my endearing qualities.

On Fridays after school, I'd head down the Old Narrandera Road and stay with Bob and Jenelle on the farm they were renting at Malebo. However, I didn't go to see Brianna, a fact I'm not very proud of. We had left our relationship up in the air and no promises had been made, but I felt it was a bit weak of me not to have even tried to make contact with her. Brianna had written to me during the holidays, but I was afraid that if I visited her, I'd be obliged to pick up again from where we left off at the end of the year. In a way, I had moved on and, as I had done in the past, when a door closed, I left it closed and didn't try to open it again.

Another factor I didn't fully understand was that people were interested in my life. One time, Ron chastised me for not keeping in touch with some college friends. I was genuinely surprised that people would be interested in what I was doing. Self-deprecation was fine, unless it became a problem. Mine was more of a problem than I realized, and it would soon surface again, much to my detriment. Still, I knew I had a lot of growing up to do, something that my past girlfriends would probably have agreed with, but being my own person at my own school gave me the opportunity to do some more growing and make a real contribution to my school community as well.

Don used to tell me I needed to get a better car when he first set eyes on the Hillman. (I wondered what he would have said about the Skoda.) His words proved prophetic on the Coolamon Road one Saturday morning, as I was approaching Wagga. A loud clattering sound came from under the car, and it wasn't a happy sound either. I managed to clatter into town and head to a garage, where I was informed I'd done a big end bearing, and it would cost a hundred and twenty dollars to repair, if repairing it was possible. So what happened? Ron took his Hillman back, and we went to a dealer, and I got a better car—a 1968 White Holden Kingswood with a bench seat, a 186 motor, and three on the tree, but, unfortunately, with the heater taken out. It cost just under two thousand dollars, and as I was now on four thousand dollars a year, which included a small schools' allowance of four hundred dollars, it was eminently affordable.

I looked forward to receiving mail from home, so I was pleased when I received a letter from my old schoolmate Robbo. I hadn't heard from him for a while, but he used to write long, detailed letters to me when I was at college, so naturally I was keen to read what he had to say. It didn't contain the usual news about what he was doing or about friends or Christian topics. The whole tenet was very different; it was very political. Robbo said he was involved in the anti-apartheid movement at the university, and he wanted me to make a public statement saying I would refuse to play rugby against South Africa, if selected, because of their government's apartheid policy. I was pretty ignorant about South African policy and, like most sportsmen of that era, believed that politics and sport shouldn't mix, and sport was a means of keeping the communication channels open. But what disappointed me was the tone in his letter—it was all about supporting his protest and had nothing of the warmth and camaraderie of previous letters. Besides, I was a smallfry in the Australian rugby scene, only playing with Country the previous year. I could just picture the headline: "Country rugby union nobody publicly rejects apartheid." The subscript to the headline would be, "Country nobody marked never to be chosen again to play for Country by selectors." That's how it worked.

With the football season approaching, I found out I was playing for Wagga Waratahs when I read it in the *Wagga Advertiser*. I hadn't decided whether to play for College, as old boys were now allowed to, or the Waratahs, who Bob had joined and who had shown some interest in me. I ended up following Bob to the Waratahs, a former great Wagga club, trying to rebuild itself.

The cricket season finished on a high note, with Lake Albert winning the final. We played the second week on a damp wicket and soon rolled Leagues Club for very few. I picked up four wickets, and our other opening bowler, Derek Rogers, picked up five. As they were well short of our previous week's score, the match finished early, so I allowed myself a trip to the pub with the fellows to celebrate. Three nights later, I was back in Wagga for my one and only training run with the Riverina team before heading up to West Wyalong to play against Central West-South West the following Saturday. Less than fully fit and with a gammy ankle I finished the match with a concussion after my bone-jarring (my bones), try-saving tackle in the corner. After the match, I socialized with some of my Country teammates from the previous year and then drove straight back to the farm, where later I was sick and deposited the contents of my dinner into the garden outside my room. The following Thursday, I was up in Sydney with the Riverina team for Country Week, still feeling lethargic from the concussion and with a bad ankle to boot.

I must have played as badly as I felt, because I wasn't selected for Country that year. *Little wonder* I thought. I remembered attempting to run around an opposing player when we played against the ACT, (Australian Capital Territory.) I stepped one way, then the other, and then I ran into him, and we both fell over. Not a good advertisement for a speedy, elusive winger.

My weekends were spent down at Malebo and consisted of rabbit shooting with Bob on Friday night, walking up and down Baylis Street the next morning, and playing rugby with the Waratahs on Saturday afternoon. It turned out to be a disappointing, albeit shortened, season, as apart from scoring a few tries, I didn't contribute as much as I wanted to Waratahs' year. I found I was unable to side-step, swerve, and accelerate, (strong features of my game) and driving down to Wagga on Wednesday night for a one- night-a-week training run was hardly going to be sufficient, especially as they were pretty shambolic affairs when players couldn't get away from their farms and get to training.

Saturday nights usually found me at the pictures, or the Way Inn, or across the road at the Mari, or down the road at the Leumeah, drinking tea and eating raisin toast—by myself, the least of both worlds. Then at lunchtime on Sunday, I'd drive back and turn out for the mighty Grong Grong–Matong Magpies Seconds, empowered by my Tuesday afternoon training run at Grong Grong football ground. It may not have been terribly exciting for some, but I was content, as all the important things in my life were happening back at Cowabbie, where my main focus was. I had joined the local Australian Rules club after Grant Kirby had talked me into it. Grant was a third-year- out teacher at Matong's two-teacher school. We became teammates with the Magpies second-grade side, and he taught me all he knew about the game—which wasn't very much. He did introduce me to the Young Rotarians in Narrandera, though, which provided me with some semblance of a social life. We went to their midweek meetings, where we had a dinner and a good talk about things. One night on our way back from a meeting, we raced each other along the Newell Highway through the fog, but we regretted our foolishness afterward and never did it again. I did go to a few meetings, but being a loose cannon, I remained a visitor and didn't officially join them.

Although I didn't have anything to do with the college now, I did drive there one Saturday night to see the new education center that we had watched being built the previous year. A dance was being held there, so I went in for a look. I didn't see anyone I knew, only students I didn't know or only slightly knew. As I watched the students dancing, I felt out of place there, even though it had been my home for two years, and I had been very involved in college life. Life had gone on, and although I still had a sentimental attachment to the place, I couldn't just duck back to my old room, because now it wasn't my room, and I didn't belong there anymore. Despite knowing that, I was having trouble letting go of the past two years, even though I had physically moved on.

I was about to leave when I noticed one of the girls I remembered from the previous year. I didn't know her very well then, but whenever our paths crossed, she had always caught my eye and given me a big smile. I was friendly with a number of first-year girls back then without forming any close attachments to any of them. But there, at that moment on that night, I found her very appealing and on her own. As I was feeling a bit sentimental, I thought, *Why not?* It was obvious she had the same thought in mind, so we left the dance, and drove up to Willans Hill, and parked for about an hour. We talked a bit and kissed and cuddled a bit more—and then I dropped her back at the dance before heading back to Malebo. I didn't think too deeply as to why she came with me, but I knew there was an attraction between us, our paths had crossed, and we were both obviously fancy free. I liked her but also, I respected her. There was always a fine line between what I felt was acceptable behavior for a Christian fellow and what wasn't acceptable, even though I knew I didn't always get it right. But spending time alone with her and doing little more than holding hands appealed to the romantic in me, as long as I was considerate of her feelings, because her feelings were just as important as mine were.

After that night, I felt I had gotten something out of my system. I didn't see any point in coming back to the college, so I didn't expect to see her again. I hadn't made any effort to contact Brianna either, so I felt I'd burned my bridges with Brianna and all past relationships at college. It really was time to move on.

I was enjoying my life as a country teacher so much that my sporting disappointments seemed unimportant. I found the responsibilities and variety of tasks that came with the job stimulating. Mundane things, like spending nights alone in my room writing up programs and preparing lessons, tests, and exams for six different classes, were time-consuming but satisfying and never boring. Educating young minds could be a daunting responsibility, so a teacher had to be able and committed. But when there were six classes operating at the same time, I was conscious of the organization needed to adequately cover all classes. For some, it could become too much to handle, but for others, it could be the makings of them as teachers. I really felt I'd found my niche at this time of my life, and it was going to be the makings of me as a teacher.

I liked the order of the classroom. It had a sense of security about it, and I enjoyed the responsibility of working on my own and being relied upon to give the children the best I had to offer. I had a good relationship with my district inspector now, after a pretty ordinary start. I was good mates with Barry, the P3 (Principal of a two teacher school) at Grong Grong, and his wife, Cathy, and with Grant and Mal at Matong, and I had enjoyed my first small schools conference at Temora. I had also enjoyed my first term, boarding with the Evans family. They were a welcoming, generous family who, I believe, appreciated my commitment to their boys' education. Yes, things were looking up. I had run the gauntlet of life insurance salesmen, mended bridges with the Irish priest (who I sent packing in the first week after he turned up unannounced and wanted to take the Catholic kids for Scripture), and was feeling comfortable within the community of Cowabbie West. I was content and had a lot to look forward to for the duration of my tour of duty at the school.

In the second term, I moved further up the road to Sunny Plains, Turnbull's farm. There, my room was out on the veranda, separated from the rest of the house. It was quite Spartan, with only a bed, wardrobe, and desk, but was sufficient for my needs, as I always ate with the family. Peter was in fifth class, and we would often play table tennis. He was a nice boy but was sometimes lacking in confidence. Each time we played, I beat him, and it seemed to dishearten him that little bit more, so I encouraged him to keep at it—until one day I relaxed too much, and he beat me. After that, he was an absolute pain in the neck. I should have kept him down while I could, because he became insufferably cocky. It was a good match to lose but made the next matches all the more harder to win.

Winters in the district were cold, so the P&C (Parents and Citizens Association) organized firewood to be cut and stacked next to the water tank. Inside, we had a wood heater that radiated heat all through the room and warmed all the corners, as long as I continued feeding its ravenous appetite. It wasn't a problem—all I had to do was chop up enough firewood into manageable sizes each afternoon, put it in the bucket, cart it inside, and leave it next to the heater for its next day's meal. Mundane? Not really. I was my own man there and it was part of the job and a responsibility I enjoyed doing. I suffered from jabs and small cuts from handling the firewood but thought little of it—until my finger became infected. An angry- looking abscess formed on the first finger of my left hand and became uglier over the next few days as my whole hand began to swell up. After school, I drove to the medical center in Narrandera and was disappointed when the doctor said I couldn't play football for two weeks. Then he handed me over to the nurse to do all the nasty bits and try to clean it out. Despite the medical treatment, it took two weeks before I could get back on the football field again, and even then, the finger still had an angry look about it.

We played Wagga City and had just lost when I made a comment to one of the opposition players, a Riverina teammate, a breakaway of all energy but little science. I told him he had just played the best match I had ever seen him play. When he thanked me, I quipped that it was the *only* good match I'd ever seen him play. It wasn't something I was proud of having said, not so much for what I said, but because I said it after the match, as we were coming off the field. Most things said to unsettle a player were fair game during the match, especially from spectators, but not after the match. I regretted making the comment and regretted it more that I didn't go to see him and put it right. Strangely, I had better relationships with ag college students than with the City club, who teachers traditionally played for. Maybe that's why I felt more inclined to play for Waratahs, a club of graziers, than City, a club of 'chalkies' as teachers were called.

A few weeks later, I was down in Wagga, helping Ross and Ron take an engine out of a VW. My role in the proceedings was that of an unintended spectator, lending a hand if asked but generally of no real use to car boffins who were toiling away at a task in which I had little interest or expertise. Try as I might, the workings of an internal combustion engine just didn't spin my wheels, so I was there basically to kill time with my mates. As it was, my most enterprising moment came when I passed someone the grease gun.

Afterward, I drove back to Turnbull's farm later than I meant to and didn't reach their farm road until dark. It had been raining, and the road was greasy. As I was driving up the road, I had a sudden urge to relieve myself, but in braking sharply, I found the car sliding off the road into a table drain. After I did the deed, I surveyed the scene and could see I was seriously bogged. The house was half a mile away, so I trudged off down the road in total darkness on a cold August night, until I saw the lights of the house. Then, early Monday morning, Mervyn took me back to the car in his tractor and pulled me out. I drove back to the farm for breakfast and then headed off to school.

At recess time, I walked out onto the playground and kicked the football to the boys. As I kicked it, I felt a sharp pain in the center of my back—a pain that just wouldn't go away and that became worse as the day wore on. That night, I couldn't lie down flat and had to sit up in bed to get any sleep. The only relief I had was when I had a hot shower. By Tuesday afternoon, the pain drove me back to the medical center to see my "favorite" doctor. His examination was cursory and his diagnosis brief: a strained back and three days off. Once again, his condescending manner left me cold. I took two days off and spent the time sitting up in bed, missing the children but feeling too miserable to do anything about it. By Friday, I'd had enough and felt that if I was going to be miserable, I might as well be miserable back at school with the kids. I spent most of the day sitting next to the wood heater and allowing the heat to warm my back. It was the only way I could get any relief from the pain.

After school, I drove down to Wagga, with the intention of continuing on south to Shepparton the next day to see a chiropractor who I'd been told treated the VFL players. I was staying the night with the family that Ron was boarding with—a lecturer from the college— rather than stay the other side of Wagga at Malebo. I was feeling pretty exhausted from the pain and lack of sleep, so I went to bed early. It was still dark when I woke suddenly, feeling pins and needles in my legs. I assumed I had a pinched nerve in my back, so after bouncing my feet up and down on the floor, I went back to sleep.

Some hours later, with the sun coming up, I awoke to find I couldn't move my legs. I was fairly calm about it, until I realized my bladder was full, but I was unable to get up and go to the toilet. I called out to Ron, who seemed surprised to see I was still in bed.

At this stage, I still trusted the doctor's diagnosis, so I presumed that somehow, all this was just a complication from a strained back. My view of doctors was a bit colored by my sister's training in alternative medicine and the attitude of the doctor who had treated me in Narrandera, so I was hopeful that it would be quickly fixed up when a chiropractor was brought in to see me. The chiropractor, however, said he couldn't do anything until I emptied my bladder. Then, after a second visit around midday, he left and didn't return. Before he left, he told Ron I was in a bad way and needed immediate medical attention. By now, I had no feeling in my legs, and my bladder had become painfully distended. Lying there, unable to move, left me feeling helpless, but paradoxically, I also felt surprisingly calm.

I lay there for the next few hours as Ron made numerous phone calls to a medical center, the ambulance service, and even the hospital. Unfortunately, it being Saturday afternoon in a country town, the lack of urgency was palpable. Most places were closed in sleepy old Wagga, and Ron wasn't able to get a helpful response from anyone. The best offer was a vague promise that an ambulance would be sent in forty minutes or so, after they finished the job they were on. It was only when Ron was able to get hold of a doctor that things started to happen. In hindsight, it seems bizarre that so much time was lost, and none of the people Ron contacted seemed aware of how serious the situation was.

1972 Cowabbie West via Grong Grong my one-teacher school.
The farm where I first stayed is off in the distance behind the school.

PART 3

GOOD-BYE, WAGGA

CHAPTER 8

We Have a Problem

"I have to operate now." The doctor was agitated, and then added ominously, "And you may never walk again."

He left the room to prepare for surgery and gave me a moment to myself. The significance of his words hadn't really hit home, which was hardly surprising. How should a twenty-one-year-old react when he has just been told that his world has fallen down, and his life has been irrevocably changed? What was clear to me, though, was that I wouldn't be back at school on Monday.

Left alone, I squeezed out a tear but felt it was forced, so I resolved not to do it again. Instead, I would keep my feelings in check. I hadn't had a difficult life by any means, but over the years, I had taken enough knocks to know if I reacted badly to them, it was a sign of weakness, so I learned to take disappointments on the chin and not to complain but just get on with it—whatever "it" was. The present situation was confusing and shrouded in so much uncertainty that there wasn't anything to be gained by thinking long term about school and my children. The only certainty was that in a few seconds, I would be wheeled into an operating room, my back would be sliced open and, hopefully, the cause of my paralysis would be treated. And all before my condition deteriorated even further. I felt I was fortunate to be heading off to the OR and not straight to the morgue.

127

I woke the next morning in Intensive Care, lying on my right side. I glanced over my left shoulder and saw a plastic tube that I supposed was coming out of my back, depositing blood and pus into a bottle. One look was enough, and I was back to sleep until the pain woke me later that morning, and my groans brought me a pethidine-led relief—and the world seemed a nicer place once more. I woke up mid-afternoon to a feeling of acute discomfort. I became aware of a dull ache in the center of my back, which seemed to increase in intensity and spread all over as I became more and more awake. Very soon, the pain was so bad that I called out to the nurse again. Again, the mighty pethidine was summoned, and the relief, the feeling of well-being, was almost instantaneous. As they turned me on to my other side, I dreamed of climbing mountains and running that 200-meter race.

The tube stayed in my back for a few days, until it had drained the abscess. Some time later, the stitches came out. By then, I had been weaned off pethidine and was alert enough to start looking around the room. I remember seeing my observation chart some days later and was annoyed to read the comment that I looked depressed. I knew it wasn't so—I was just taking it all in, adjusting to what, for me, was a totally foreign situation. I was just quiet and reflective, not thinking too far ahead, but my feelings were guarded at this point. It might have been a strength, or it might have been a weakness, and I lacked an emotional connection to my changing world. Then again, it might just have been the way I reacted to change—by withdrawing, internalizing, contemplating, and then accepting the situation, as I had with past disappointments. Or maybe it was just the fact I had a simple faith in God. It was not a situation anyone would want to be in, but I believed that God was with me, and it would all turn out for the best in the long run.

I took that line when talking to the nurse in charge of the Intensive Care ward. Her response was to harangue God for reasons she wouldn't explain to me. I was put off by her supercilious tone and the suggestion that she had a superior knowledge of God than I did. I didn't see God as a benevolent Santa Claus who played favorites but as a holy, loving God, whose creation was perfect until we messed it up. I didn't believe that God ever got things wrong or that He was the architect of our problems—we were, by our own choices. Nor did I ever think that God had abandoned me. He was always there, all those days leading up to and following my operation, even if He allowed things to happen that weren't of my choosing.

However, I wasn't particularly interested in pursuing my thoughts with her, as she seemed to have a closed mind to God. I did wonder what might have caused her reaction to my initial comments about my faith, although I remembered she'd had a run-in with the doctor earlier, when she had taken it upon herself to have a plaster cast fitted around my lower legs to hold my feet up, because I apparently had "drop foot." When the surgeon next did his rounds, he was not happy. He spoke to her quite sternly and told her to have the plaster removed. She had been businesslike, rather than friendly, before that incident, but afterward, she was even more distant. A curious incident and a reaction I found quite strange.

My surgeon turned up on Monday with his entourage, hoping for some improvement. Unfortunately, I couldn't oblige him, as hard as I tried, when he touched, scraped, and tapped different parts of my legs and abdomen with his little rubber mallet (even though my brain had convinced me I was moving my legs). Despite our best efforts, my legs remained numb and lifeless. I felt sorry for him, because he seemed so disappointed, and I knew his disappointment wasn't for his handiwork but for me.

About a week after the operation, the stitches were removed from my back and the surgeon told me what he had done. He had to get into the spinal column by taking the tops off four or five vertebrae, which he repaired with bone fragments. The exposed abscess extended from T4 to T8, so the paralysis actually started at mid-chest level and had crushed the spinal cord so it resembled not a thick cord but a sliver of ribbon. The good news was he had gotten it all out, and there was little chance of its recurring—maybe one in a million?

My parents came down on Monday and then drove back on Tuesday, as my father had to work. It hurt me to see the distress on their faces. I was my father's hero, and to know he was in tears was upsetting.

I felt sorry for them, as they didn't deserve to be put through more grief, considering the difficult times they had already been through with my sister. I told them not to come down again but to wait until I was able to come back to Sydney. They didn't listen to me, of course, and drove down again the next weekend.

I was becoming more aware of my surroundings each day. I noticed one of the IC nurses on a step-ladder trying to reach up to get something from the top of some shelves. The higher she reached, the more her uniform rode up, revealing more and more of her legs. I watched with considerable interest as to whether she'd reach the offending article before I saw more than I needed to.

"Higher," I called out from across the room, much to her amusement. I can't remember her name, but I remember how friendly she was and that she had a boyfriend who worked on the Gundagai newspaper, whom everyone called "Scoop." She was a small, pretty girl, whose easy charm made my less-than-exciting stay in IC more bearable. I suspect she reported that incident as, "He seems to be getting better." Obviously, I looked forward to the times she came on duty. Having friendly faces was very important to me in those first few days.

Visitors were limited in IC, so one day when Ross came in, I waited until he was close to my bed, and then I started groaning and whimpering about the pain, just to see the horrified look on his face. His expression was priceless when I said, "Gotcha!"

Bob and Ron were the others allowed in during those early days, and although I wasn't always fully with it, I really appreciated their visits, as brief as they sometimes were. What I didn't appreciate, though, was the nurse with the gloved hand. It had been eleven days since the operation, and my internals were unmoved by every effort made to clear them. The last resort was the lubricated gloved finger up my backside. I can't say either of us enjoyed it, and I was too embarrassed to ask how she had gotten the job. However, that and further humiliations showed me how helpless I was and how much I had lost. Disappointment came in each visit from the doctor, when my legs stubbornly refused to obey our commands to move, despite my best efforts.

Two weeks later, I said good-bye to intensive care and was moved upstairs to a ward. My new roommate was Larry, a local lad and rugby league player, ten years my senior, who had played half a match with a broken neck. He had been told that I was the young bloke who would never walk again but that he shouldn't say anything about it to me. His somber expression when I was wheeled into the room told me that he knew something I wasn't to know. Inside my head, I knew what I knew—and that was that I would walk again.

There was a lack of movement in those early weeks after the operation, both internally and externally. I loathed the next visit from the nurse with the gloved hand. It was humiliating for a healthy young man to know that he had absolutely no control over his bowels and a young nurse's aide was about to give him what was charmingly called a "manual evacuation."

"Lie on your side," she said, seemingly unfazed by what was to follow. With some effort, I obliged and then endured a few minutes of misery as she went to work, picking away with her gloved finger. During all this, I found Larry a good roommate, as he was full of good humor and bad jokes—just the right sort of company I needed, despite our vastly differing views on certain matters.

CHAPTER 9

Yippee!

It was Wednesday morning, September 15, 1971, a week after my twenty-second birthday and a little over five weeks since my operation. Each visit from my surgeon and his poker-faced entourage had ended in disappointment. Despite my grandest efforts, messages were not getting from my brain down through my spinal cord to my legs—and time was running out. In my mind, I had moved the two impostors, just as amputees felt movement in their phantom limbs, but the reality of it was that my legs remained stone, motherless still.

But then…

They came, both stern and unsuspecting, With expressions unexpecting,

As would harbingers of woe.

His tone was full of resignation, He was lacking inspiration,

When he said, "Let's give it one last go." "See if you can move your foot," he said.

Today's the day, I thought. *I'd better start performing.*

I strained and sweated and then suddenly, the big toe of my right foot twitched. The mood in the room changed dramatically. Faces came alive, people were grinning, and my doctor was jumping around excitedly, encouraging me to try the other leg—so I did and amazed everyone in the room with a knee flicker of the left leg. There was pandemonium, the room was in rapture, and I was exhausted. How chuffed I was to see how very chuffed they were, just by tiny movements. *Imagine how they'll react when I get up and walk*, I thought.

After sanity returned, it was said what we knew—my spinal cord wasn't completely shot and there would be a recovery ... of sorts.

I felt optimistic and knew that I'd do whatever it took to walk again. I was a person who thought in the short term and didn't have great long-term goals. I lived for each day and trusted God for the next. The damage to my spinal cord was severe, so the extent of my recovery was unknown. All I could do was to work hard at what was there before me. In my case, my short-term view on life protected me from unreal expectations and allowed me to focus on each new challenge I had to face each day. What I was able to draw on, though, was the same thing I drew on that night as a teenager with a tape recorder. And that was patience, because I was going to need an awful lot of it over the next few years.

One night, we had a bit of excitement when Larry said to me, "I think your leg has fallen out of the bed."

For some reason, my left leg had jumped out of the left side of the bed and was dragging the other leg with it. I grabbed the hand bar above my head and held on tight, as my upper body started to follow my legs. Falling out of bed on to the floor wasn't the problem; it was just an amusing sideshow. The problem was that the urine bottle, to which my catheter was connected, was on the floor on the right side of the bed. And it was full and heavy and immovable.

As I continued sliding, my catheter started stretching—all the way back to the bottle. I felt a painful tug inside me as my grip on the hand bar tightened. Momentarily, that held my upper body in check, but it didn't stop my absolutely useless legs from continuing their descent. Being the dead weight they were, they started dragging the rest of me with them. I was part horrified at what was happening to my catheter and part amazed that I couldn't do anything about it. It was like watching a train crash in slow motion. Larry's frantic cries brought two nurses running. They saw what was happening and whipped around to the far side of the bed and lifted my legs back on to the bed, before my catheter was ripped out of me. It was a great relief when I was safely back in bed, but enough damage had been done so that I passed blood for the next few hours.

Being completely paralyzed meant that it wasn't just my bladder that didn't work. This time I had been constipated for only a week, so all manner of potions were inserted in both ends to move things along a bit. And move they did one day—with very little warning.

"Loz, I've gotta go," I said desperately. And go I did—copiously, continuously, completely. Larry called for a nurse, but it soon became too much for him. Despite his broken neck, he was up and heading for the door, holding his nose and muttering, "Poo! Poo!" as he left. I was shocked with what was happening, but there was nothing I could do to stop it. Another slow-motion train wreck in progress. A nurse poked her head in, grimaced, and looked grateful when I told her to go away, as I'd take care of it myself. Fortunately, I had plenty of bed pads in the drawer, and by the time I was empty, I had filled three of them and done my best to fold them up. I felt sorry for the poor nurse who had to take them away, but at least I had cleaned myself up and was feeling much better. Eventually, Larry returned, still sniffing the air suspiciously before telling me it was the worst smell he had ever smelled. I can't say I didn't disagree with him, as it even disgusted me, and I was the cause of it.

An occupational therapist came in one day with some craft material. She stood at the foot of my bed, told me she had a weaving activity for me to do, and waited for me to accept it. When I declined, she said something about knowing what was best for me, before huffing out of the room, never to return. Her whole demeanor was rather baffling. She didn't seem to understand it was a child's activity, something I could have done with my infants' classes at school, or it was constructive therapy for a brain-injured person. It seemed as if she had plucked something out of her magic box and said, "That'll do." But it was her attitude that I resented. It was so impersonal and pushy, and it contrasted with the sweet-naturedness of the nurses I saw daily. I appreciated their human touch in all their dealings with me, but I didn't appreciate someone making a judgment about what was good for me without knowing anything about me. It reminded me of a certain doctor in Narrandera.

Over the next few weeks, more movement came back to my legs. Each day, I was put into a warm bath as a form of hydrotherapy. Nurses clustered around to watch as I tried to move my legs and do other satisfying things. Each session left me quite exhausted, as I expended a lot of energy and put a lot of effort into sometimes achieving tiny movements. Some days there was noticeable improvement from the previous day, while other days were frustrating, and there seemed little change.

Hard work characterized those early days—the effort needed to move paralyzed limbs even a tiny bit left me feeling as exhausted as if I'd just spent an hour on the squash court. Over the weeks, I sweated a lot and used up all my reserves of energy at each session. The downside was that while all this was going on, I was lying in the bath, stark naked, in front of all the nurses, with nothing to hide behind but a protruding catheter. I found it embarrassing, so I asked for a towel to be placed over me—"Ken's modesty towel," it became known as. It was another aspect of my condition that was hard to accept—my physical deficiencies, my helplessness, and my loss of independence was bad enough, but lying naked in a bath in front of a group of young girls, irrespective of the fact they were nurses and had "seen it all before," was one humiliation too many. It didn't help that one of the nurses clustering around the bath was Miranda. I wondered what she was thinking under her nurse's stony expression.

Needing a catheter brought its own problems. When the catheter was changed one time, it was incorrectly reinserted, so that the bubble was filled with water while it was still in my urethra. It caused a painful blockage, and my bladder soon filled and became distended. A few painful hours later, another doctor came and correctly reinserted it. For my troubles, I passed blood for the next few hours and picked up my first of many bladder infections.

I found that the harder I worked, the more improvement I made, and the more improvement I made, the harder I worked. At the same time, I was encouraged by the positive attitude of my doctor and the nurses, and I know they were encouraged by my willingness to work hard as well.

When it was time to try to stand up, I was bought a new pair of shoes to wear. I gazed down on the nurse as she pulled on my socks, fitted my new shoes on my feet, tied up my shoelaces, and then prepared to help me to see how well I could stand. Not well at all, and after a few tense moments, I was glad to be sat down again. My first time up was quite scary. I didn't feel light-headed, just completely helpless without the attending nurses. They were so good to me and were very supportive (pun intended). When crutches were thrust under my shoulders, they hovered around like mother hens and seemed as delighted with my first steps as I was. Each day saw a bit more improvement, a bit more strength returning to my legs. Soon, I had progressed beyond my room and was out into the hall, and then down the corridor a short distance, and then back to the safety of my bed. A few days later, I was put into a wheelchair and taken downstairs to my first slope. It wasn't steep, but when I tried to walk down it with my crutches I felt helpless, totally unbalanced, and with the sensation I was going to topple over at any moment—a sensation that followed me down every slope I tried to negotiate in later years as well. Thankfully, my supporting nurses were there this time and gave me a lot of confidence. I think that helping me walk again was infinitely more appealing to the young girls than manual evacuations.

As I became more mobile, two positives occurred. The first was that I could wheel myself across the hall to the bathroom, go to the toilet, see what worked, and shower myself. The second was when my catheter came out—for good. That was both good and bad: good to get rid of the foreign intruder inside me, and bad, as I had limited bladder control. It also ushered in the age of wet pants.

My days there were days of adjusting to new circumstances and a new life. So it was predictable that one of my visitors, a fellow student from college, decided to give me a pep talk and started with, "I suppose you've been saying, 'Why me?' ever since it happened."

I listened in silence, because I knew his comment was well intentioned, but it still annoyed me, because I didn't say it. In fact, I never said it or even thought much about it.

Having a pity party had never entered my thoughts. Rather, my immediate thought was, *What now, Lord?* I did resent what had happened, but that's where it ended. The victim mentality had no place in my thoughts for any longer than was reasonable. Otherwise, it would start to undermine my thinking and my state of mind and would limit any positive response I might make to my present situation.

I believed that trusting God meant accepting the good and the bad and looking for positives in both. I never expected a life of ease. It was a test of my faith, but I knew my faith wasn't so shallow that it would collapse under the first real test that came my way. I knew others had survived far worse, and I could draw on their experiences for encouragement. Besides, I had been toughened up by the knocks I'd already taken in life up to that point. I knew I wasn't alone, because Jesus said He would never leave me or forsake me; He would always be with me, and I would never be tested beyond what I could bear. And even when my faith and resolve would be tested and stretched to the breaking point, I could still hang on to that truth and would ultimately come through the crisis.

One of the patients who came into the ward was a doctor who had worked at the hospital. He had become a paraplegic and was in a wheelchair. It must have been difficult for him, and I occasionally heard raised voices coming from his room. A nurse confided in me that he was the worst patient you could have—sharp-tongued and always complaining about something or, annoyingly for them, playing the doctor and not the patient.

A patient up the hall from me was Terry, a popular and cheerful young man who was about my age. He had a badly broken leg from a motor bike accident, which stubbornly refused to heal. It caused his doctor great disappointment when he removed the pin, and the bone popped out through the skin. Terry was sent home later for Christmas, with his leg in plaster and a bone graft planned for the New Year. I never heard Terry complain or utter a bad word, despite what he was going through. On a positive note, though, I found out, years later, that he had made a good recovery from his injury.

CHAPTER 10

The Next Stage

For a change of scenery one Sunday afternoon, a nurse took me outside in a wheelchair and left me on my own. I was able to wheel myself down toward Edward Street, where I sat for a while, taking in the afternoon sun and watching the world pass by. While sitting there I realized that everything I saw as normal was happening out there beyond the hospital grounds, while my "new normal" was sitting there, with me locked up inside. As I sat and watched, three college girls I knew walked by. They knew I had seen them, so it was hard to ignore me. They rushed over and pretended to be concerned before hurrying off, never to return. On another day, I heard a group of students from college singing outside before coming upstairs. I half expected to see them come through the door, but it soon became apparent that they had stopped down the hallway and were visiting someone else.

Throughout the course of life, these were fairly minor events but at the time, I felt disappointed when I realized they really didn't care. With all that had happened, my self-esteem could have been better, so any effort to show concern would have been helpful and very welcome. That's why I was grateful for Bob's, Ron's, and Ross's regular visits, not because of what they said but by the fact they came, and were there, and showed they valued me as a friend and as a person. That was all I really needed at that stage.

Another mild disappointment was that none of my old girlfriends ever dropped in to see me. Then there were visitors I could have done without like the group of ag students I knew from church. One of them was going out with Brianna at that point and related to me in detail what she had told him about our relationship. In particular, he mentioned our time in the park after the college ball and that she had told him nothing happened. I found it strange and in poor taste that he would bring up such a private matter in front of everyone. It was hardly going to make me feel better, and he should have known that as Christians, nothing was ever going to "happen" between us on that night. It didn't show much faith in Brianna's morals—morals I took for granted in a Christian girl. Still, I didn't blame Brianna for not coming to visit, because I was the one who didn't contact her. However, back then, I still held her in high regard and would have appreciated a kind word and just seeing her again.

Bob and Ron were constant visitors on whom I could rely. When Ross came over from Murrumbateman to meet up with Pauline, he always dropped in. Others came once or twice and then dropped off, seemingly satisfied they'd done their duty. No one from Lake Albert cricket club ever came near me, nor did many of my old College or Riverina rugby teammates. Even my Waratahs teammates were just occasional visitors. Wickets and tries, friendships don't make.

Another visitor I could have done without was the teacher who replaced me, a fellow of about forty who seemed to delight in telling me that he had changed everything I had done at school before leaving, never to return. Another was the local Pentecostal minister, who came a few times only to preach his own particular brand of Christianity. I initially welcomed him but soon had enough of his loveless proselytizing. I didn't get enough, however, of the occasional visits from people I knew at the Baptist church.

One visitor I welcomed, though, was the beautiful Kathy, a slim-hipped, shiny-eyed, horse-loving senior nurse from Gregadoo, a farming community a few miles south of Wagga, who I arranged to question about Catholicism. I wasn't really interested in Catholicism, but I was interested in talking to Kathy, who indulged me one evening when she was off duty and came in for a chat. She looked stunning in her civvies, and although I didn't allow my interest in her to extend far, because she had a boyfriend, I found that just looking at her was very therapeutic.

I discovered she had a boyfriend earlier, when I was kidnapped by some of the nurses and taken to a party. A number of ag students I knew were there, so I introduced Kathy to one of them and his younger brother, much to their amusement. I was quickly made aware that Kathy and the brother had been going together for some time, which made Kathy off limits for all but the mildest flirting. A line had been drawn in the sand with her, a line that only a self-centered cad would try to cross.

We wrote to each other a couple of times when I was back in Sydney. Her interest in me was purely medical, so after letting her know that things were fine, our correspondence came to an end. It would have been easy to develop strong feelings for her, but I didn't want to carry any emotional baggage with me when I left Wagga, as I had to keep everything intact for the next part of my rehabilitation.

Two one-time visitors were very welcome, though—one was Peter West, an English lecturer from college, who came, said hello, said I should write a book, and then left. And the other was Celeste, who was passing through Wagga on her way back to Albury. She had just driven in from Broken Hill, where she was teaching and had just heard what had happened to me. I was very happy to see her, and before she left, she reminded me why she was the best kiss I'd ever had.

A number of my students and their parents made the more than sixty-mile trip from Cowabbie West district to see me. I was really pleased to see them but couldn't get over the look of bewilderment on the face of Debbie, my dear little first-class girl. Some of the fathers, too, didn't know what to say and hovered in the background. Even so, I appreciated seeing them, especially as I'd only been with them for two terms.

Still, as my visitors waned, I gradually accepted the fact I wasn't a particularly interesting commodity anymore, despite a number of articles written in the *Wagga Advertiser* about my condition. It was also a salutary reminder that relationships only last when you invest time and energy into them. So in all honesty, I wasn't really surprised. I had been content with my life at my school, and the Cowabbie West community, and my weekends at Malebo with Bob and Jenelle. I had cut myself off from much of the past. But at a time when I needed all the support I could get, it did disappoint me. One minute, a rooster; next, a feather duster—that certainly applied to me.

Miranda dropped in from time to time to see how I was doing, although I wondered why. I certainly didn't want her feeling sorry for me. Then one Sunday, dressed in civvies, she bowled in with another nurse and announced they were taking me out for the afternoon.

They drove to Oura Beach, a stretch of sand on the Murrumbidgee River, eighteen miles from Wagga along the Nangus Road. I had to be helped in and out of the car and supported as I "walked" over to a place where we could sit down. Although it was a lovely spring afternoon, the memory of my last visit to Oura, when things were so different, was painfully fresh. As well, there was Miranda now seeing me in an entirely new light—helpless and stripped bare of any of the macho trimmings fellows tend to hide behind. Today, she was my nurse and a friend, giving me an afternoon away from my prison, supportive and prepared for any embarrassing moments (which thankfully didn't occur).

After a couple of hours, they dropped me back at the hospital and helped me upstairs. Having to be helped was something I had to get used to, although I was having difficulty in accepting it. At some time, I asked her about that awkward moment from last year, and all she said was that it was her fault, as she was just being silly—a nice gesture that I appreciated, as it removed any lingering tension there might have been between us.

Over the years, I've had a number of falls as I've tried to work around my lack of balance. A few were painful, some downstairs; while others were more gentle, where I could almost choose how I

was going to land. Injuries have been minor, although in one seemingly innocuous tumble down four stairs, I sat up at the bottom and noticed the first joint of my forefinger was bent in the opposite direction. It was an impressive-looking dislocation, which I knew would be painful if I left it, so the only thing to do was to push it back into place with the thumb of my right hand.

As falls became regular, I became annoyed with the overreaction of people (especially my mother) whenever they saw me take a tumble. Falls to me were an unfortunate but unavoidable part of my life, and if I was willing to treat them as such, then I expected others to do the same. I didn't want people rushing to help me up either, as my life, with all its limitations, had to go on. Sympathy, I didn't need, nor did I seek it—understanding, yes, but sympathy, no.

As I continued to make progress, I used to take myself up the hallway and around the corner to where there was a set of parallel bars. I used it as a walking frame, spending up to an hour after dinnertime, clumping up and down between the bars, night after night after night. It was tedious, monotonous, and boring, but that was the price I had to pay if I was ever going to walk again. My legs felt heavy and clumsy, like heavy weights had been tied around them, so I always worked up a sweat before I'd had enough for the night. The night staff knew what I was doing and understood. They always turned a blind eye to the lateness of my endeavors, leaving it up to me to decide when I'd had enough.

It was a struggle, but every day was a struggle, and every other day after that was a struggle as well, because even at that early stage, I had set the bar high and intended to walk again. I liked the nurses. They were young, friendly, and respectful, although one or two of them had higher opinions of themselves than I thought warranted. One of those was a nurse's aide whom I found hard to like. She was younger than I was and was forward and pushy. She often crossed the line of familiarity that none of the other nurses presumed to have with me. On one night, I was doing my thing between the bars, and the nurses were doing their thing down the other end of the ward,

leaving me in peace to continue doing my thing. Then the aide decided to assert her authority and ordered me back to bed. I found her tone insulting, so I told her I would finish soon, when I had done enough, and I continued my laps. That didn't go down well with her. She showed a lack of maturity and broke that element of trust and respect that had existed between the staff and me. By the time the officious head nurse came bustling up the hallway to tell me I was being a "naughty boy," I'd had enough. The child in me was offended, so I headed back to my room. I knew after that, something inside me had changed. The first bloom in my relationship with the staff had passed, and now I was just another patient.

I didn't want to go but I had to...

As a long-term patient in need of intensive rehabilitation, it was obvious that I needed more than I could get at Wagga. Despite the dedication of the staff and the skills of my specialist, they had limited resources and insufficient expertise for such a program. Besides, they were making noises that it was best I go, so after nearly three months of being under their care, I accepted the inevitable and flew up to Sydney in the air ambulance for further treatment at the spinal injuries unit of the Royal North Shore Hospital. And so I left, but it was with the mixed feelings of one who had to leave a life unfinished, a job not done, and a place he had grown to love, in the knowledge that if he ever returned, it would not be as the same person as the one that injury had left behind.

When I left, I took with me fond memories of a touching farewell by the staff and the wonderful nurses who had looked after me. I assumed my popularity with them was due to my age. I was young and not a grumpy old fellow or a walking vegetable, entirely dependent on care. They had seen me at my lowest point, and I suspect it was more satisfyingly for them to witness the progress I made from wheelchair to crutches. We had shared laughter, my humiliations, some triumphs, and three months of drama while I was there. I know they were genuinely happy for me and of the part they'd played in the process, so for a time I wrote long letters to them—one of sixteen pages—inquiring about the goings on at Wagga Base, detailing what was happening with me, and sometimes saying the things I always found hard to say to a girl's face, albeit tongue in cheek and with a humorous tone.

I heard later that my letters were well received, eagerly read, and constantly passed around among staff in the ward.

I also received letters from some of the nurses, my students, parents, college lecturers, friends, and now ex-teammates, which helped fill two boxes and a school case. It was touching to read how people felt, but Wagga quickly receded into the background as I was so determined to get back on to my feet. Now, it was Sydney that would become a new series of chapters in my life, some of which would have very few pages.

CHAPTER 11

Life at the RNSH

My recovery continued at the RNSH Spinal Injuries Unit under the direction of Dr. John Yeo. I stayed at Glenwood Convalescent Home down Greenwich Road, about half a mile from the hospital. I would be picked up each morning by a hospital car and dropped back later that afternoon, after completing my daily rehab program with physiotherapists Stephanie and Helen and strength work with Don, the jolly wardsman.

The first thing Dr. Yeo did when I arrived was to take away my security—my full-size, shoulder-length, armpit-chafing crutches and swap them for half-sized, wrist-holding Canadian crutches that I found immediately compromised my balance.

"We'll have you on a walking stick soon," he promised, terrifying me.

A short time after I started physio in earnest, my Canadian crutches, which had given me good arm support and balance, were taken away from me and swapped for quadrapods, which gave me no arm support but had a four-prong base for good balance. After a short time, they swapped my quadrapods for two walking sticks and let me loose. The walking sticks provided me with absolutely no arm support and little balance. My first few intrepid steps with the walking sticks were accompanied by feelings of terror—I felt I was going to topple over at any moment. When it inevitably happened, all I could do was pick a spot and hope for a soft landing.

After a few weeks, I had made enough progress to sally forth around the hospital's pathways with Peter, another incomplete paraplegic, all in the name of exercise but what was really adventure. We both used two walking sticks now, and I suspect we made a comical pair as we clumped around the hospital grounds, laughing and insulting each other along the way and generally acting like two naughty little boys. Conscious of our personal needs, we were out just long enough so we were able to get back in time for toilet relief.

After Peter went home, Klaus and I continued the tradition. Klaus had a penchant for telling jokes while we clumped around. However, I found that I could do only two out of three things when he told a joke. I could laugh and fall over and not wet my pants; I could stay upright and not laugh and not wet my pants; or I could stay upright, laugh, and wet my pants. So on this particular day, Klaus was delighted when I laughed at his joke and stayed upright. When we got back to the unit, my ambulance was waiting for me. I explained my embarrassment to the two ambulance officers, my understanding mates, and they said they would walk in front of me past the group of waiting visitors to the ambulance and save me some dignity. They were great fellows, so when we reached the group of visitors, they both stepped aside, revealing me cowering behind in all my wetted glory.

One of my friendliest, most helpful drivers was Paul. In one of our conversations, I discovered that his mother was the matron of the small maternity hospital where I was born and had, in fact, nursed me through those first few rocky days of life. That relationship, I suspect, was a topic of conversation back at the station, so even when a new ambulance officer (they disliked being called drivers) picked me up, he already knew who I was.

Their good-naturedness, though, contrasted with what I thought was a selfish attitude by my hospital driver when I was at Glenwood. I thought we had a good relationship until the day he left me behind. It was a cold morning, and I was waiting outside for him. He was late, and after half an hour, I went back inside, out of the cold, just as he arrived.

147

Instead of coming inside and getting me, he just drove off, as though he couldn't be bothered. Next time, I told him I'd waited for him in the cold and then asked him why he didn't come inside to get me. He just said, "You weren't there, so I wasn't going to bother myself with looking for you"—even though I was his daily pick-up. When I thought about it, all he ever did when he picked me up was talk about himself. His accent begged an inquiry, so when I asked, he told me he was called a Manx, as he came from the Isle of Man. I was interested and didn't mind listening to his stories about himself. In my situation, however, it was easy to see myself as less than a man. Someone who had daily interaction with someone in my situation should have had a basic understanding of that; instead, he reinforced the stereotype that a person with a handicap is a second- class person, not worthy of being treated with respect. After that, my relationship with him was never the same, but I doubt if he even noticed.

Peter was a twenty-six-year-old Qantas engineer from Sutherland. His lower back had been broken when part of a wing fell on it and paralyzed his lower legs. He needed calipers to keep his feet up and to stop them from flapping around like duck's feet, a comical feature we would often laugh about. The other fellow I got on with after Peter went home was Klaus, a German from Adelaide. He was about twenty years my senior and used to tell the crudest jokes imaginable. He was always jovial, and his good-natured wife, Pam, was there each day, supporting him. Eventually, he too was released and went back to Adelaide to continue rehabilitation. He wrote to me, but for some reason I didn't reply. I have a sneaking suspicion that although I valued their friendship at the time, I didn't want to maintain a relationship afterward, possibly because I didn't see myself as an invalid. I also tended to be resistant if I felt I was being forced into anything, relationships included. The old me would have been able to choose his friends—people I felt comfortable with—but at the hospital, I had little choice. I was reluctant to let go of the things that identified me in the past, and I secretly hoped the new me would only be a product of the injury and soon pass. At the back of my mind, I always had, *This isn't going to be permanent.*

It didn't stop me from thinking about Peter and Klaus over the years, as they were there at a bewildering time in my life. But it wasn't a period I wished to dwell on, as the transition I was going through was hard to work through, let alone understand.

Generally, I was pretty laidback, slack even, but I could be stoic and strong-willed (or was that stubborn?) if I wanted to be or if I thought a cause worthwhile. That was helpful in accommodating the frustrations and humiliations of each day, but it wasn't enough to survive what would be a lifelong journey down that confusing, often bumpy road to recovery. I needed to tap into a greater power for that, and I believed that greater power was God, who was always with me, as He promised He would be all through that journey.

My time at Glenwood was quite an eye-opener. The men's ward was a large open room of about a dozen beds plonked around its perimeter. Opposite me was a gravelly voiced dwarf named Clem. He used to appear in pantomimes in his younger days and had a consistent number of visitors. His major preoccupation at night was tipping urine from one bottle to another while accompanying the sloshing sound with grunts and groans. An older fellow, who was only known as Mr. Greener, had the bed next to Clem. One day Mr Greener went home, and I never saw him again. Another fellow was a quadriplegic, made totally immobile after falling off a house he was building in New Guinea. He was constantly attended to by family and friends, and despite the tragedy of his situation, I never heard him complain. He looked to be in his fifties, although I wouldn't have been surprised if his condition had aged him and he was much younger. Kerry was another wheelchair-bound fellow who had an intellectual handicap, while the character of the ward was Bourke Gibbons, who had cerebral palsy, was wheelchair-bound with twisted limbs, and had a face full of laughter. Members of Bourke's family were always visiting him, and there was always love and laughter coming from his corner of the room. He had an engaging personality, and although you had to listen very hard to understand what he was saying, he wasn't adverse to requesting special favors. One time, he had me on the floor with a spanner, tightening up the leads to the battery of his motorized wheelchair, now lying on its side. It was only later that I noticed that battery acid had spilled on my legs, blistering my feet and ruining my shoes. That was a small price to pay for doing Bourkey a favor.

Elsewhere, the place was inhabited by old ladies, who seemingly had given up on life. The smell around them was of oldness and decay, quite an interesting place for a young fellow to find himself in. Bladder infections had become a concern, as regular as wet pants, and for a while I was on a chocolate-looking tablet called Mandelamine, which looked a lot better than it tasted.

Each day, a car would pick me up from the hospital and take me up to the spinal injuries unit, where I would do my stuff. The unit was made up of old, decrepit buildings that had bedrooms, a gym cum exercise room, and an office. The doctors and nurses were inspiring, committed people who delighted in seeing any improvement in the patients' condition. Most of the patients there had suffered complete spinal-cord injuries and would never leave a wheelchair. One of the saddest was a fifteen-year-old high-jumper who became a quadriplegic when he broke his neck at a school athletics carnival.

At lunchtime, we would sit around in the warm sun, get fed by the nurses and the pink lady, and sometimes talk about our levels of spinal-cord injury and how to cope in the post-hospital period. One story I heard made me shudder. It concerned a complete paraplegic who came home from hospital, expecting sympathy and understanding from his wife. Apparently, she told him she wasn't going to be his servant and do anything for him; he had to do it all for himself. When he fell out of his wheelchair, she made him drag himself across the floor and get himself back into it. Talk about tough love. It apparently worked, and he became very self-reliant, but it wasn't a position in which I would have wanted to find myself.

Then there were the short-termers who'd been here before and only came in for treatment for bed sores and infections. They were old hands at life in a wheelchair, and it was one of those who looked me up and down and told me that I was one of the "lucky ones." Such was the burden an incomplete paraplegic had to bear. I didn't tell him I didn't feel particularly lucky, because as low as my bar had been set, his was much lower.

But lower still were the quadriplegics, some still with their trachies in. When I looked at them, some still quite young but aging prematurely, I didn't feel I was too bad off.

My main physios were Stephanie and Helen. They were both professional but informal and friendly. Each day, I found myself in the pool, doing hydrotherapy and trying not to look down the front of Helen's swimsuit. Then it was down to the exercise room to do a series of floor exercises. We would do a variety of "patterns of movement," as they called them, to wake up and strengthen muscles that had been—until quite recently—dormant. It was a bit like waking up the dead. One of the problems I had was the disparity in strength between my adductor and abductor muscles, which caused my legs to want to meet in the middle and stick together. That affected my walking, as legs sometimes crossed over, and then I'd stumble forward. If I couldn't catch myself in time, I'd fall over. Or I could end up stuck to the spot, when one foot trod on the other and neither would move. Then I would either fall over, when my upper body kept going on ahead of my legs, or I'd fall in any other direction, when the sensitive nerves in my feet exploded, and my foot yanked itself out from under the other foot and deposited me on to the ground. It was quite amazing what my legs were capable of doing and annoying that I had absolutely no control over any of it.

I also found that the fine movements that muscles perform naturally for balance were lost. I would stamp my way around with plodding, clumsy movements, while my ankles were almost frozen, and my calf muscles were non-functioning.

Spasm was another little problem that affected the muscles in my legs. As the nerves were reawakening, certain movements would irritate the electrical discharges to the muscles and cause my legs to shake violently, especially if a particular pattern of movement provoked it. To stop the spasm, I was prescribed Valium but I found that with the warmth of the sun and the soporific effect of lunch, I was nodding off to sleep every lunchtime, along with all the other Valium users. I was a bit alarmed, so I took myself off Valium, leaving my happy hour behind, and just worked around the problem. It soon became predictable which movements would cause spasm, but although it was always present, I was able to avoid the more violent and uncomfortable episodes. Quite often on the exercise mat, Stephanie or Helen would pause during a movement and either stop it completely or alter an angle slightly to alleviate the spasm when it began. And many a time on the floor, they would pause while I had to take myself off to the toilet.

When my physios finished with me, I'd be up and down on the parallel bars or down in the gym with Don, doing bench presses to build up my upper-body strength. Over time, we increased the weights, and I was soon pressing over two hundred pounds, which meant that if I fell over on my face, I could lie there and do push-ups.

CHAPTER 12

Going Home

While I was at Glenwood, I picked up a nasty internal infection, as one did. The cure was twenty-six intramuscular injections of a thick globular substance, into whatever part of my anatomy was available but preferably not the arm. My sister-in-law Emily, being a former nurse, volunteered to give them to me. Twenty-one ended up in my right buttock (because my right side had little feeling in it), and only five into my left. Even so, it was a bruising, uncomfortable experience, and by the end, we were both fed up with injections. Despite feeling like a pincushion, I was able to go home for Christmas. Then, a short time later, I left Glenwood for good, only coming back to visit everyone there, especially good fellows Bourkey and Clem.

Nothing much had changed at home, except that after sixteen years, my father had had enough money to put a room on the back of the house. It had been financed through the money he and his sister had inherited from their older brother, Matt, who had died three years earlier while I was still at college. Apparently, Matt and his "wife," whom who we called Aunty Elsie, had neglected to do two vital things: write a will and get married. So even though they had lived together for many years as husband and wife, she had no legal right to his estate. My father felt that he and his sister should share it with her, but Elsie didn't like that idea—she wanted it all. But soon after, she died, leaving my father and his sister to share the lot.

With all the legalities settled, my father had a sunroom built and continued to plan for the trip of their lifetime to Britain. It had been his desire to take my mother over to see Scotland and the area where her forebears lived. She knew more about Scotland than she knew about her own country, due to the influences of her aunt Janet, a Scot to her bootstraps, who had filled my mother's head with romantic tales about Scotland, rather than the poverty that drove the family to Australia. The trip, though, was delayed when my mother refused to even consider it while I was recovering at home. She wasn't at all placated when my brother's wife said I could look after myself and that they would drop in to see me from time to time. While all this was going on, my father continued planning for the trip, despite his own failing health. He had suffered more from my injury than anyone else. He lived for my successes and found solace for his lost years through them. He came to all my matches, just a shadow in the background, a rustle among the trees. On a charitable day, I'd look for him, but other times, I cringed with embarrassment when I saw him there. Who would go to support the cricket team that his son had been dropped from on the morning of the match, after the captain rang and said he didn't need to turn up? My father would—because it was a matter of honor to support the team, even if I wasn't playing. So the personal grief he suffered through my injury exacerbated the harm his body had been caused by stress, the years of handling lead proofs, and the years of passive smoking he put up with because of inconsiderate chain-smoking workmates. He had suffered a mild heart attack while I was in hospital and never fully regained his vigor and health—another reason my mother wouldn't go. Yet still he planned.

My old bedroom was still the same. The faded gray wall paint was still cracked and peeling, and the round depression in the plaster next to my bed that matched the shape of my head still spoke of youthful wrestles with my older brother in the days he could throw me around like a rag doll. Now, with Geoffrey married and gone, I had the whole room to myself. And each night, in my private world, I could fill my urine bottle, wake to turn myself over, and disturb no one.

Each day I would be picked up from home by ambulance and transported to and from the hospital. The drivers were generally young, blokey fellows and very supportive. We used to chat on the way home and even had a bit of excitement one day when we received an emergency call to attend an accident in Dee Why.

"Want to go for a run?" he asked.

"Sure," I replied, thinking it sounded like a bit of serious fun.

So with the siren blaring, we hurtled through Collaroy and up past Long Reef, scattering cars before us as they dived out of the way to let us through. And all the time, I sat perched up in the front, regal- like, my disability hidden, empowered by a siren that announced that two knights were on their way to bring comfort to the broken-hearted and rescue for the injured. As it turned out, a lady had slipped on a gutter and hurt her ankle, so after attending to it, the ambo, with Walter Mitty in the front seat next to him, drove somewhat more sedately back to my castle.

For a time, a kind-hearted older fellow used to pick me up in an ambulance bus and take me to the hospital. He was very deliberate in his movements, plodding even, especially his driving. One morning we were powering up Spit Hill with the siren wailing—for what reason, I can't remember—only to be passed by a double- decker bus, with curious passengers peering into the ambulance to see what was going on. I kept looking straight ahead, trying to be invisible, while making sure I didn't catch the eye of any of the bus's passengers.

Then one day, it happened. Despite being under medical care in Sydney, I had felt my real world was back in the country at my school. But over time, that started to fade as my condition became the focus of all my efforts. The nights preparing schoolwork in my room at the farm and the days playing with the kids on the playground took on a more distant feel. My world of independence and authority was now a world of dependence and subservience to anyone in a nurse's uniform or wearing a stethoscope. I never let "my kids" go, but little by little, they were taken from me until one day I knew they weren't mine anymore—

those wonderful country kids were someone else's. And that was hard to take.

I met some interesting people during the time I was an outpatient at the spinal injuries unit. One was Angela, a senior nurse with whom I had a most peculiar relationship. Angela was passing by one day as I was exercising on the parallel bars, and she stopped and started talking to me. She was friendly, if a bit guarded, but she was easy to talk to—maybe too easy. A few days later, she stopped by again, and during our conversation she "confessed" to me that she'd had sexual relations with a fellow. Back then, there was a bit of a stigma attached to girls who had sex, so I was surprised she told me—I didn't know her very well, nor did I think her personal life was any of my business. She stopped by over the next few days and then suggested we go out together. She even offered to pick me up, so I thought, *Why not?*

Over the next few weeks, we'd go somewhere and park for a while and talk. I enjoyed her company and our often deep and meaningful conversations. One night, we parked just off the Wakehurst Parkway at Deep Creek, and she opened up about some problems she was going through. I talked about my Christian faith and the problems it had helped me through. Everything she told me was unsolicited. It seemed like she was desperately trying to unload and get things off her chest, and I was a good listener.

When she dropped me at home, she seemed to go cold and said she wouldn't be seeing me again. I had given her a friendly hug, so I wondered if she had misunderstood it. After that, we spoke a few times in passing, but I could see her mind was elsewhere, and she never suggested we go out again. In the end, she stopped coming by, and for my part, I wondered why she had initiated a relationship and then ended it so abruptly without any explanation. I suspected she just needed someone to talk to, and I seemed like a safe place to go, or maybe all the issues going on in her life were pressing and I was a distraction from them.

Still, I remembered her as a nice girl whose company I enjoyed briefly, but with whom I'd had a most peculiar relationship.

I wasn't interested in a flirtatious relationship with Angela, but the delicious Sienna was an entirely different matter.

Sienna was a trainee nurse and had to walk past the unit on her way to the unit where she was working. I was exercising on the parallel bars, as usual, when she stopped to talk to me. She wasn't pretty, like Angela, but was attractive and had a sweetness about her that I really liked. She also had a sense of humor and introduced herself as the "lowest of the low," meaning she was just out of high school. I wasn't a chatty person, more of a listener, so I let her do most of the talking.

She was never in a hurry to leave after that, so I had a feeling there was some interest—so I asked her out. I was a bit surprised when she accepted my invitation, as I half expected her to politely decline. Later, she said that when she told her friends, their reaction had been something akin to enthusiastic. Again, it surprised me, as it hadn't occurred to me that the nurses might see the patients not just as patients. Then again, the young ones were still free spirits with less responsibility and fewer inhibitions than their more senior "sisters" might have.

Fortunately, I had been down to Wagga and had brought my car back to Sydney, so I was able to pick up Sienna outside the nurses quarters. I had arranged to go to the pictures with ambo Paul, so I drove to Manly Wharf to meet up with him and his lady friend. We waited outside the Odeon picture theater for a while, until it became obvious he wasn't coming. Sienna wasn't really interested in seeing a film but was happy to go for a drive up to North Head. We found a spot to park, and before I'd turned off the ignition, she was out of her seatbelt and had slid across the bench seat of the Kingswood and was resting on my shoulder. Talk about initiative. She was so quick off the mark, I didn't have time to undo my seatbelt. I'd have to say she was up there with Celeste as the best kisser I had ever come across. It was the sort of evening I liked—a pure, chaste, romantic evening, where we both felt completely comfortable.

I went out with Sienna a number of times and then she invited me back to her place to meet her parents. I was a bit uneasy about meeting them so soon because of my condition and because I wasn't sure what she had told them about me. I hadn't thought about our relationship as being any more than a pleasant distraction, because I really wasn't in a position to see it in any other way.

157

If I wasn't sure how I would be received, I soon found out. They were English, and while Sienna's mother was pleasant enough, her father seemed to be deliberately antagonistic and ready to criticize anything I said, as well as making disparaging comments about Australia. I had more important concerns in my life than worrying about what he thought of me, so as much as I liked Sienna, I didn't feel the same about her parents. We had gone out because I'd thought we were attracted to each other and enjoyed each other's company. But after meeting her parents, something changed. I didn't feel comfortable enough to ask her about her feelings for me, as it was an area I wasn't prepared to visit. If I wasn't ready to let anyone into my life before, then I was even more reluctant to do so now. I certainly wasn't going to lead her on, just to satisfy some personal need. Sienna was a decent girl, but I felt that at eighteen, she was far too young to be part of my complicated world. I never stopped liking her, but she was becoming a distraction I didn't need, so I stopped seeing her and kept my focus on the road to recovery that was still there before me.

Over the years, I found that I liked talking to girls rather than fellows. Girls liked to talk about things in depth, and I could be the objective, slightly distant friend, listening. But when it came to feelings and emotional issues, I was far happier hanging with the fellows, whose sole counsel on broken relationships was usually, "Get over it."

One day my father showed me a letter he had just received from an official of the Manly Cricket Club. It came as the result of a previous letter he had sent to my father, inquiring as to my whereabouts and noting I hadn't played for Manly in the cricket season just past. In reply, my father had detailed in a letter an explanation about my situation. A reply quickly followed, expressing shock and sympathy. He went on to say that he wasn't aware I was teaching in the country and had written to ask me to rejoin the Manly Club, as I was someone of ability they didn't want to lose. It seemed to me it was a bit too late to be showing interest in me now.

Soon after, a sympathetic article appeared in the *Manly Daily* that was mostly factual. I wrote to the sports editor, the father of one of my former teammates, purely out of courtesy, which prompted a second article that stretched the bounds of truth as to the cause of my condition. I was embarrassed when I read it, as he quoted some private thoughts I'd shared with him in his column. Then, out of the blue, a few months later he wrote a third article, more nostalgic than the others, because by now he had forgotten the facts, as well as generously promoting me in it into past Manly rep teams for which I hadn't been selected. I thought it must have been a slow news day because I hadn't contributed any more information since my first and only letter. As much as I liked seeing my name in print, I felt any further stories would descend into banality and was thankful when the sympathy articles had run their course, and I was out of the public eye.

During the first year of my recovery at home, I made a number of road trips. The most significant was my first trip back to Wagga to pick up my car. I went down with my father, Grahame, and cricket mate Paul. We met up with Ross in Wagga, and then we drove home.

Apart from picking up my car, two visits made the trip worthwhile. One was to the hospital, where I saw some of the staff who had looked after me. Then afterward, we drove up to Peter Dewey's house to see him. It was a short but important meeting, which was quite emotional, as he related to me the extent of my injury, his concern for my well-being, and his pleasure at seeing me walking again. I was glad I was able to give him that satisfaction, as well as thanking him for not only his efforts but also the human touch he brought to my case. When I left, he wasn't a reserved and starchy Englishman but a caring friend who had grown up in London during the Blitz and learned the hard way how important the life of each individual was.

We left Wagga and drove sixty-five miles northwest, past Grong Grong and up the Newell Highway, to see my school at Cowabbie West. We stopped and walked through the grounds and took pictures, and then we moved on, passing through places with memories still too raw for me not to feel my loss. As much as I felt I still belonged there, I was glad to be on my way. The months in Sydney had brought a disconnect with the area, as I had begun to realize the fit young man who had taught there a year ago no longer existed, while the person who was left behind just wouldn't have been able to do the job satisfactorily anymore.

The second trip came at the end of the year in December. Ross had been conscripted and was on leave when he rang me and said, "Pack the Kingswood. We're going bush." Compliant as ever, I did.

I picked Ross up at his Greenacre home and then we headed south down the Princes Highway to Nowra, where we stopped for lunch. Ross became annoyed with the looks people were giving me as I stumbled along the footpath to the RSL Club, so he said, "Put on a show for them." Compliant as ever, I did, and just about scared the next person to death with a robust and highly exaggerated display of silly walking. In the club, Ross nodded toward me and said, "Vietnam," thus ensuring free drinks and the concerned attention from the patrons at the bar. If anyone asked what had happened, a helicopter and parachute had a good chance of getting a run, but thankfully, no one did, as I knew I couldn't lie about something like that and keep a straight face.

We continued south to Bega, where we were able to see Ken Kermode, our mate from college. After staying a couple of nights, we headed up from the coast to Cooma and then continued up into the Snowy Mountains until we reached the car park just below the summit of Mt. Kosciusko. Although we arrived safely, we had had a minor scare on the way. I was driving, and as we approached Nimmitabel, we came over a rise where the road suddenly dipped and darted off to the right. My foot became caught under the brake pedal, as I tried to negotiate the sudden change in direction and free my foot at the same time. It became just too difficult, so I headed off into the bush until we were able to yank my foot out from under the brake and stop the car. We lingered for a few moments, recovering from our little adventure, and then I handed the keys to Ross, and he drove the rest of the way until we reached Mt. Kosciusko.

At the base of Kossie, we parked next to some cars and then started up the track to the top. Although my balance had improved and I could walk without a stick, it was still a daunting climb for me. Ross tried to piggy-back me, but after staggering on for a short distance, the altitude of seven thousand feet got to him, and he had to put me down. We rested for a moment, and then I said to Ross that we'd come too far not to make it to the top, so I was prepared to give it a go. I was pretty sure I

160

could make it, so we set off again, this time both walking. It didn't prove too difficult, but when we reached the summit, we were greeted by an icy wind blasting across the high plateau. The sheets of ice and the cold conditions up there certainly gave lie to the fact it was early summer. We stayed there long enough to stand on the highest point of Australia and see the view (What view? Kosciusko is no alpine peak) and for Ross to take some photos. One showed me sitting on the cairn on the summit, with my hair blowing backwards and a grimace on my face.

After leaving the mountain, we drove back down to Cooma and then north along the Monaro Highway, stopping to check out the school at Michelago. That became a pattern of behavior during my country trips—checking out schools in places I happened to be passing through, as well as looking for toilets. Although I had a lot more control over my bodily functions, it was, at best, tenuous and necessitated sudden stops and furtive darting behind bushes. As we approached the outskirts of Sydney, we stopped at Leppington to see an ex-college mate and then continued up the road to Greenacre, where I dropped off Ross and then went back home.

The third trip at Easter took Paul, Ross, and me down to Humula in southern New South Wales, where Mick Millard's family owned two properties. We went to the first property but Mick wasn't there; he was over at the other one, Miowera, so we headed there. We passed the pub and dropped in, and we found him there, having a drink with his mates. His expression was priceless when he saw me—a welcoming smile to an old mate. Bob and Jenelle were staying there for the Easter weekend, so we slept in the shearing shed. It was cold but not so cold that it was uncomfortable. We went out rabbit shooting one night and then sat around a fire afterward, listening to Mick narrating "The Man from Snowy River" and other Australian bush poems. It just reminded me how much I felt at home in the country.

I received letters and cards from nurses over the months, but that too faded over time. When I left Wagga, I hadn't expected to maintain any but occasional contact with anyone from the hospital. I did appreciate their interest, but then, during the year I started to receive letters from Miranda. She was now working in Melbourne, and her early letters were friendly and newsy telling me about people we both knew. I replied to her, telling her what was going on up my end, the improvement I had made, and that I was now back at home. It was all very chummy, I thought, and much as I expected, until the tone of her letters started to change. They became more personal and affectionate, and she said she thought about me all the time and was coming up to Sydney to be near me. That was unnerving. As much as I liked and respected her, I didn't have any romantic feelings toward her, nor did I see myself, at age twenty-two, having a serious relationship with anyone.

She came up to the northern beaches, and I visited her at a house where she was staying. I was pleased to see her, and she was pleased to see me. It would have been easy for me to say things and take advantage of the situation, but I couldn't. Miranda was emotionally vulnerable, a friend, and too decent a girl to even contemplate it. I stayed for a while and when I left, she knew there wasn't going to be anything between us.

After that, I lost touch with her. I wondered if she had misunderstood my letters where I tried to be positive and humorous. As a way of coping, I found it better to hide behind a joke, and keep my feelings to myself.

I continued having a busy year with girls. Ross and I visited Marie from college at her family home in Haberfield. She had finished college and was back teaching in Sydney. I hadn't seen her since I left college, and I didn't see her when I was in hospital. She was her normal self, though—effusive, friendly, and very stylish. We visited her another time, but it was obvious my relationship with Marie had moved on, and she had other interests—and probably people—in her life.

Then, some time later, Sarah contacted me and came over for a visit. I wasn't sure why, and I didn't even have the sense to ask. Did she just want to see how I was, as old friends do, or was I flattering myself into thinking she still had feelings for me and was looking to rekindle that spark that existed between us two years before?

We went out a few times, but it became obvious that the attraction we'd had for each other was lost in the past. Back then, it could have been the basis of a relationship, but in deference to Marie and their friendship, it was never allowed to grow. I felt Sarah was looking for something more in me now, but I knew I wasn't the same person she had liked back then.

I wasn't surprised when she stopped coming—I almost expected it. She didn't really know me now, whoever "me" was. I was caught up in an entirely different world from the one we had shared a couple of years before, and the adjustments I was still in the process of making didn't strike a chord with her now. It did remind me that a lot of the attention I received from girls in the past was for pretty shallow reasons, based more on my profile and what I did than who I was.

But even that had changed now, because I wasn't sure who that person was anymore.

Christine was another nurse from the hospital in Wagga. She came from a small country town in the Riverina and was one of the nurses who looked after me when I was in the general ward. When she was on night duty, she would spend time in our room doing physio on my legs and avoiding Larry's overtures. She was tall and attractive, and after Larry's forwardness, I used to sing to her the first two lines of "Hey Jude," just to keep things light and friendly between us. I continued this until she started to give me strange looks. I thought I'd better stop then, because the looks seemed to be asking questions I didn't want asked. I was friendly, even flirty, at times with the nurses, but I was careful not to say anything that could be misinterpreted or even taken seriously—so I thought.

After I came back to Sydney, we wrote a few times. Then her letters became more personal and she wrote how upset she was because of the unwanted overtures she had received from a former patient. I felt sorry for her, because I knew from the many raunchy things he had said that he was pretty keen on bedding anyone who was available, and now he had his eye on her.

One day Christine came to my place with a nurse friend and met my parents. It was a friendly visit, I thought, nothing more than a kind gesture. The friend was overly familiar with my father as they were leaving—an embarrassing experience for him, as he held the nurses who had looked after me in high esteem and was quite taken aback by it. After that visit, I didn't expect I'd be seeing Christine again.

It was quite the norm for young teachers, especially males, to start a degree by correspondence after graduating from teachers college. Then they could work their way up from primary school and become a high school teacher. In 1972, I began an arts degree at UNE (University of New England) by correspondence. With an unsure future and the need to continue medical treatment, I chose to start my degree with one subject: English. I was pleased there wasn't a residential school in Armidale for first-year English, so I approached the year with confidence. I could be anonymous and do it all at home. I was put in touch with Penny, a fellow student who lived farther up the peninsula at Newport. Penny was a few years older than I was and had completed English the previous year. She was only too happy to help out in any way she could. I paid her a number of visits; met her husband, children, and in-laws; and generally sailed through the course. I did well with my essays and did the final exam in a church hall in Dee Why, along with a number of other correspondence students. It was no surprise to me to receive a credit for the course—it had been that easy.

I continued at the unit until the beginning of 1973, when I was pronounced fit to resume work by the education department doctor. As much as I didn't like being a full-time patient, the hospital had been my security blanket, where I didn't have to step outside my comfort zone. My walking had improved to the point that I could get around with one walking stick or waddle around with an acceptable level of balance with none. The damage to my spinal cord had affected the motor ability primarily on the left side of my body, from my chest down. Dr Yeo calculated I had 60 percent function for the right side and 50 percent function for the left side. It wasn't so obvious back then—I was able to regain enough mobility and strength in my lower back and legs through therapy and exercise that I got by with just a hint of a limp. I was thankfully able to avoid a "hitch kick," as it was called, with my left leg, or a pronounced "halting step" until years later, after aging saw continual deterioration in my condition.

One of the peculiarities of the physical anatomy is that while the left side of my body suffered more motor damage, it suffered less sensory impairment than the right. The right side was basically numb—hot and cold didn't register, I could barely feel sharp objects, while soft touch would occur without my brain having any knowledge of it. The left side, though, had a semblance of normal feeling, if normal was feeling through a couple of layers of clothes. I could feel hot and cold as well as sharp objects, while on the right side of my body, they only registered high up on my chest.

After three to four years, apparently there was no more nerve regeneration, so I had to spend the rest of my life working hard to maintain the recovery I had already made. Still, I always believed in miracles and that God could heal me and restore my legs to their former days.

Although my legs grew stronger, they always felt heavy, like lead weights had been tied to them. Because of that, I used to become tired dragging them around as I walked and found I couldn't walk long distances. They were always sore, without being painful, and at times there was tingling in my feet, which were so sensitive I rarely went barefoot. If I trod on something sharp or abrasive, my foot reacted and my leg was liable to fly up and almost knee me in the face. Amusing to watch but irritating when it happened.

At times, I would lose my balance and stumble. On bad days, that meant a stumble and a fall; on better days, a stumble and I'd catch myself—or a railing or someone with me would intervene before a fall. With practice, I became adept at picking my spot and preparing my body for a landing. "Fall gracefully and land softly" was my motto. I failed miserably one day when I had nothing to stop my fall other than a brick wall. And it did ... with my head. I lay on the ground for a few minutes, stunned, until I was able to lever my way back to my feet and with a new respect for the hardness of brick.

While I was young and had a legacy of good health and robust fitness, my body was able to accommodate the physical changes, but the psychological effect it had on me was another matter. It would become a constant theme I had to work through. Many a time my thoughts wandered off to the final bend of that 200-meter race and pictured myself pushing just a bit harder in trying to finish third.

At night I had the twin problems of having to wake up to turn myself over and making a number of trips to the toilet. Bladder infections would exacerbate the problem, and getting up three or four times a night to go to the toilet and the ensuing broken sleep would often leave me feeling tired and washed out the next day. But again, it was just another quirky consequence of my condition to which I had to adjust to and work around.

Three oddities come to mind that made my life more interesting. One was that I became uncomfortable in tight spaces with other people around me. It inhibited my sense of balance, as movements and corrections I needed to make were often frustrated by people standing in my space.

When I was sitting down, I became uncomfortable because of the constant pressure on one spot. I soon worked out the best position to sit in, so it would relieve pressure on my back. I would plant my body in that position and adjust it slightly when I needed to.

The other thing I found, which became worse over the years, was when my foot wouldn't move. It seemed to hesitate as though it hadn't decided whether to come with me or stay behind. It was only the left foot, and while I was young and strong, it wasn't a major concern—just an inconvenience. The older I got, the more holes I wore in the big toe of my left-foot shoes, as walking became more of an effort and, at times, a bit of a drag.

CHAPTER 13

My New Normal

My father had an upstairs room built over our outdoor patio. The patio was turned into a family room, and the upstairs was built ostensibly so that my brother and his wife would have a place to stay when they came back from overseas. When they came back, however, they moved into Mamre, Emily's family's property at St. Mary's, on the western fringe of Sydney, and the upstairs room became a retreat for my father to read the paper and gaze out over a world that was passing him by.

Mamre took its name from the plains of Mamre in the Old Testament and was built and owned by Reverend Samuel Marsden in the early 1800s. I stayed there one weekend, and lying in Marsden's four- poster bed, I listened to a radio broadcast of Bob Massie taking 16 for 137 against England in the 1972 Lord's Cricket Test. Mamre had such historical significance about it that it hosted a parade of visitors: my parents and sister, of course; my father's sister; my mother's sister; my cousin; my friends. Heck, I even took my physiotherapist there for a visit, such was the unique quality of the place.

Robbo came back into my life when he appeared at my parents' place one day. He said he had just heard about my mishap, or he would have come to see me sooner. Much had changed since we were last in contact. He was at Sydney University now and had moved away from his

167

peripatetic lifestyle on the northern beaches to grow roots at Annandale, an inner-city suburb. He was renting a house on Johnston Street and then moved farther down the street to a corner house, which he shared with other university students.

He introduced me to a different crowd of people than the ones I was used to. In Robbo's eyes, he was doing me a favor and giving me a real education as to what life was really about. To Robbo, real life was now defined as a product of the enlightened world of university—its education, its melting pot of ideologies, and its offsprings of social change and political activism. It didn't take into account my own perceptions and experiences, especially my most recent ones, and it suggested that my Christian beliefs were unenlightened and naïve. By this stage, any pretense of Christian belief that Robbo had espoused just a year or two earlier was gone, replaced by a political activist, an angry ant railing at the system and with a decidedly pinkish worldview.

Still, for the next year or so, I often made a beeline—sometimes with mate Paul and sometimes without mate Paul—to Annandale to meet a lot of interesting people whose views were often diametrically opposed to mine. I did enjoy my education, because rather than undermining my Christian faith, rubbing shoulders with uni types only confirmed it. One night I met a number of Robbo's friends—rugby players who had toured South Africa with the Australian Rugby Union team just a few years before and were now publicly advocating boycotting South African rugby, because of their government's apartheid policies. They were intelligent, urbane, highly educated men, with a moral conscience that put most to shame and who took a public stand that cost them their places on the Australian team, but whom history ultimately proved correct.

I also saw the social revolution going on through the pot-smoking, free-love lifestyle operating in Robbo's house, a lifestyle he had embraced. I suspected it was a glimpse of the bigger picture going on on university campuses around Australia at that time. His type of activism saw off the Vietnam War and the South African Rugby team and ushered in the Whitlam years on the Australian political stage. It was an amazing world to be part of for the short period we maintained our relationship.

However, while I found my time there educational, I did feel it would be short lived. For me, there were questions with no answers as to what my life was about and where it was heading. For that, God had to be at the center of everything I did, whereas with Robbo, God was out of the picture, nowhere to be seen—actually, obliterated by revolutionary Marxist philosophy. When I questioned Robbo about his new beliefs, he said, "I want to do what I can now, before I become like everyone else who gets a job, worries about his mortgage, and becomes part of the system."

I did lose a girlfriend over my interest with the Annandale household. Linda was a girl I had met through my sister about five years before. She used to go to the World Evangelical Crusade (WEC) meetings I regularly attended with my sister Jane. She was a sweet, pretty young girl who had finished university and was now an occupational therapist. I met her again on a hospital visit to Mt. Wilga rehab center, where she worked. We hit it off straight away and went out for a few months. In the end, she didn't like the Annandale crowd and their lifestyle and indicated to me that it was either them or her. Sadly, it was them, which wasn't really fair on Linda. She was the right sort of girl for me but of course, it was the same old problem— lovely girl but an unwillingness from me to commit, so I was reluctant to give it a go and see if things developed. She reminded me of Brianna—small, dark-haired, pretty, smart, and a Christian with a lively sense of humor. I couldn't fault her, but there were no bells ringing or skyrockets going off, and I wasn't going to string her along either.

I hadn't seen Christine since she visited me at home the previous year. Then one night, when Paul and I were at Annandale visiting Robbo, she turned up, unannounced, with her younger sister. It was a bit of a shock seeing her, so we ended up talking outside on the footpath, because Christine didn't want to come inside. Paul came out for a look, so her sister reasoned it had to be more interesting inside than outside, where our labored conversation was taking place. Christine made it plain she only came to see me, so we sat in my car to talk—or so I thought. I can only surmise she was lonely because she gave me that same look she had given me back in Wagga hospital. My feelings for her

169

weren't of a romantic nature but were the affections and appreciation of a former patient. I didn't mind girls I liked taking a bit of initiative—at times, I was so slow they had to—but not when they threw themselves at me. It was quite unnerving, and I could only surmise she was looking for a relationship with someone and came up to see if it might be me. I didn't know what her feelings for me were and quite frankly, I didn't really want to ask. That would have opened up an intimacy between us that I hadn't encouraged or entertained. Despite my less-than- robust emotional state, I wasn't willing to just 'drift' into a relationship with her either. Still, I didn't think it was fair to ignore her, so I saw her over the next few months, if somewhat half-heartedly.

Then Christine dropped out of my life, only to reappear nearly two years later under circumstances I found quite bizarre. I had left the flat where I was living at the time and moved back to my parents' place. Some weeks later, the owners of the flat rang me to say Christine wanted to move in, and as she had mentioned my name, they wanted to know a bit about her. So Christine moved in and then rang me a week or two later and asked me to come down to see her. I came down after dinner to find her getting ready for bed. We talked briefly, and she mentioned offhandedly that she had a fiancé somewhere, but she didn't say why she was at Collaroy or where she was working. It was all a bit confusing, because she went into the bedroom and said she was going to bed. That was a confronting moment, because Christine was an attractive girl and her invitation was obvious. I did what I thought was the right thing to do and left. Sometime later, I heard from the house owners that she had left the flat, and I never saw her again.

The whole episode had shown me that I liked girls but found I could get into a relationship I didn't really mean to, and then I didn't really know how to get out of it either. I respected women but had sometimes missed the warning signs to stay clear because I didn't want to hurt their feelings, only to regret afterward that I had, in fact, hurt their feelings.

I certainly had a lot to learn about girls, but with such competing issues in my life, I wondered if I ever would.

CHAPTER 14

Life—What Is Lost or What Is before You?

I was excited, although a bit apprehensive, when I started back at school. It was eighteen months since I'd been paralyzed. I had made a lot of progress, with at least another eighteen months of hoped-for improvement before me. I wasn't back at my bush school, surrounded by wheat paddocks, nor was there a dirt road out the front, silent except for the occasional car shrouded in dust thundering by. Nor was I running with my kids, kicking the football to them, wielding a hockey stick, or swinging a cricket bat. This was the Correspondence School, where, legend had it, only teachers dead above the shoulders ended up. No wonder I felt like a lesser man, if my life had come to this.

In my view, there are two ways of seeing loss. The first is to focus on what has been lost. The second is to look forward to what is to come. The former, I suppose, looks at the world through a glass that is half empty, with constant reminders of what once was. The latter looks ahead, with confidence that God is the rock on which all hope is founded. I would like to say I moved seamlessly into the second phase but in truth, I vacillated between both, as my daily reminders of what had been lost always had an unyielding, inescapable presence. Still, to trust God and focus on the next step helped me to see that the glass was half full—and filling, more times than not.

The Correspondence School was situated at the bottom of William Street in Sydney, just before it made its way up the hill to Kings Cross. I was able to park at the rear of the building, from where I could go through the back door and up the lift to the third floor. It was a door through which I only ever would have gone through misadventure. The old me would have stayed one day and then would have been on his bike, straight back to the country. The stifling and insipid atmosphere said it was a place for losers from the vast education system, and now I was one of them. It wasn't helped by the overly protective fawning of some of the motherly types there, one of whom informed me breathlessly one day, "We've all taken you to heart." *Yuck!* I thought.

Despite my initial misgivings, it was the right place for me. I soon found the staff there were a mixed lot. Some were talented educationists who thrived in the protective atmosphere of the school. Others saw it as a place where they could still be a teacher, enjoy the holidays, put in minimal preparation, and rarely have to see their students face-to-face. And still others missed that contact with students and endured all the frustrations of not being in a "real" school during their time there.

I soon realized that to stay too long would become a life sentence, and some in the school "family" fully expected it. "That poor young fellow. We'll look after him," the building seemed to say. But it was different now. I was no longer a patient but a young schoolteacher, still wanting what I once had—that lazy drive to school down the track and across Cowabbie Creek; weekends at Malebo; late nights hiving around paddocks in Bob's station wagon, shooting rabbits and missing foxes; the freedom, independence, and responsibilities of a country teacher juxtaposed with the bittersweet feelings of going into town, looking for familiar faces but having no one to share my time with.

But to hold on to those memories, I would have to work my way out of the place, and when it was time, be prepared to forsake its security and go.

In 1973, I started there as an illustrator in a room staffed entirely by women, some of whom were art teachers and some of whom were trained illustrators—and one who was me.

I could always draw, but without any formal training, I'd have to say that as an illustrator, I was barely average. I learned quickly, though, and listened to advice, and was a much better illustrator when I left than I was when I first started there.

It must have been a bit of a shock for the girls when I turned up for my first day, but despite any reservations they might have had about me, they were very welcoming and made me feel right at home. Having me there didn't inhibit their lively and often ribald conversations either, some of which were slyly directed my way. Nor was I spared the personal bits about their lives or the things that are probably only spoken of behind closed doors in the ladies room.

The work was interesting, and there was always a buzz of energy around the room. Very soon, I felt my macho rugby persona slipping away and being quietly replaced by another side of me I both embraced and loathed. Gone was any boys talk as I entered a "classroom" completely dominated by female sensibilities.

I was there for the rest of the year and became friendly with Anne. She lived out my way and soon became my passenger and a welcome change from the tedium of navigating Sydney's peak-hour traffic on my own. Anne was open and friendly and talked incessantly about her husband and her two children. However, she was good company for the years she was my chief passenger. She paid the harbor bridge toll, and as time went by, my number of passengers increased and allowed me a quick trip down the transit lane and an occasional full tank of petrol.

The Illustrators were a tight group, though, supporting each other through difficult—and in one case, tragic—circumstances. I observed all this in silence, like a fly on the wall, intrigued by other people's dramas being played out in front of me. Still, they were all kind and friendly and, after we became more familiar with each other, flirty even, so when I moved on, I had a healthy respect and good relationship with all of them.

Despite being a tight group, tensions often surfaced on every second Thursday. That's because it was payday. Teachers and illustrators were paid under a different award, which saw teachers paid more than illustrators. Marge, our supervisor, was an older lady and a trained illustrator. She was generally affable, except on paydays. She was paid less than all the teachers and would let us know when giving out the checks, while railing on about the injustice of it all. I happily received my check but not the commentary that came with it.

Some lunchtimes, I would go for a short walk up William Street for a bit of exercise. I wanted to be more independent, so I would often go out without my walking stick. If I fell over, I was able to get back up, although I tried to avoid crowds, as any sudden jostling could send me tumbling. On one such occasion, I was returning to the school when I saw Daryl Harberecht, my country rugby coach, walking up William Street toward me. I hadn't thought of him as a city person, dressed in a business suit, but rather as a country rugby coach, dressed in his tracksuit. But like many of the country officials, he lived and worked in Sydney. When Daryl saw me, his expression changed from instant recognition to one of shock and concern. As for me, I felt embarrassed that he had seen me, not as a fit and healthy footballer, but as I now was. My embarrassment was partly my concern for his feelings and partly for my own. I explained what had happened, and he offered his sympathy, but when we parted, all I could see in his eyes was pity—another painful moment and a reminder that I had lost another family, this one being my rugby family.

I moved out of the illustrators—friendly, supportive people—into a classroom situation with more friendly, supportive people. I soon found they were a mixed bunch too—talented contributors, survivors, casualties of the system, an alcoholic, malingerers squeezing out every benefit they could until retirement, and later, my first exposure to a mistress who was an ideologically driven feminist.

It was a good place for me, though, as I could keep my head down, learn the routine of working with isolated children, and rebuild my confidence. I was very focused on doing the best I could, so I tried to ignore any teachers federation business or school politics going on around me, or I let go over my head.

At this time, I was going through a period of contentment, as I felt close to God. I knew He was with me, protecting me, and softening my pain—the pain of missing the country, the lifestyle, and my school and friends. Still, good things were happening, although I still found myself dreaming of running that 200-meter final again, straining just a little bit harder on the final bend, and finally, coming third.

My new workplace proved to be rich in potential and opportunity, if you were looking for it. It was a place where I could use up a lot of creative energy and learn new things, which would have been unlikely if I had still been back at my one-teacher school. A ready source I could rely on was the wealth of experience of the older teachers around me, which I was able to adapt for my own purposes. As well as having my own class I was asked to take over writing the school magazine's weekly reading sheet from one of the older teachers. After that, I worked on *Outpost*, the primary school magazine, for two years with another experienced teacher. She had been doing it for years, but no one wanted to work with her. I did, and to everyone's surprise, we got on brilliantly. My view was when working with older, strong–willed women, one should be compliant, and everything will turn out fine.

My classes allowed me to renew my relationship with children but on my terms. The distance meant they would "see" me through the content of my comments, my insane cartoons, and my spontaneous humor, all designed to make learning fun and exciting and bridge the gap caused by that old tyrant, distance. Comments coming back to me from parents and students led me to believe that that approach was largely on the right track. But I still had to be on my guard that I wasn't overcompensating.

I also found it to be an instructive period, as it allowed me to be a student as well and to receive a thorough education into what life was like for isolated students and their parents.

I had my favorites, of course—perky little Louise, the bright-as-a- button sixth-class daughter of a doctor from Coonabarabran. She was doing correspondence work because of a medical condition, but whatever therapy I might have been for her, she returned it to me in bucketloads. We had a riotous time, but when she came down to Sydney with her mother for a visit, I wasn't emotionally ready to meet this bubbly little mite, standing in front of my desk and grinning at me for all her worth, because finally, she was able to meet her crazy teacher. Now, she was seeing me as I was—handicapped both physically and—in her case—emotionally. In that moment, I lamented that this wonderful young girl would never meet the real me—the other me, the sportsman, the teacher who would come alongside his students and share in the triumphs and disappointments of their day, and who I still considered to be better than the person I now was.

But Louise and her mother hardly noticed. They were so generous and appreciative, and when they had gone, I was still that mad person in the post who was her teacher. When Louise was back at home, we resumed our anarchical relationship as if nothing had happened. But then I realized, nothing *had* happened. We had met, and how I looked didn't matter to them, it only mattered to me.

Another student who made an impression on me was a young girl in a wheelchair who had cerebral palsy. Anne McBrien lived with her parents on a farm on the Hume Highway, just north of Holbrook. Over time, I built up a good rapport with Anne and her mother and told them about my own situation, so they would know I understood what they were going through. I decided to fly down to Wagga on the holidays, hire a car, and drive down to see them. My secondary reason of visiting old friends in Wagga became less important after I visited the McBriens. It was a very emotional experience, meeting them. Anne was very excited, and her reaction let me see how much it meant to them, as well as how important it was for children in her situation to have personal contact. I stayed for lunch and headed back to Wagga later that afternoon, feeling mentally worn out by the experience and wondering if I was out of my depth with handicapped children. Things hadn't been easy for them. John had suffered a heart attack, farm income was down, and Anne was difficult to manage. They hoped to get her into a school for crippled children next year, which meant selling and relocating to Melbourne.

The next day I looked up old friends in Wagga and then flew back to Sydney. Anne was in my class for the rest of the year but after that, we lost contact, and I don't know what became of her and her family. I'd been such a small part of her life but wouldn't be a part of her future.

I became friends with a bright, young, dramatically trained teacher who was sent to the Correspondence School as her first appointment, when nothing else came up. Her abilities and creative talents could have been wasted there, but fortunately, when we first locked eyes, we knew we were kindred spirits. By pooling our ideas, we were able to collaborate in producing educational tapes for the correspondence students. At that time, I was writing language leaflets, so Bernadette would trundle over to my desk; start the conversation with, "Say, Ken"; ask my opinion; and write the scripts. Then we would troop downstairs to the recording studio and record them. It was that easy. Our wicked senses of humor made for a rollicking good time, while we hoped the kids would get as much fun out of the tapes and the information they contained as we did making them. We had a productive relationship for the year she was there, but Bernadette wanted to teach in a real school, so she was happy when she was transferred to Harbord Public School.

A year later, she was back. Unfortunately, she found that in that one year at the Correspondence School, when she didn't have a class, she had lost her edge. It happened that easily. Harbord School was a plum appointment on the northern beaches, but Bernie told me she soon found she was out of her depth in a very competitive environment and was verbally abused by two of the female teachers as being "unprofessional" because she needed just a bit of encouragement and help. She would have made a brilliant teacher with the right support, but instead, she was back at the Correspondence School, trying to pick up the pieces and restore her self-confidence.

Soon after, we resumed our working relationship, and soon after that, she had a smile on her face again. I loved working with Bernie; she was a lovely girl, as well as being a real hoot.

After a few years I was relieved from class duties and put on writing (and illustrating) language leaflets for the new language syllabus. It was all very therapeutic, as it released a lot of creative energy that I had locked up inside and improved my drawing and graphic-design skills to no end. It also opened up an opportunity to write for Reeds, publisher of educational books. It all happened because a fellow writer—the flamboyant, eccentric teacher/author Isobel—was impressed by my writing ability and introduced me to a friend of hers from Reeds, who was trying to enlist her again to write for their new series of reading books. The series was called Bunyip Books, and with the gifted Pat Edwards as editor and author of six of the books, I found myself authoring three out of the twelve books of the series. To do it properly, I spent many hours researching and gathering information from the microfiche files at Macquarie University Library. It was from all the information I gathered that *Ned Kelly*, *Galahs and Cockatoos*, and *Let's Go Bush* had their origins. Most interesting I found was all the extra information I gathered which I couldn't use, such as Ned Kelly being a distant relative of Annie Oakley. Still, I enjoyed the experience of collecting, sifting, and editing my way through copious amounts of material and squeezing just enough of it on to the pages in very simple language, which took me a while to get used to. I enjoyed the meetings with Pat, the other author, and our gorgeous illustrator, Esther. I was pleased to see Esther used some of my rough drawings as a guide for her illustrations in a number of the pages of *Ned Kelly*, but I wasn't too pleased when the Australian Tax Office decided I was now an author and should pay provisional tax on my new stream of income. This led to an exchange of letters, until the tax office saw my side of the argument and treated my authoring as a once-in-a-lifetime anomaly and taxed me accordingly. *One small victory for the little man*, I thought.

An interesting sidelight to writing language leaflets was that most of the teachers I worked with were older and closer to the end of their teaching careers than the beginning. I gleaned things from their well- traveled minds, especially in the area of the English language, with its confusing rules and idiosyncrasies of grammar, punctuation, and syntax—points that were strangely neglected in the new language syllabus. Instead of a prescriptive syllabus to follow, we had to be creative in interpreting the spirit of the new syllabus and putting into the leaflets the things we felt were important. I had a "grammar upbringing" at

Collaroy Plateau Public School, so I made sure I sneaked some of it into my leaflets, even if I did talk about adjectives as "sparkle and fizz" words. I did feel some disquiet, though, that some of the grammar I had learned never entered the picture for the next generation of primary school students, and that girls in my leaflets, at the insistence of our feminist supervisor, had plum jobs of using hammer and saw.

CHAPTER 15

Paul

Paul and I had grown up playing cricket and rugby together. We were mates, or "cobbers," as his mother would say, using the then- common if fading Australian vernacular, but Paul was quite erratic in his relationships with his mates. True, he had appeal—he was a talented sportsman, especially at cricket, where he played first grade for Manly while still in his teens. He was quick, intelligent, and had a good singing voice, singing in Gilbert and Sullivan productions at school and was the lead singer in a rock band. He also had an extroverted, larger-than-life, and sometimes assertive personality, which attracted young people to him, especially young kids. As a teenager, it was obvious to those of us who knew him that Paul copied the persona of those who could hold a crowd, and Paul thrived in a crowd. Paul had everything going for him. But on the down side, he craved attention. He was self-indulgent, narcissistic, and unable to empathize with people or understand that the world didn't revolve around him. He was jealous when I received public acclaim for my sporting successes, during the primary school years of our relationship, although he did mellow a bit in his later teens.

Paul, though, was a free spirit, hardly noticing that other people also inhabited planet earth. If only there had been one law for everyone and a flexible one for Paul, he would have been happy. With all his strengths, he should have made a great teacher—his chosen profession. For the first year after teachers college, he was doing what he loved best and being paid for doing it—working daily with children.

It was strange that our relationship was so firm, as we were mostly opposites, and although he professed to be a Christian, he had a dark side that he spilled to Grahame and me one night. He told us that he didn't resign from teaching; he was dismissed—and the reason was that he was a pedophile. He had an intense attraction to prepubescent boys and girls and had picked up hundreds over the seven-odd years since, as fifteen- and sixteen-year-olds, we had coached the boys cricket team together. He even laughed about one time when he should have been on the football field, but he was chatting to two young boys behind the change shed. I remembered the match—I'd looked around vainly for my center partner, just as the referee was about to blow his whistle to start the match, and Paul was nowhere to be seen.

If I said we were shocked by his confession, it would have been an understatement. (I was probably less shocked than Grahame as I'd seen more of Paul's eccentricities over the years.) Telling us about that side of his life, because he thought we were mature enough to handle it, and then trying to justify his feelings for young boys left us unsure as to how we should react. He talked about the purity he saw in boys that needed protecting, and he was the one to protect them, like he was a "catcher in the rye." His reasoning, though, seemed to be more of self-indulgence, like the misguided brattishness of Holden Caulfield, than a noble quest for someone with a Peter Pan complex.

After that night, it wasn't just me who needed support from his mates. Paul was asking us for the same, as he was facing a life of not only broken dreams but notoriety and public shame. Paul's parents—quiet, respectable church people—were bewildered by events that led to many court appearances, public exposure, public humiliation and ultimately, incarceration. They implored me to stand by him, as I was his one true friend, and he needed my support. It wasn't a situation I particularly needed, but I often wondered how Jesus would have handled it. In the end, Paul's friends were few, as there was nothing more ignoble in people's eyes than someone who interferes with children.

Over the next few years, there were numerous court appearances, although I only came to the more serious ones in the District Court,

as well as visits to Parramatta, Long Bay, and Bathurst jails. All this was happening while I was trying to get back on to my own two feet.

Then one day, I was summoned to the primary school principal's office to take a phone call. It was from the police, and the conversation went something like this:

"This is Constable So-and-so from Such-and-such Station. Is your name Ken Little?"

"Yes, it is," I replied, wondering where this was heading.

"Do you know a Paul ...?" (They often used the indefinite article when referring to Paul.)

"Yes, I do. We grew up together. What's happened?"

"Did you know he has been using your teaching diploma and passing himself off as you?"

That was news to me. He could hear the incredulity in my voice, so he asked if I wanted to speak to Paul. I did, so he put Paul on.

"You know why I did it, don't you, Ned?" Paul said, using my high- school nickname. Then he insisted, "I didn't mean to get you into trouble. I'd never do that to you. You know that, don't you?"

Nothing surprised me about Paul anymore, but I did believe him on this occasion. For all he was, Paul would never intentionally hurt me

—or anyone else, for that matter. But Paul was a ticking time bomb, and when a ticking time bomb goes off, the situation is out of control, and you never know who's going to be hit by flying shrapnel. I learned that on one of Paul's visits, he'd asked to see my teaching qualifications, which were in a drawer in my bedroom. I didn't suspect him of anything sinister, so I showed them to him. Then afterward, he excused himself to go to the toilet but instead, he sneaked back into my room and took the graduation certificate I received from Wagga Teachers College, with the intention of copying it and heading up to the Northern Territory to get a teaching position there. So mixed up was his mind, he couldn't see the wrong in his actions, other than he got caught.

That was the first of many occasions Paul used my identity. Years later, when Paul was at his active worst, my brother told me I had a police record more than thirty pages long. Hundreds of offenses of indecent acts with children, as well as multiple traffic offenses, were recorded in my name, as one of Paul's aliases. As Paul explained later, he knew everything about me, so my name conveniently tripped off his tongue as he tried to hide his real identity when he was pulled over or arrested. Paul's reasoning was that I should be prepared to accept this in the name of friendship, and as I was such an upstanding person, I could easily show that it wasn't me who had committed all those offenses. He had no idea how much trouble this caused me over the years, but despite it all, I didn't feel angry with Paul, although I did feel distaste for what he was doing. What was obvious to me was that Paul was one sick puppy dog.

Paul would drift in and out of my life over the next few years— sometimes he'd be in jail, other times he'd be surviving the best way he could. I knew he used to buy cheap cars, fix them up, and sell them. I knew he bought and sold shares, and had jobs with pretty dodgy people, and sang in a rock group, but I didn't know what he did other times, nor did I think it was always legal. But whatever his activities were, there would always be a cloud hanging over our relationship.

In some ways, we were similar, but I suppose our responses were different. We both had a handicap. Mine was physical, which became a mental and spiritual battlefield, whereas Paul's were centered in his Peter Pan world and fed by his physical impulses— he chose to abandon normal moral standards and rational decision making, just to satisfy his immediate needs.

We both found it difficult to have a deep relationship with girls but for vastly different reasons. Paul willfully walked away from God's laws. I found myself, by choice, moving closer to God. Adjusting to life was too much for me to handle on my own, and I didn't want to become a person who had lost something, had no direction in life, and was just trying to survive each day.

Paul's humiliations were played out in the public arena—in the courts and the newspapers and even on television—whereas mine were played out in my own private world, where wet pants or uncontrollable bowel functions often left me in despair. Of the latter, one time I was 'saved' by the kindly art supervisor who covered for me and provided support so I could clean myself up sufficiently to drive home and then clean myself up more. On the drive home, I prayed I wouldn't have a car accident. If I had, it certainly would have highlighted the wise advice mothers gave to their sons, "Always wear clean underpants in case you're in an accident."

CHAPTER 16

The Old Has Gone

I changed churches about this time, moving down to Dee Why Baptist after feeling I needed a completely new start. Dee Why had an established young people's group, as well as a few people I had known years before at the Plateau church. I soon felt comfortable and was able to slip into church life there anonymously. After I'd been going there for a few weeks, I noticed three sisters sitting down the front with long hair down to their waists. Although they were only teenagers, the oldest caught my eye. She looked to be about eighteen or nineteen, had a fresh appearance, a lovely smile, and was very attractive. I made a mental note to keep away from her.

When I left the hospital, I had to take on more responsibility for my own rehabilitation. The daily exercise programs were a thing of the past. I had entered the next phase of my recovery, just as I was now entering a new time of my life and stepping into new situations to which I would need to adjust. There was no gradual move from one thing to another; it was all sudden, final, and quite confronting.

First thing I did was to join a gym down at Collaroy and have an exercise and strength program designed that would take into account my limitations and needs. Most of the machines I used were static, so my lack of balance and lack of strength in my lower body wasn't a major factor. I went there three times a week and worked on my upper-body strength, so it would be easier to get myself up after I'd had one of my inevitable falls. I did floor exercises as well, for stretching and flexibility, thus beginning years of continual—although not always continuous— physical activity, partly for my ego's sake but mostly to provide the physical outlet my body needed, as well as much-needed cardiovascular work.

The squash center at Mona Vale, where I used to play squash with Grahame and Paul when we were teenagers, had an indoor heated pool. I knew the owner quite well, and when I turned up with requirements other than a racquet and a ball, he was more than willing to let me swim and exercise in the pool when it was available. I used the pool in the daytime until I went back to work at the Correspondence School. Then I used it at night on occasions, while continuing my gym work at Collaroy.

I visited the unit at RNSH for checkups, to see people, and for some internal probing through intravenous pyelograms (IVPs) and cystograms. The former made me nauseated, when they injected the dye into me intravenously; and the latter made me feel full, when I was catheterized and another liquid was injected into my bladder. Not terribly enjoyable experiences, but as someone whose urinary tract functions were impaired, the tests were standard procedure to determine the health of my kidneys and to preempt any future difficulties that could arise as a result my spinal cord injury.

I also managed to catch up with Helen, one of the physiotherapists, and took her to Mamre to visit my brother and his wife—or more correctly, she took me, chauffeuring me there in her Mini, a popular car of the time. Helen was one of a number of independent career- minded girls I got to know over the next few years. My muses about clingy females, barefoot and pregnant, seemed destined for the garbage pile, among other dinosaurs that lay there. We kept in touch when Helen was in Bourke for a short period and in San Francisco for a year. Our relationship sat uncomfortably between strictly professional and a bit friendly, but I was so half-hearted about pursuing relationships that nothing was ever going to develop between us anyway.

Overall, it was a time of both hope and despair. I remember nights down at Griffith Park, Long Reef, praying fervently to God to heal me and then setting off on a stumbling, clumsy run, half expecting to break into my normal running style halfway around the oval. It never happened. I remember tumbling over and spilling my car keys and driver's license out of my pocket onto the ground and searching for them in the dark. That's all I had in my pocket, thankfully, because that's all I needed. That's all my life was—simple, with not much going on outside my own small world.

That year saw a serious lack of success in my uni studies as I took on two subjects: modern history and psychology. It soon became apparent that I had taken on more than I could handle at that stage of my recovery, and psych wasn't a particularly good fit for me either. I found myself revisiting old territory from the psychology course I did at teachers college, and despite passing the first few assignments, it was draining my enthusiasm, rather than motivating me to press on. My reality was that life was unpredictable and not a system that was neat and orderly, as the theory I was studying suggested it should be. I was trying to adjust to a confusing new world with new norms, as well as accepting life changes, the loss that went with it, and my often total lack of control over everyday events. Among all this background noise, I now had to seriously consider the behavioral habits of stickleback fish and their bubbly little eccentricities as part of my coursework. At the same time, I was receiving copious amounts of reading material for Modern History, so much so that I was starting to feel overwhelmed by it all, much like a ship floundering in oceans of information.

During the May holidays, Ross and I drove up to Armidale for a residential school I was dreading. Two years before, I would have looked forward to it as an equal—a week of lectures, meeting new people, checking out the girls, embracing uni life—but instead I was a spectator watching as people rushed by, excited and full of energy, chattering on like children at the zoo. Ross left me at our table one time to talk to people he had just met, while I sat on my own, feeling isolated and self-conscious—and distracted by the pressing concern of my next toilet trip. I felt disconnected from the world of carefree, able-bodied people and more comfortable with my hospital world of invalids.

Back home, I pushed on, and although my Psych lecturer tried to encourage me, I found it hard to stay motivated. The work wasn't hard, and under normal circumstances, I would have walked through the course—but that only added to my frustration. When I pulled out of Psych, I was coldly informed it would be recorded as a failure. I hoped it would free me to concentrate on history. It didn't—and I started to get my history assignments in late. When I tried to explain the situation to my lecturer, he was encouraging, but his words seemed mechanical and unhelpful, because they didn't address the underlying problem that was still there, which I didn't fully understand and which left me feeling dissatisfied and depressed.

In the end, I forced myself to finish all my assignments, even though they were late. The last two were returned with solid marks but had 100 percent taken off for lateness. I did my final history exam at the same venue as the previous year. I passed the exam but was informed I'd failed the course. It was quite dispiriting, but in hindsight, it was the wrong time to be doing the wrong course. It seemed to be more representative of my old life than the reality of my new one. The desire of becoming an English/History teacher began to recede as I started to think that I had already missed the boat. It had also put my state of mind into question, as the confused effort I'd made suggested I'd fallen short of my own standards and really needed to do things better. As much as I hated giving up the degree course I had started, I felt I had set myself up for failure, and in that, I had succeeded.

Once a week I'd drop Anne off at her place and then drive a bit farther up the road to a Balgowlah Osteopath for a pretty vigorous treatment. One of the trainee osteopaths was a former high school rugby opponent and the boy wonder who kept me out of the CHS rugby team. He had strong hands and was delegated with the task of giving me deep massages before my treatment. While massaging my legs, he would drive his thumbs into my sciatic nerves and work his thumbs up and down the backs of my legs. Normally, that would have had me hanging from the ceiling, but so insensitive were my sciatic nerves that it only just registered in my brain. I went to acupuncturists as well, all in the hope of finding the magic bullet that would wake up slumbering nerve connections and return normal function to my legs.

I was always looking for answers, so during one dark period, I read the book of Job from beginning to end in one hit. I was hoping to make some sense of things but instead, I didn't find any convenient answers, just more questions. I did find, though, that it reinforced what I believed, which was that life can be hard, so trust God and get on with it. When I did, I found that God was always close by, a fact that I was reminded of one day on the way to a Navigators conference in Canberra.

While at high school, I had become involved with the Navigators, an evangelical para-church group with a worldwide mission. In the year I started at the Correspondence School, I went to a Navigators conference in Canberra during the May holidays. As well, I provided transport for four girls who were attending the conference.

It was a wet day, and I was following a truck along the Federal Highway, but it was throwing up so much water that it was affecting visibility. I kept close to the truck, so that when a straight stretch of road came up, I could safely pass it. Moments before, I had looked in my rearview mirror to see a car way back in the distance, so I assumed the road was clear when I pulled out to pass the truck. Just as I pulled out, I found myself looking into the shocked face of the other driver, who had come speeding down the other side of the road, trying to pass both of us. She hit my side door and went off the road onto the grassy verge, as I tried to cut back into my lane behind the truck. Unfortunately, it was too close, so to avoid running into the back of the truck, I pulled sharply on the steering wheel and felt the car sliding sideways and about to roll over. I turned the steering wheel to straighten up, but the car veered off the side of the road into a grassy culvert. It started to roll over but amazingly, it got halfway into the first roll and then settled back down on to its four wheels.

We sat there for a few moments, trying to catch our breath but very relieved. The girls were quite upbeat and said it had been a great piece of driving. I didn't feel so generous about my effort as they did, as it had been my fault we were sitting there in the culvert. The other driver was parked on the other side of the road. She said she and her passenger were okay and there had been no damage to her car. And apart from frayed nerves and a large dent in my driver's side door, we had escaped unscathed as well. Meanwhile, the truck had continued on, completely oblivious of the near carnage behind him.

We continued on to Canberra and had an enjoyable time at the conference. A few days later, we were safely back in Sydney. Back home, I looked at the dent in my car door and reflected on the near accident. I could only put it down to God's providence protecting us, rather than my driving skill. I squeezed back into an impossibly small space behind the fast-moving truck, traveling at about 55 mph without hitting it. Then the car began to roll over in a table drain until an unseen hand intervened and settled it back down on its four wheels. It had to be God, because I'm sure the laws of physics would explain why that maneuver was impossible and should have resulted in a very serious accident.

At this time a rather unfortunate period for my parents began, a time they could have done without, considering what they were already going through with me. My sister Jane was in the Northern Territory, teaching aboriginal children in remote areas. The very macho frontier mentality of the territory was harsh and uncompromising, which made for a difficult environment for a young, single female teacher. She suffered from the mental stress of living in isolated places, such as Maningrida and Groote Eylandt, and seeing, as she put it, "abominable things going on and nothing being done about it."

While training, she had to sign a confidentiality clause, agreeing to keep quiet about what she saw in the welfare settlements in the Northern Territory. On top of that, she caught tropical diseases and had other serious health issues, due to the lack of fresh food. After three years, she left the territory with an undiagnosed post-traumatic stress disorder and came back to Sydney in a less-than-robust mental state. Then she went to Melbourne and studied art. After a difficult year there, she came back to Sydney, with issues still to deal with. She also had issues with my parents, which stemmed from her active teenage years and were aggravated by that fall from a horse six or seven years, before which had left her in a coma for two weeks. It was then that Mrs. Clark, a well-meaning lady from our church, stepped in and pretty well took over Jane's life.

Mrs. Clark considered herself an expert after years of dealing with her own difficult daughter. My parents were sidelined and were spectators, as the decisions made about Jane's life were taken out of their hands. It exacerbated the strained relationship Jane had with my parents, especially when Mrs. Clark convinced her to marry a fellow who had followed her up from Melbourne. My father felt he wasn't the right person for her, but such was Mrs. Clark's hold over Jane. She went ahead and married him.

Initially, he seemed a loving fellow, but he had a violent streak in him. Over time, he assaulted her and hurt her quite badly. While their marriage was disintegrating, Jane started third year at the osteopathy college, picking up from where she had left off while she was doing her teacher training. The marriage finally ended after ten months, and she came back to live with us. The result was that Mrs. Clark's influence over her waned, and her relationship with my mother improved a bit, although there was still some tension with my father. Stung by all that had happened, he retreated into his own world of planning for an overseas trip. His health, though, was all the worse for that experience and other recent episodes.

My sister moved back to her old room briefly and continued her course. After completing four more years of training, she graduated as an osteopath-chiropractor. She also carted me off to hyped-up meetings with Christian friends, all aimed at getting me healed. I went to one meeting at a house church in Epping, where I was prayed over and then spoke in tongues. It was a strange experience, but it encouraged me to look deeper into the charismatic. I was comfortable with Baptist theology, because they were so strong on the authority of the Bible, and I always found a deep sincerity and love of God there. Despite all this, I was open to the possibility that there was more to having a relationship with God, because after all, it was God, and who could ever fully know Him? And as my life seemed surreal anyway, it wasn't such a big jump into the charismatic world, which also seemed a bit surreal.

After a short stay with us, Jane moved out with friends and soon found her way to the Correspondence School in '74. She started there as an art teacher before joining my old girlfriends in the illustrators' room. When she came back home to live, it gave me an extra passenger and a permanent run down the transit lane. It also gave me a window into Jane's world, which at the very least was always interesting.

CHAPTER 17

Footy, Ivan, and More Girls

I was on my way out one night when Ian Jeffereys approached me in the driveway. Ian was the coach and manager of the Collaroy Cougars subdistrict rugby football team, which he had formed from some of the leftover players from the church team I'd played for back in my school days. Some years before, I had played a game for his team when I was on my college holidays. Apparently, he had remembered me from that one game (I suppose I did run the length of the field to score a try), so when he heard that I was back on the Plateau, he came visiting and asked me to help him coach the two teams. He had told his players I was a hotshot country rep, so I must be a hotshot coach as well. I was hesitant at first, but Ian was such an enthusiastic and engaging person, I agreed to come down and have a look.

Thus began a most satisfying period of my life, where Ken the sportsman was in demand once again. I could start with a clean sheet with a group of fellows who didn't know me before my accident, and so my handicap didn't diminish me in their eyes, despite my often negative feelings about myself. Instead, it added to the mystery of who I was—this great prospect so cruelly struck down, who had helped NSW Country in their mighty win against Sydney and had a storming game against New Zealand Services (which somehow was confused with the Junior

All Blacks, not that I bothered to correct them. Nor did I mention the two tries I gave their winger in that match.)

Still, the way I was accepted by everyone was important to me. It forced me to be more outgoing than I had been as a player and get closer to the fellows than I ever had with my former teammates. What I used to see as a shallow lifestyle was, to some extent, based on my social immaturity, as well as my personal choices. However, I was able to see the good side in the fellows (despite some of them having better skills at drinking and sexual adventurism than football), and in a way, it was mutually beneficial, as it allowed them to see how I lived and coped with life as a Christian.

I drove down to Griffith Park at Collaroy to meet the players, just a bit concerned about what sort of impression they would have of me. Ian, however, had been generous and had given me such a buildup beforehand that the players had already accepted me before I arrived. I soon found they were good-hearted fellows—some a bit rough around the edges but ready to accept me as someone who had reached a higher standard of football than they could reach and someone worth listening to.

The players were a cross section of the northern-beaches set, aged anywhere from late teens to mid-thirties. There were tradesmen (who proved a great help to me over the next few years); students, both school and uni; professionals; businessmen; and unskilled types. What they had in common with so many sportsmen I had grown up with was that they all liked to have a drink—some too much—and much of their social activities revolved around drinking and the club. I had avoided that lifestyle in the past, but now I couldn't avoid it any longer.

Some fellows, though, were a mystery to me. One was a Vietnam War veteran, who had obviously suffered through his experiences over there. He was quiet, reserved, and well protected by his mates. I regretted never getting to know or understand him in his short stay with us. Then there were fly-by-nights who turned up one week, played, and then disappeared, only to surface again some weeks later, before finally drifting off to another planet. One of those was a fellow I only knew as Fang—and "Fang" is what I wrote down on the players team sheets.

194

When he grinned at me, I could see why he was called Fang. He was short and skinny and looked like he'd be blown away by a northeasterly, but he threw himself into the action with almost suicidal abandon. I wasn't surprised when he only lasted a few matches before giving it away when his body took one hit too many.

Other players were known mainly by their nicknames, such as Clackers, Hairy, Bear, Chuck, Noddy, and Midnight (a pale-skinned New Zealand Maori, who added so much color to the team). Midnight was a nuggetty, thick-legged, dicky-ankled center who worked at the Hilton hotel. He told us of the time he was in the lift with some Welsh rugby players. It was quite amusing as he described how they entered the lift and crowded him into a corner. All he could do was cower there until the giants of Welsh rugby reached their floor and got out. Still, such was the informality of subdistricts rugby that Spanner and Greyhound turned up for a game one week with a mate and stayed for five years.

One of the consequences of my rise in the players' eyes was Ian's demise, so partway through the season, he left the coaching to me, virtually handing me the club. (That had been his plan all along, as he wanted to ease his way out and concentrate on his water bed business.) To his credit, though, Ian stayed involved, hosting barbecues at his house and becoming club patron when a fully constituted club was formed a few years later. For the next season, though, I found myself coaching and managing two social subdistrict sides. We were always struggling to fill both teams, and I had to prevail on the good graces of my players to double up each week, when they'd rather be standing on the sideline drinking beer. It was hard on those whose lives revolved around uni and careers, but apart from a grumble or two, they always obliged and filled the gap.

As coach and manager, I had a lot of new responsibilities to learn. Even so, I fell short when I failed to register the club for the new season—not an insignificant oversight. One of my players knew the ropes and made a phone call to the subdistricts' administrator, and I followed it up with some further groveling. The result was that both teams were reinstated into the competition.

195

It wasn't a good start for me as manager. The shock of almost missing out on the competition that year left me feeling chastened and realizing I had to do better. I set about organizing myself, just as I had three years earlier at my first school. Every week, I had my trusty clipboard and pad with me, with names, comments, team sheets, registration forms, other bits of useful information, and enough pens to sink a battleship.

During matches, I wandered up and down the sideline, on to the field at halftime, and then off somewhere with the second team to prepare them for their match. All that while trying to stay upright, get to the toilet, take notes, write down observations, and hopefully not become physically spent and have my legs stop in protest or my back seize up on me.

Football got a degree of normality back into my life, though, and as challenging as each Saturday afternoon was, it was a challenge I enjoyed. I wasn't operating in a protective environment anymore; it was a world of normal people, so I had to adjust to it and work around any deficiencies I had.

As the weeks passed, more things found their way into my pockets, along with my wallet and keys, until I wished I had more pockets to keep all my goodies in. That was a good sign, though, as it showed I was becoming more confident and able to involve myself more and more in the real world.

Over the next few years, one of my players became my assistant, as well as creating the position of statistician for himself. He supplied me with all sorts of interesting facts and figures for our weekly newsletter, the *Cougars' Growl*, to go in after my weekly match reports. I had started the *Growl*, as it became known, because I remembered how much, as a player, I looked forward to the weekly match reports when I played in the churches' competition. The *Growl* soon became very popular with the players, as they could read about themselves and their team's heroics and then muse over Wayne's interesting (albeit confusing) statistics.

One of the highlights of the year was the Grafton 500. It was a knock-out carnival, held in the northern New South Wales town of Grafton at the end of the season, for teams from all over the state and even some from Queensland. The first year, I flew with Ian, the players, and their wives and girlfriends to Coffs Harbour and caught the coach up to Grafton. Results were not important; it was the trip that mattered. Then the following year, when I was both manager and coach, we hired a coach (bus) to take us all the way to Grafton. We were to drive all through Friday night, sleeping if possible, and play on Saturday and Sunday afternoons. Once again, wives and girlfriends came along, as well as friends and friends of friends.

That's how I met Nancy, a young PE teacher from America and the flatmate of a friend of a girlfriend of a player. She was sitting in the front of the coach on her own when I got on board, because her flatmate had had a better offer up the back. She looked a bit lost, so I sat next to her and had a far more enjoyable trip up than I had expected to have.

The weekend went well, and the players were generally well behaved, except for one incident when I was woken up by a commotion coming from Nancy's room next door. Three of my players had blundered into it—by mistake, they assured me—after having had a few too many drinks. Nancy was on her own again and looking quite anxious, so I told them to leave. I became her hero, friend, and protector for what I assumed would be only the rest of the weekend.

When we arrived back at Brookvale early Monday morning, Nancy said she wanted to see me again. We had gotten on so well over the weekend, and as I hadn't been out with anyone for a while, I thought it wasn't such a bad idea. We went out for a couple of months, but although I enjoyed her company, I knew it wouldn't last. She had told me things about her life back home, and it soon became apparent she was a free spirit—with a wandering eye as well. When I went to a party at her flat, I felt out of place with the party spirit and the crowd of people who had been invited. She was surprised to see me there, and when she told me she had met another fellow, I knew it was time to leave. I closed the door on a brief relationship I knew I'd never try to open again.

It took a few weeks to stop thinking about Nancy and for any feelings to wear off. Although there was pain I could have done without, I knew I'd met a lonely girl on a bus without knowing anything about her. I wondered if the old me would have been so quick or even bothered to try. He surely would have known that if he was looking for the right girl, a football trip to Grafton wasn't the place to find her. Still, I was quite amazed by how shallow people could be when it came to relationships, ever ready to flit from one person to another, even if it meant running two motors at the same time.

I first met Ivan the following year when he turned up at the Correspondence School one day with his wife, Pam. It was August 1975, and they had just come over from New Zealand at a time when teaching positions in New South Wales were scarce. Being a fairly quiet person, I was bemused by Ivan's exuberant behavior when he was introduced to all the teachers, for reasons I only found out later.

We hit it off straight away, possibly because we both had rugby backgrounds but more probably because of something else we had in common. My first impression of Ivan was of a happy-chappy who was both friendly and sincere but with a more complex character lurking under all that politeness and good humor. Most of the chat among the teachers was genial but shallow, so you didn't really get to know anyone with any depth unless you made an effort. Ivan was different. He seemed curious and genuinely interested in you. He didn't just look at you when he talked to you; he seemed to look into you. Maybe he found me the most approachable because he kept coming over to my desk for a chat. Sometimes it was for advice or information about something, but other times, it was obviously just to make contact. At that time, the Australian rugby team was touring Britain, so every Monday I would tell him of another win, and he would respond that it was the same match I'd told him about the previous week.

As Ivan began to open up more, he told me of his excitement at being in Australia and having a job at the Correspondence School. I hadn't seen the position that way. Instead, I'd taken it for granted and always considered it second best to what I'd previously had. Still, he seemed to be someone I could trust, and we used to chat to each other like old friends, even though he was about eight years my senior.

Then one day, when we were down in the men's restroom, where we fellows used to go for relief, a chat, and to take turns at looking out the window at the Domain, Ivan asked me somewhat cautiously what I was doing on the weekend. When I told him I went to church on Sunday, there was an excited response from him. He told me he was a Christian too and that he had been led by God to Australia, for what reason, he didn't know, other than starting a home group. After that conversation, our relationship was cemented and would be an important part of my life for years to come.

Later, Ivan told me about that first day at the Correspondence School, when he seemed to be jumping out of his skin. Earlier that day, they had just arrived in Australia, and Ivan had been to the Education Department's head office but was told there were no teaching positions available. He was about to leave, he said, when the official seemed to have a change of mind and told Ivan to come back in five minutes, as he wanted to make a phone call. Ivan said he stepped out for the five minutes, on a high, thanking God in anticipation of a job.

When Ivan walked out of the Bridge Street office that day, he walked along Macquarie Street and then straight down William Street and into the Correspondence School to meet his new colleagues. No wonder he was on a high. Miracles tend to do that to you.

In 1976, the subbies team had been strengthened by an influx of players from surf club members, who played league on Sunday while dabbling in union on Saturdays, as well as mates of mates. After performing quite well the previous year, we found ourselves promoted into the highest division for three team clubs, where the football was just a bit more serious. We had one and a half teams (two, when everyone turned up or when I could prevail on one or two of my players to double up), while our third team was a St. Augustine's team, which played against the other clubs' third-grade sides.

When Ian left, running two teams on my own had its problems, as apart from the on-the-field coaching, I was also team manager. Filling out forms, registering players, registering the club, writing match reports for the *Manly Daily*, sending team result sheets to the powers that be, and fixing up any other bits and pieces that might arise was just part of a football manager's normal duties. Forgetting to register the club two years earlier, though, wasn't, and I could just picture Frank Russell, my old inspector from Cowabbie West days, shaking his head and saying, "At least he was only a day late for me."

New players joined the club from Harbord when it folded, so the dynamics and culture went through some subtle changes. As part of this change, we moved our training ground from Griffith Park up to Plateau Park on Collaroy Plateau. My relationship with the new players was embryonic, while they, in turn, seemed to be trying to work me out. I was a handicapped former representative player who was both their coach and manager. Apart from that, I was a bit of a mystery. I thought they possibly were ambivalent as to whether I was physically up to the task of coaching two teams, which was frankly quite a handful.

At training, I always tried to position myself as close as possible to the action, but that tended to put me in the path of rampaging forwards, and sometimes I had to hurry to get out of their way. If there were ever any misguided feelings of sympathy for me, it ended one night when Steve, one of our new players, ran into me and sent me flying. The players stopped and looked horrified, possibly wondering how I would react and whether I'd be able to get up. For my part, it felt good having physical contact again, so I yelled at Steve to stop worrying about me and to get after the ball. That seemed to do the trick, as they realized I was able to handle the knocks and look after myself. It also did wonders for our relationship, and any distance between me and the new players ended that night. After that, Steve deliberately bumped into me a few more times, just to cement our new understanding and keep me on my toes.

At the end of the season, some of the key players came to me and said they wanted to get serious and form a fully constituted social football club, with elected officers, patrons, and a coaching director. It was a step forward from the loose organization we had and would take the worry of club management out of my hands and allow me to concentrate solely on coaching. So after our first fully constituted club meeting, I was made coaching director, which let me and my wacky ideas loose to develop a particular style of play and playing culture for the club—something that satisfied both the teacher in me and the footballer in me. All our fringe players committed themselves to the club, so we were very optimistic about our chances for the next season.

When the new season got underway, I was still looking around for more players, so I thought of Ivan. Ivan had only stayed at the Correspondence School until the end of the year before transferring to Lindfield Demonstration School, which was not far from where he was living. We had talked about my football involvement the previous year, so I rang him and asked him to come along and lend a hand. Ivan was not surprised with my call but remained dubious before agreeing to come. He played in a couple of games, but it became obvious that his best playing days were behind him. Despite that, I knew he had the character and maturity the club needed, so I asked him to stay on as my assistant coach. That created a problem. It's often those in the most need who don't recognize it or when that need is being met. Ivan was just the person the club needed, but he was still finding his way and didn't have the players' respect as a footballer, let alone as a coach. He found their attitude frustrating and had second thoughts about staying.

One night at training, it all came to a head. Halfway through a lackluster session, I became fed up with the attitude of some of my players and the lack of respect they were showing Ivan, so I called them together in the center of Plateau Park. I had rarely raised my voice at anyone, but I was about to do so now. I knew something had to be said, and I had to be the one who said it. I had never considered myself a leader, especially of footballers—nor had I ever wanted to be—but that night, I had to push aside any doubts and inhibitions and be not just a football coach but be a leader. I ripped into them, and the effect was quite startling. There was absolute silence as they listened, stunned but mostly embarrassed, as I told them a few home truths about themselves. Not all deserved it, but I felt it was important that they know what I expected from them, which was for each player to take responsibility not only for his own attitude but the attitude of his teammates as well. I set rules for attendances at training, for selection, attitude on the field, and for each other and especially for Ivan, who, I said, had my total support as my assistant coach.

Up until then, I had been coaching both sides. One team had most of the dependables—players who were there when I started with the club but weren't the tough nuts like the players in the first team. They were the newcomers, talented fly-by-nights, Sunday league players, mates of mates, and some of my original hard heads. They had the toughness but not the commitment to each other to be the strong team they easily could have been. All that changed after that night. I took the second team and pointedly gave Ivan the first team. From then on, they had an identity—they were Ivan's team, and he molded them from a bunch of individuals into a team that performed heroic deeds for the rest of the season and gave the best teams a real fright, even if they didn't actually beat them. It also established Ivan's position and his positive influence in the club and with the players. They took on a siege mentality for the rest of the season and carried the mantra, "Nobody cared for us except Ivan," into each match. Most teams that came up against them were happy to hear the full- time whistle. While Ivan's input was considerable, it also showed the character of the players. When their pride was hurt, they didn't sulk and make excuses; instead, they took it on the chin and came back stronger and better, both as players and—for the time since I'd known them—people.

My players were talented, so now I could concentrate on them, toughening them up and getting the best out of them. To their credit, they committed themselves to my methods all the way to the grand final. I had picked up a lot of ideas from my playing years and from the best coaches I'd had. My plan was quite simple: get the best out of each player and have each player contribute that best to the team on match day. It wasn't complicated. I remembered what had gotten the best out of me and what hadn't. It wasn't only about football, as some of the fellows caught on to, but it also was about them. It worked because the goodwill in the club was so strong that they stormed into the grand final, beating the leading team on the way. It was a grand final that everyone came to see—Ivan and all the players from our first team, my father and his camera, and heck, even my girlfriend.

It was halftime in the grand final, and we held a slight lead, so I gathered my players into a tight group around me. They paced around like nervous thoroughbreds, sniffing the scent of battle and waiting for the right words to be said to fire them up for the second half. "Talk to us, Ken," the team captain said. So I talked quietly to them and reminded them what each person's job was: to do the simple things well, to stick to our plan, to control the momentum of the match, and when the opportunity came, to take it. They were so ready when it came, they took it. They put on our special "Benny and the Jets" move—our "take it this way, send it back that way and then go the other way" move—pulled it off to perfection, scored a try from it, and the grand final was ours. It was, as my players often said, "magic."

That win topped off a year that had seen positive signs of change in the club. The club culture moved from that of a social club first to football club first; from a drinking culture with modest effort to a drinking culture (some things never change) with maximum effort. The ideals of camaraderie rather than drunken revelry, commitment and teamwork rather than grudging obligation, and peer pressure contributed to the positive direction toward which the club was moving. Ivan had prospered as well, winning the respect and affection of the players, who were often bemused but comfortable with the fact they had two coaches who were both Christians.

The positive changes in the club were good for me as well. True, it was nice to be appreciated by your players, but that was secondary, as it helped soften my own frustrations somewhat, because I was able to be a teacher and mentor to players who were basically at school and still learning about life. If I couldn't be a teacher who could run fast, I could at least be a teacher who was listened to.

The following year, we moved up to the top three team division and again, Ivan took our firsts. I continued with our seconds, who were playing so well they were favorites for the premiership. Our success had seen a further influx of players, and we had enough players to have our own third team with its own coach. Our thirds were always game and feisty, always up for a scrap, and always giving a good account of themselves. However, nothing is permanent, and just when things seemed to be moving smoothly along, it all changed and my life was turned upside down ... again.

I had two lines of thinking when I left Wagga hospital. The first concerned my lifelong belief that at the right time, I would meet the right girl and marry her. Now, though, I had serious doubts about the fairness, as I saw it, of burdening anyone with my disability. I wanted "her" to know the sportsman who I was before— who, with so little effort, could run fast. In short, I wanted it to be the old me, not the person I had become. I felt he was a much better prospect than the stranger in transition who even I didn't really know.

The other thought was to accept what had happened and who I had become, accept the frustrations and limitations, and trust God totally for what was to come. But letting go of the past wasn't easy, because it meant letting go my identity—a free spirit who could run fast—and making a new one who, barring a miracle, couldn't.

But while trying to get on with my new life - all the hopes and aspirations of my old life kept intruding and rubbing up against my present reality. I'd be watching an international match, and I'd see someone I'd played against at school and think, *That might have been me out there*, or I'd feel full of nervous energy and not be able to release it through a walk along the beach or a run around Edgecliff Boulevard.

The other challenge was to not allow my self-confidence or feelings of self-worth to be determined by my physical state but by my relationship with God and the knowledge that He was caring and interested in my life and understood my needs. Knowing isn't always doing, but even though I trod a narrow path of often competing tensions, I wasn't lacking in determination or unwilling to put in the effort to get the best possible result out of my present situation.

And so, life moved on.

Sometime after my brief flirtation with Nancy, I felt like a change, so I moved into the flat at Collaroy. Six months later, I'd had enough of independent living, so I moved back home again. Then, to my surprise, Christine appeared on the scene and moved into the now- vacant flat. She wanted to see me again, I suspect to see if there was anything between us. There wasn't, and by that stage, I had moved on and had met another nurse, in whom I was becoming quite interested—an interest that had started a couple of years earlier at Dee Why.

1976 Collaroy 'Cougars' Rugby Team.
I'm standing with my players after we won
the premiership for our competition.

CHAPTER 18

Church Life—Starting Again

When I left my church on the Plateau to start again at Dee Why, it seemed to be the right time to go. I soon found there was an active young people's group there that met in the "dungeon," a downstairs room under the Sunday school hall, on Sunday nights after church. There was always music playing, with ABBA hits popular with the young teenage girls. They would jump up with little prompting and perform the songs, while the rest of us sat around at tables, drinking tea or hot chocolate and trying to talk.

I was twenty-three, one of the oldest young people there, and when the girls performed, I felt even older. Ralph Parnwell was the associate pastor and a man deep into his thirties who had had an epiphany and went into the ministry later in life. He and his soon-to- be-wife, Helena, ran the youth group, so I was pencilled in with Ralph and Helena at the pointy end of leadership in the group. Having a decent car also helped when it came to Friday night outings, as the teenagers suddenly became friendly and respectful, according to who was giving them a lift. There were a number of lively young girls in the group, but one, Andrea, a recent arrival with her brother, was quiet and seemed to be a bit of a loner.

One Sunday night near closing time at the dungeon, I found myself chatting to her. Andrea was concerned that one of the fellows was showing too much interest in her, and she was trying to avoid being offered a lift home by him. She seemed to be wary of the older boys, which, thankfully, didn't include me. When I told her I could drive her home, she eagerly accepted my offer.

For one so quiet, she became very talkative on the way home, as though she wanted to unburden herself. When we arrived at her house, she asked if we could go somewhere quiet and talk, so I drove on to Long Reef and found a spot next to the golf course overlooking the water. We talked for at least an hour about a number of things that concerned her, and while it felt good to be trusted by a seventeen-year-old, I felt she was dealing with some fairly deep family issues. The personal matters she raised were not the sort of thing you'd share with just anyone, so when I dropped her off at her home afterward, I was glad I'd been the one to talk to her and that she had seen me as someone she could trust and confide in, much like Angela had the previous year.

Andrea came along to the Friday night youth nights more regularly after that. When we all went out, she came in my car, but I felt that to be alone with her again, as we were that night at Long Reef, would have been inappropriate, so it never happened again ... except for one time. I drove her home one Sunday night after church and then said good night and let her out. She had seemed distracted on the way, and I wasn't surprised when that was the last time I saw her. A year later, I heard she'd become engaged. She was still young, only eighteen, so I could only muse on what else had been going on in her life.

I continued my involvement with the youth group, providing transport when it was needed. Two of the sisters with the long hair were now regulars, while the oldest came only occasionally. Still, I enjoyed being there and helping out, as well as being somewhat of a mystery man, a bit older than the others but still young enough to be comfortable around them. Ralph and I used to sit at a table and watch the group during those times down in the dungeon. Ralph was often amused by the way the teenagers behaved and especially by the younger fellows' bumbling efforts at being cool and "sophisticated."

I had been out with girls over recent years without feeling any desire to form an attachment to any of them. At church, though, it was a safe place, and I did have a regard for the girls there, much like an older brother casting a protective eye over his frisky young sisters— not that they would have listened to anything I said anyway.

Away from church, I had been spending time at Annandale and down at Collaroy, at the flat at the back of a house where Grahame and his girlfriend were living. Going there made me feel I needed to stretch my wings a bit and get away from my parents for a time. The chance came when Grahame and Michelle moved out of the flat, and I promptly moved in, cutting some apron strings and having some time on my own. It had the trappings of independence, but I always allowed my mother to do my washing for me. I cooked for myself and on Tuesday nights drove up the road a little way to Griffith Park for the Cougars' training night. I even invited a girl called Jenny over for dinner. Then, when I decided I'd had enough of flatting on my own, I went back to my parents' place and to my good old room and waterbed.

CHAPTER 19

Jenny

As mentioned before, I had first noticed Jenny a couple of years earlier at a time when I was trying to get some normality back into my life. I had just graduated from the "theater of dependence," (a place where hospitals, doctors, nurses, and physiotherapists had been the main players in my life), when I started going to the Dee Why church. Then a few weeks later a new couple came to the church. They had three young teen-age daughters and always sat together as a family up the front of the church.

Although my defensive walls were still up, it didn't stop me from admiring the oldest sister—young with fresh-faced innocence; pretty with a natural, quite dazzling smile. I felt she was far too young so I kept my distance, although I believed there was no harm in looking. And what I saw over the next few months, was someone who was shy but friendly, coy but not flirty, modest and with that certain something that most girls I'd been out with didn't have. Jenny came to church when she could, as she was living in the nurses quarters at Camperdown Children's Hospital, where she was doing her training. But when she started coming to the dungeon more regularly, it was hard to avoid her. Because she was just that bit older than the teenagers, she gravitated toward the older young people's group. Of that group, the boys, late teens mostly, were socially incompetent and had no idea how to approach a girl, so by

209

default, I ended up talking to Jenny while they watched, twiddling their thumbs. Initially, I tried to keep a distance between us, but she soon had me intrigued when her certain "something" started to show through. I had a lot of newly hatched theories on a number of things, and she surprised me by listening patiently as I expounded some of them to her. I don't know what she made of them, apart from learning snippets of quite useless information, or whether it really interested her. However, I found her quite appealing, and the more I talked to her, the more unsure of myself I became. The more unsure of myself I became, the more I talked. So apart from overdoing it and bombarding her with my all-embracing theories, I annoyed her by reminding her of our ages— me, a mature twenty-three, while she was a mere child of eighteen. I was probably sensitive to the fact that the "competition" were all able-bodied fellows, so I overcompensated with a barrage of useless facts. Eventually, I felt she deserved more than the Kentucky Fried Chicken the group sometimes had after church or pizzas at the Pizza Hut on Friday night, so I bit the bullet and asked her out, half expecting a cool response.

I knew a number of trendy eating places, such as Sorens in Woolloomooloo (if trendy means having peanut shells all over the floor and being painted a gaudy red), the Volunteer at Balmain, and an eatery just off Broadway on City Road, although I didn't know Jenny had her own bevy of eating places near the hospital that she and her nursing friends had made their own. After our meal at Broadway, I made a fuss of needing help to keep my balance as we walked back to the car. It gave me an excuse to put my arm around her, and as infantile as it was, it was more about my trying to be amusing and making light of my situation than trying to make a move on her.

Nothing really happened after that between us, and I didn't think it ever would. I felt I'd fired off too many bullets and needed to back off a bit. In other words, I'd blown it. Jenny was having a different effect on me than other girls I knew. I wasn't looking around for the exit door with her, which must have meant something. Still, I wondered if the old me would have felt the same. I really needed to be myself and not try to be someone I wasn't, but then, that was half the problem—who was I, anyway?

Jenny's other life at Camperdown limited her involvement with the youth, while I continued providing transport for the Friday night activities as "older person with car." I didn't see much of her socially for another year, as our lives moved in different directions. Then, in '74, with summer approaching, a pool party was held at one of the church leader's houses. I wasn't there that night, but when Doug, one of the young blades, started talking about the two sisters in their bikinis, I became a bit more motivated to do something about it before he did. (After all, I'd left him enough rope so he was bound to start trying to reel it in sometime.) I'd had enough of Grafton trips with the football team by this time, and although I still had reservations about myself and relationships, I was comfortable with the fact that Jenny and I at least knew each other. However, I was still concerned about starting something that might not end well. Over the years, I had seen too many shallow relationships form in church youth groups that ran their course and then ended, leaving one party upset and the dynamics of the group fractured. Then, too often, I'd seen one of the parties start up with somebody else in the group, and the already delicate situation would become further strained. I didn't want to be part of "musical chairs" relationships, which might have been the norm for an unchurched world but was inconsistent with the Christian values we espoused. With that in mind, I was cautious in my dealings with the young people, so it was with a degree of wariness that I considered testing the waters with Jenny.

The church leaders were keen on having the young adults play a bigger part in the church. That saw plans hatched to run church services that summer at the beach. A grassy area was staked out next to Dee Why Surf Club, and a large tent was erected, much like the ones used on beach missions. There were day programs for children and night meetings for the teens and adults. In one of the night meetings, Jesus was put on "trial," accused of being the Son of God. We had a prosecutor and a defender—Chris and Kevin, two law students in the church. They presented their cases, and the judge tidied it all up when they had finished. I was the judge. I had no idea what I was doing—it was all a bit ad hoc and unrehearsed—but I tried to look as if I did. At the completion, I summed up the evidence with the utmost brevity, sidestepped making any other theological statements, and simply told everyone that as they were the jury, they should examine the evidence presented and decide whether Jesus was guilty or not guilty of being the Son of God. *Brilliant, Little*, I thought. *What a clever face-saving cop out.*

Another night, I gave a brief testimony, after which Ralph informed me that my views were Calvinistic—not that I knew what that meant. (It did set me thinking I should do some theological study sometime.) It also opened up opportunities for some of the other young adults to speak at Sunday night services, although I hesitated to call it preaching. It was more like rambling on.

During that week, church groups took turns sleeping in the tent overnight to guard the "church" and its equipment. At this point, I was quite chummy with Jenny, and my interest in her was becoming stronger, so on the night that it was the young adults' turn to stand guard, I decided it was time for me to stand guard over Jenny.

I could feel there was something sparking between us that night, so I took her outside into the darkness of Dee Why Beach. When we came back sometime later, we were a couple. I was quite surprised I'd actually done something about her, because I knew it would mean crossing a line I hadn't been willing to cross with anyone before. But on that night, my resistance—or was it my reluctance?—had been completely disarmed. Instead of holding back, I opened the door and let Jenny into my sometimes-confusing world. I knew I was taking a risk, but she was someone special, so I took a step in faith and had to trust she was ready for it.

It had been more than three years since I was paralyzed. I had worked hard during those three years to get to where I was, but always, in the back of my mind, I had the hope that if that wasn't enough, there was always God's ace in the pack—His miracle card. I had no doubt that God could heal me but was unsure if He would— or that maybe He already had, and what I had was all I was getting, so I should be grateful I wasn't in a wheelchair, thank you, Sonny Jim. The other possibility was that maybe further physical healing was second best, and any further healing would be emotional and spiritual, whatever that meant. I went to healing services, trying to find reasons why God might overlook any lack of faith I might have by noting that I had bags of it, just by turning up. Besides, I reasoned that even those healed in the Bible didn't always show an abundance of faith and often seemed to be healed more because they obeyed a command than because they believed. It seemed more about God's faithfulness in those cases and, as always, for a higher unknown purpose. If I'd heard the voice of God saying, "Throw your stick away and walk," I would have. To throw it away, however, and try to walk seemed foolish if I hadn't heard His voice, or only imagined it, or tried to drag up faith from a place where there may have been doubts. Would God honor that, or was I completely missing the point about faith and healing? If some with questionable faith were healed due to God's faithfulness or for a higher reason, could God squeeze me into that category as well?

So with all that bouncing around in my head, I went to healing meeting after healing meeting, got prayed for, and got pushed over, except I didn't play the game and fall over. Then one day, I went to a mass healing at the Opera House through the sterling efforts of Rex Humbard, who then entreated us all to contribute money so his family could make another trip to Israel. Obviously, I left the Opera House unhealed, although I wondered what might have happened if it'd only been a headache.

During those years I was prayed for by the faithful, the charlatans, the newly converted eager to exercise their spiritual authority, and the ridiculous. They all had a go. Then there were lessons from Job and the more recent Dietrich Bonhoeffer and Richard Wurmbrand, both stars in the suffering-for-Christ stakes, as I looked for something to fill that hole when the unexplainable comes into your life. And all the while, fragile emotions of self-worth were bouncing around inside my head like a pinball machine, as I tried to find that all-elusive reason for how I felt about myself and what God really thought of me. So many thoughts swirling around—no wonder I was reluctant to have anything other than brief relationships. Detached from all that, I got on with life and did what I had to do. Then, when Jenny came along, it blew all my resistance away.

The first time I invited her to that tiny little flat I was now living in at Collaroy, I went into my tiny little kitchen and cooked the biggest meal I could for both of us. Then, over the next few months, she was a frequent visitor. My cooking never improved—or changed. It was always chops and vegetables, with sausages and steak thrown in as well. I was never one to confuse quantity with quality, which is why Jenny soon took over the cooking until the time when I decided I'd had enough flatting on my own and went back home.

Now I was back home I had to change my routine if I wanted to see Jenny during the week. And did I ever. I'd get home from the Correspondence School before five, recover, then zoom off to Camperdown at six to see Jenny, only having time to scoff down half my dinner, which I now allowed my mother to cook for me again. I was punctilious about time and made sure I would pick her up at the time I nominated—I felt Jenny had to be able to trust me and take me at my word. I wasn't going to be like other fellows who would say one thing and do another, and expect the girl to meekly accept it. Not surprisingly, I lost so much weight over the weeks and months of half dinners that I found my favorite bone-colored trousers kept falling down. The snug fit of trousers from my football days was certainly a thing of the past. I had taken a sabbatical from the gym and kept up my fitness by walking up and down the sidelines with my football team, so there wasn't any bulk being lavished on to my frame.

Jenny took on a lot with me. I didn't talk much to her about my mental battles and frustrations. I just made her aware of my physical limitations. But she did share my experiences in a supportive way, as well as being open to learning about my world. Every payday, Jenny would give me twenty dollars, which would go with my twenty dollars into the far corner of my wallet and be our "going out" money for the fortnight. And it was always enough, as we weren't big spenders and often just liked being with each other and our friends. We did everything together—dinner, church life, parties (where I first discovered the vertical tendencies of my bone-colored trousers), and the pictures. A new picture called *The Other Side of the Mountain* had come out. It was the story of Jill Kinmont, a young American downhill skier who, in the fifties, had become a quadriplegic after crashing into trees during a downhill run. We saw it together, and although my intentions weren't about looking for the right formula for handling life-changing events—because everyone handles adversity differently—it was both educational and inspirational. It also reinforced to me that my reactions and frustrations were quite normal for someone with an abnormal complaint, while confusion of the old and new me was a product of my largely contented old life. It was helpful for Jenny to see it as well and see what Jill Kinmont's life in a wheelchair was like. And of course, I met her nursing friends.

I never felt entirely comfortable with that age group, as nice as the girls were. They were all able-bodied, as were their boyfriends. They were young, lively, and full of ambition and were planning things in the nursing world, in which my involvement had primarily been as a hopelessly dependent patient. I stood uneasily between both worlds, as an observer and often a participant but never a full member of either. I was disconnected from that confident sportsman and wondered what he would have done. I didn't feel I had any right to say anything to Jenny about her choices and her ultimate desire to go to Scotland to do midwifery. If I did, it might have been this new me being selfish, wanting to hold on to something that wasn't his to hold on to. Jenny had her own growing up to do and a life to experience, and at this stage in our relationship, I had no idea if I was going to be a part of it.

Jenny and her friends went on a two-week Pacific Islands cruise to celebrate the end of two years' training. It worried me, because Jenny was a very appealing girl. Although she wasn't naïve, she had a trusting innocence about her, while I had little trust in the innocence of young fellows on a cruise.

I was down at Griffith Park on that Tuesday night, training my football teams, when the liner sailed out of Sydney Harbor past North Head. I didn't see her off but could see its lights approaching and then, with a toss of a capstan, turn east and head away until it disappeared over the horizon, taking Jenny with it.

A few weeks later, my fears seemed to be realized when I went to the overseas terminal with her parents to pick her up. The ship had docked and as we waited for the passengers to disembark, I watched a parade of young men come up on to the deck, where Jenny and her friends were waiting, to say good-bye to them. It was obvious that friendships had been made, as the tearful farewells seemed quite genuine. I'm sure my face looked exactly as I felt. I shouldn't have been there, because I knew the contrast between what she had been doing and what she was coming back to would be absurdly obvious.

On the drive back to her parents' place, the atmosphere in the backseat was distant and cool. For the next few weeks, I felt empty and emotionally spent, as our relationship hung by a thread. I hung around her like a lovesick puppy, hoping for some crumbs of favor, but I could see that she wished I wasn't there. The boys had done what I had feared—the excitement and romance on the high seas had led to a marriage proposal, and for a twenty-year-old, sought- after girl, it was a lot to deal with and think through. Having me hanging around didn't help. How could I compete with that?

Over the next few months, back in the real world, when romance waned and memories faded, life got back to normal. Things improved between us, although photographs and the odd comment reminded me of how close I'd come to losing her. But although things had moved on, I still had a nagging fear I could lose her to the next big event. I wondered how I would handle another breakup with her again. The problem was, I had lowered my guard and let Jenny into my life and into a world that I knew I couldn't really expect anyone but a very special person to understand. And by doing that, I had taken a risk and had become captivated by her.

Soon after, Jenny had her twenty-first, and the next year, when I brought Ivan into the football club and friendships grew, we started going to Ivan's place for a midweek home group. Later, we went camping with Ivan and Pam and their kids, drove down to Wagga to stay with Bob and Jenelle, and went to a Sunday afternoon study group on, of all books, Leviticus. But always in the background, Scotland lurked. We were both very involved in the church at Dee Why at this stage. I was superintendent of the Junior Sunday School, and it seemed our relationship was very tight. Jenny even came along to see my football team win the grand final, something my players said later was pretty cool. Everyone who met Jenny immediately liked her and treated her with respect.

One Sunday morning at our youth meeting, we heard that our elderly minister had died that morning. Ralph took over in the interim until a more senior minister could be found. Then Ralph and Helena relocated to the church at Schofields, an outlying suburb in the northwest of Sydney, while a new minister came in with his wife and two grown children. We soon found out they were a family of talented musicians. The children were opposites, the son being confident and extroverted—if a bit cocky for my liking—while the daughter was much quieter, like her mother. The son had a clouded past, a failed marriage, but seemed to be accepted by everyone and brought a high level of music and showmanship to the church scene. Meantime, Jenny and I visited Ralph and Helena at Schofields, maintaining a relationship with them.

We often went to meetings at my mate Jim's place as well. He was heavily involved with the Full Gospel Businessmen's Association and brought business associates to parties at his home, where he would deliver a gospel message in his own entertaining style. They were all dry meetings, and it amazed his guests that they could have a good time without drinking alcohol. It was a style of evangelism in which Jim excelled, and I found it intriguing to watch. There was a certain irony about the situation, though, because Jim was sales manager for Kaiser Stuhl, an international wine company.

By this time, it had become accepted that Jenny would be going to Scotland with her friend Wendy for eighteen months to do midwifery at Bellshill. I had little say in the matter, nor did I think it fair to try to stop her from going. As much as I was in conflict about it, it was something that I knew Jenny had to do. She wasn't ready to settle down just yet, a position I could fully understand. When she came back and had—I hoped—gotten it all out of her system, then the "M word" would be firmly on the table. But now, I had to take the risk of losing her, so I let her go. We had already committed our relationship to God, so I had to trust it was all part of His plan for us.

To be eligible for the course, Jenny needed six months experience in psych nursing, so she moved to a house in Ryde with Wendy to be close to the hospital. It meant an out-of-the-way drive and less opportunity to see her, and without a car, it was difficult for Jenny to come to the meetings at Ivan's place. Still, it was the best we could do under the circumstances, because in a few months, she would be gone, leaving me on my own with Ivan, Jim, and the football team.

Well into the 1977 season, it all changed. The football club and my team were doing well, but my world was suddenly turned upside down when I lost Jenny to another fellow. The pastor's son had been seeing her behind my back, something I was completely oblivious to.

One night, I went to see her at Ryde, but when I arrived, he was sitting on the lounge with Wendy and Ian, looking quite at home. I was surprised to see him there, until I saw the pained expressions on everyone's faces. Then I understood. There are times in life when something happens that causes your world to suddenly darken, and then everything that happens after that feels so surreal. For me, this was such a time. It felt like a cold wind had blown right through me, causing an emotional numbness to set in. I didn't know what to do, but I did know I didn't have any rights over Jenny, so arguing wasn't an option. The same went for complaining—there was nothing noble about playing the victim and looking for sympathy. It would have betrayed everything I'd worked through over the past few years, so I didn't even consider it. Instead, without even getting past the front door, I turned and left with an empty feeling in my stomach, while sparing all parties any further embarrassment.

Over the next few weeks, I shared my sadness with Ivan and Pam, Jim and Pauline, and my mother, who had been my rock over the years since my mishap and whose gentle Christian faith had steadied some dark moments.

I continued at Dee Why church, as I was still in charge of the Junior Sunday School. It was hard, though, seeing the awkward looks from some of our friends and hearing whispered words of support. What followed was a time of emptiness and sadness, as I found myself just existing from day to day. But paradoxically it was also a time of grace, where I felt close to God, knowing He was sharing my hurt. It's a funny feeling, being heartbroken. You feel consumed and not able to see much beyond your own sad little world. But as bad as I felt, each day had its own challenges that had to be met, so I just had to get out of bed each day and meet them, mechanically, robotically, devoid of emotion but always sustained by a fellow traveler, my companion called hope.

One day at school, I heard about a scheme to bring education to children in the outback and that the architects of the scheme were looking for a teacher who could start the pilot program straight away. One had already been running from Nyngan since the beginning of the year, but this second program was to be based in Bourke, five hundred miles northwest of Sydney, which was just about as far enough away from Sydney as I felt I needed to be. I needed a change, to step away from my situation and have a new vision, so this was a godsend to me. In the past, I had been keen about visiting students in their homes, so it was easy to say to our principal that I was interested in the position.

After that, things moved quickly. I met the teacher involved in the Nyngan project and soon after, I met Cliff, the principal of Bourke High School, when he was down for a Federation meeting. Cliff was one of the key figures in the scheme, so after a chat and a cursory inquiry about my condition, he was quite happy to welcome me into the program.

Then Roger came down. He was the teacher from Enngonia whose submission I'd be working under. His enthusiasm impressed me as we buzzed around the city, buying library books and educational material that would be set up in the back of a truck as a "school," which I would then drive around the shire and visit properties near and far. Roger had already picked up the truck, a city transit van, and had agreed to drive it back and have it set up for me when I came up to Bourke a few days later. I was secretly pleased that I wouldn't be driving it back. The heavy clutch's high position meant I would have to lift up my weaker left leg to push the clutch down. Although my leg was strong enough, it would be problematical trying to manage it in heavy Sydney traffic, especially if my left leg went into spasm. I didn't want to take the risk of the truck kangaroo hopping across an intersection and getting stuck in the middle when the lights changed to red. I wasn't going to say anything to Roger, though, because I didn't think it would be a problem once I got to Bourke and the wide open spaces. Besides, they were keen to get things moving, and finding someone who was able to start straight away avoided any searching questions about my condition. I reasoned they didn't really want to know too much, so I didn't volunteer anything more—the less they knew the better. If there were problems, I would adapt and work around them. Of that I was certain.

In the meantime, I was ready to go and determined to make the most out of the opportunity. It wasn't just a means of escape for me; I was genuinely looking forward to getting out into the country again and, in my mind, redeeming some of what I had lost over the years since I was paralyzed. I would be getting back to a place where I felt comfortable, free, and more the person I felt I was, rather than someone trying to play catch-up with his life. I had done the best I could with my students, building good relationships with them and their supervisor parents. I had begun to understand what the life of an isolated student was like, while always trying to encourage them.

Now I could go out there and get a first-hand look at some of the difficulties they routinely faced, difficulties that people in the city had little inkling of, let alone understanding.

There were people I had to tell first. My worry-wart parents came up with reasons why I shouldn't go before realizing that I was going anyway. I told Ivan and the club and resigned as coaching director and then as superintendent of the Junior Sunday School. I handed in my last semi-completed draft to my editor of *Galahs and Cockatoos*, said good-bye to Jim and Pauline, and left Sydney in my Cortina for Bourke and the great outdoors. I didn't tell anyone else, I didn't think it mattered. I wouldn't be missed, and they'd find out anyway.

Before I left, Ralph gave me the name of someone he knew would be a good contact up there. So when I left Sydney, I left with bittersweet memories and the names Laurie MacIntosh and Lodebar fixed firmly in my brain. But my faith in God was strong, I knew I was resilient and had been toughened up by life's often hard lessons, so I was ready, confident, and looking forward to whatever lay ahead of me.

PART 4

ALL GOOD THINGS

CHAPTER 20

Bourke and Beyond

When I took on the position, I was seconded to the Disadvantaged Children's Association (DCA), which I understood to be a quasi- government body, for an undetermined period. I would be operating under Roger's submission to the DCA as an itinerant teacher. The other player in the program was the Isolated Children's Parents Association (ICPA), which had been the prime mover in getting a teacher (me) out to the isolated properties to work with the children of the Correspondence School and the School of Air. The ICPA had grown into a strong parent organization from its early beginnings in 1971, when Pat Edgley had successfully campaigned to keep the Bourke hostel open.

The way I saw it, the program would give me opportunity to see the children on the isolated properties, as well as fitting in visits to the aboriginal reserve at Enngonia when I was up that way and was able to visit. The teachers at Enngonia, Roger and Mary, saw things quite differently. They emphasized in the submission the needs of the preschool aboriginal kids on the reserve and expected they would hold the same importance as the isolated children did.

Both sides were passionate about their needs; both sides were perfectly correct and had clearly articulated those needs, so a compromise submission was put forward that attempted to cater to both. As preschool education didn't come under the Education Department's funding, and the ICPA represented the children who did, Roger's submission to the Disadvantaged Children's Association was necessary for the program to be accepted and funded by the government. Unfortunately, the submission had the potential for conflict over competing interests. In an ideal world, both needs would have been met, and in an ideal world, two teachers would have been employed to facilitate them. However, money was available only to fund a pilot program covering the whole Bourke shire of some 16 000 square miles, (42 000 square kilometers), and employing one teacher, who was to ascertain what would work and what wouldn't work and who would be operating, with mixed signals from different parties as to what the priorities were.

Of course, I wasn't to know all this at the time, while any potential conflicts of interest didn't seem important, as there was much hope and goodwill, so any problems would be identified and easily overcome. Or so I thought. I believed all parties were single-minded in establishing a program that would bring education to the isolated children in the bush and that all parties were pushing in the same direction.

The five-hundred-mile drive up to Bourke was trouble-free and gave me the opportunity to see a part of the state I hadn't seen before. I stopped at Dubbo overnight at Jo's place, my "foot friend" from teachers college days. The next day I continued up the highway through Narromine, Nyngan, and then the final straight stretch through Girilambone, pub-famous Coolabah, and lonely Byrock and on up to Bourke. I was intrigued by the miles of trees and vegetation pressing in on the highway that suddenly fled as the plain opened out into a huge expanse of open countryside, twenty-five miles shy of Bourke. It was both sudden and breathtaking for a city boy, on his first trip to the real bush, to see the vastness of the Australian outback greened by recent rain. I loped along, only slowing for the sweeping right-hand bend that doglegged across the train line before resuming its arrow-straight sprint up to Bourke. In the afternoon sun, I could see in the distance white roofs of what looked like a small outback settlement. Moments later, I passed the "sweet-smelling" meatworks. Then a bit further on, I passed the same white buildings I had previously seen at a distance. I followed the road, running parallel with the railway line, before turning right and finding myself in the "center" of town. My first impression of Bourke was that it was a dusty little town with wide streets, a grand courthouse, and an impressive park but a long way from home.

I found my way to the high school and met up with Cliff before being directed back to the hotel, where I spent the first few nights. Three days later, I moved to the Manston Lodge, and after a week I was relocated to a teacher's flat at the children's hostel. It was next to the high school and proved to be a most satisfactory place to stay for the duration of my time in Bourke.

My first full day in Bourke found me at the high school, meeting people and inspecting the truck. I met Tim Macartney, a manual arts teacher from Bourke High School, and his offsider. They showed me into the back of the truck they had fitted out, with bookshelves full of library books and storage boxes full of soft toys, games, and other material. The truck was given the name, the Little Outback School, a name that ticked boxes on a number of levels but sounded a little corny. Initially, I was somewhat diffident about the name, but everyone seemed happy, so I quickly got used to it. Later that afternoon, I spoke to a roomful of parents about the program and what I hoped to achieve. I was encouraged by their response and had some fruitful conversations afterward. A number of the mothers told me how much they were looking forward to my visit and offered me a bed for the night. I met Linda from Brindingabba Station, and after a friendly chat, I agreed to stay with her family when I did my Hungerford run. I appreciated their trust and—important for me—felt valued as a teacher and a person.

I soon found out that all the children lived "in" Bourke, even if visiting them would sometimes mean a trip outside the shire and into exotic places in Queensland. That was because the ubiquitous prefix "via" in the bush was no respecter of city mind-sets where distance was concerned.

Even so, by using the excellent council maps of the Bourke shire, we were able to work out five separate routes I would travel to visit as many properties as possible. Each run would keep me out for a week, except my "on the road to Tibooburra" run, which needed to be a two-

225

week sojourn, considering the distances I would have to travel and the number of properties I would have to visit.

In summary, the first route took me up to Enngonia, the reserve, and then east to Weilmoringle before heading down the Culgoa River and back to Bourke, after seeing a number of properties on the way. The second route took me up to Enngonia, again visiting three properties on the way, and then west into a maze of back roads and properties before popping out on the Hungerford Road and coming back through Ford's Bridge. Route number three took me to Louth after heading down the Kidman Way towards Cobar, then west to Belah Station, on to Louth, and then across the Darling River, up into the clay pans of the Cuttaburra Channel country, before finishing at the isolated property of Emaroo. The fourth, the Hungerford route, was a long one. Through Ford's Bridge, Yantabulla, and Hungerford, 133 miles northwest, and then along the dingo fence for about 30 miles to Waverly Gate, then back to Bourke, picking up more properties I'd missed on the way up. My fifth and final run would keep me out for two weeks and pick up properties on the way to Wanaaring, before heading west beyond the Paroo toward Tibooburra and then into the great somewhere northwest of Wanaaring, (once again crossing shire lines), where properties were measured in the hundreds of thousands of acres. A welcome addition to the truck was a CB radio, a necessity out where I would be going. I did make one trip east toward Brewarrina to visit a family at Beemery, as well as down the Tarcoon Road past Mt. Oxley, where I met up with a family in the middle of the road, where promises of a visit were made. Sadly, it was the only time I managed to come their way—another instance of too much country and not enough teacher.

One of my first acts was to go to Bourke Christian Church on Sunday to meet the mysterious Laurie MacIntosh. However, Laurie wasn't there—he and his family were down south in Tasmania, so I was put on to the next best thing, a substitute Laurie, when I was introduced to his brother Malcolm and his wife, Amada, and scored an invitation for lunch at Lodebar, the family dairy farm. I clung to Malcolm and Amada for the first few weeks, while meeting other delightful folk in the church. Two other church families who proved to be good friends and so welcoming were the Busters and the Boones, Californian farmers who together came to the district via Wee Waa in the sixties and grew cotton twelve miles out on the Wanaaring Road. Other folk I met at church were most welcoming, while I felt blessed with the friends I had so easily made.

My first run took me up the Mitchell Highway to Enngonia and then west along a dirt road to see the first properties I was going to visit. The truck was sent out in a rough-and-ready way, with deficiencies to be noted and fixed when I got back to Bourke the following Friday. And deficiencies there were. First, the single bogy rear-wheel transit van with a three-speed manual gear box and a city suspension was totally unsuited to the rough, dusty roads of the outback. We found that out over time, but the more immediate problem was the fine red dust that found its way into the back of the truck. As well as that, nothing had been set up to restrain the books on the shelves, so they were thrown around as I bounced my way along the roads, and they ended up on the floor in a red dusty heap. For the first week, when I arrived at each property, the children joined me in the back of the van, picking up, brushing down, and restacking the shelves of the more than two-hundred-book library and then sweeping out the back of the truck, which remained dust-free only until I headed out on the road to the next property. On my first Saturday back in Bourke, resourceful Tim fixed elastic ropes to the shelves and an ingenious system of overlapping ground sheets to the back, which kept out the dust without hindering my ability to open up the roller door and get into the back of the truck. Another problem was the limited range I could travel on a tank of petrol, so once again, my ingenious friends added an extra petrol tank that just about doubled my range.

And so it happened one Monday morning, when I set out dust-free and carefree along the Wilcannia Road to Louth, that the ingenious extra tank had its first hiccup. Some fifteen miles from Louth, my truck slowed down and stopped in the middle of the road and refused all my entreaties to move. Fortunately, I was in CB range and was expected in Louth that morning, so after a call, a couple of jovial fellows drove out from the garage in a tow truck to sort things out. They were resourceful and had soon worked out that small fragments of rubber had broken off from the hose of the new fuel tank and were blocking the flow of petrol into the engine. I was impressed by their ability to work all that out, more so when they had me on my way straight after cleaning out the hose.

I went straight to the pub to find a certain high school student who hadn't sent in any work for a while. I was told by the publican that when she heard I was coming, she took off—such was my impact on the local ladies, I feared.

"That one needs to be brought into line," he said sympathetically.

Still, I enjoyed my visit to Louth. Harry Marshall, a local political identity, took me on a tour of his old school, which had been closed for some years, and the racecourse, where the Louth races were held. In those parts, the Louth races were just as popular as their counterparts in Birdsville. I visited the Le Lievre family, just down the road a bit at Deerina, before pushing on the next day across the Darling, finishing up at Emaroo in the clay pans of the Cuttaburra Channel country. On the way, I visited families at New Chum and Mt. Mulya. I found the primitive living conditions of the farm worker's family at New Chum—a caravan and a tent-like structure with complete ventilation at either end—quite sad, but their spirit was strong and their hospitality welcoming.

As I clocked up the miles, wherever I went I was welcomed by the locals, who seemed eager for a visit and fully supported the program. But to get to the really isolated children out west, I had to travel the Wanaaring Road. It had a fearsome reputation, but I soon found that its reputation depended on when it had last been graded. At its best, it was a smooth, benign, dusty road, but at its worst, it was a confronting track of shifting stones and bone-jarring corrugations that caused the truck to sometimes shudder out of control and lurch across the road, with sudden bumps and jolts that loosened your fillings. I found parts both at its worst and at its best— smooth around Poison Point Plain and the approaches to Wanaaring but shudderingly bad elsewhere. Those parts were stony with a high crown and table drains down both sides. To avoid its worst, I drove in the table drains as much as possible, avoiding the crown of the road and its teeth-rattling corrugations. At each grid, I'd drive up on to the crown of the road and then back down into the table drain. One time, a road train came my way, so at the last moment, I had to dart off into the drain to keep out of its way, as the driver seemingly hadn't noticed me. Another time, when the road was less stony, another road train and I approached each other at reduced speed. As we passed, he gave me the universal sign to a fellow truck driver. I solemnly returned it and then laughed to myself. "I'm a truckie."

Hungerford was 132 miles northwest of Bourke on the Queensland side of the border and about twelve miles farther than Wanaaring. The road was mostly firm, if a bit corrugated in places, but with miles of drifting sand on top. Generally, though, the truck and I found it less stressful than the Wanaaring Road.

I stopped at places on the way and made Hungerford on Wednesday, with enough daylight to continue along the dingo fence to Waverly Gate to see the family who lived there. It was good to see the excitement in the children when I arrived in a cloud of red dust and later, when I was able to spend time with them. But the best part was when we all climbed into the back of the truck, and the children selected books from the library and toys from the toy library. They looked as if Christmas had come early.

Although they were very isolated, they weren't as isolated as the next gate. Hamilton Gate was another hour's drive farther west, just a bit too far for this trip with dark setting in. I was learning fast how slow travel could be in the truck on roads of corrugations and shifting sand and that the map could never fully explain why on those roads, fifteen minutes on bitumen was an hour in the truck. No wonder the locals went hell for leather when they could.

My visits to the Wheelhouse family at Ford's Bridge Hotel on the Hungerford Road were often amusing affairs. On the first night of my Hungerford run, I had been to two properties and was to meet John at the pub and follow him up to his Green Creek property for the night. It was dark when I arrived, so I thought we'd head off straight away. "No, she'll be right," Johnny said. "I've got dinner with me." He showed me a large bag full of yabbies (a type of fresh water crayfish), which he said we'd cook up when we got home. So I waited and starved for another hour until he was ready to go. Finally, we headed off. I was following John, and we were keeping in touch on our CBs, so I heard him call his wife to tell her we were on our way.

"Johnny boy to base," he said a number of times. "Johnny boy to base. This is Johnny boy to base. Come back."

Then a loud, nasally voice that could have torn holes in a corrugated iron roof yelled back at him, "Yeah, whaddaya want?"

We finally got back to Green Creek, and Johnny's wife cooked up the bag of yabbies for dinner, which we ate at midnight. I had no idea what the kids had eaten earlier—one of my many memorable moments on the road out the back o' Bourke. Lovely people and real characters.

When I began each run, the plan was that each property would know my route for that week and where I would end up at the end of the day. Then I'd turn up before mealtime, stay the night, and work with the kids in the morning, before pushing on to the next property. I would try to visit three properties a day, although with some of the distances and road conditions I encountered, I really had to push it to get to the next property before dark. One time it took me more than an hour to get from one house to the next, which just happened to be next door, so far back from the road were they built and so long were their house roads. I was never happy with the small amount of time I had to spend at each property, but I was consoled by the fact I was basically exploring new ground in a system that would be improved progressively as each problem that arose was fixed.

Some properties had governesses, mostly young girls from the local area or from the city. I heard a story about one young girl who had come straight off the train and, after experiencing the loneliness of one night of total darkness and isolation when the generators were turned off, was back on the train the next day, heading straight back to Sydney. On my travels, I met two governesses who were absolute stunners. One was a teenage girl I met early in my travels when visiting North Keribree Station, and the other I met at Warraweena Station on the Culgoa when she came down from Bullaroon to meet up with her boyfriend, who was flying up from Louth to visit her. She was lovely and impressed me no end in the brief time I knew her—all of five minutes. The quintessential country girl waiting for her man to fly in to see her. How precious was that. The young girl at North Keribree had seemed quite reserved when I met her earlier but some time later, I heard that she had entertained the patrons at Ford's Bridge Hotel by dancing on the tables. Somehow, I felt she had found her feet and sadly might have shed her innocence as well.

I only had to sleep out once but had an interesting experience at a couple of places. At one place along the Culgoa, the wife said her husband was away, so I couldn't stay in the house. Instead, I slept out in a shed on a narrow stretcher, which was more than three feet high. It was so narrow, I had to contort my body to stay on it and worried that I might fall off on to the concrete floor during the night if I woke and rolled myself over too vigorously. Obviously, I didn't get much sleep that night.

Another bed at another property was a double bed pushed up against the wall. Good so far, but unfortunately, the springs had collapsed on one side, and the mattress sloped that way, so I found myself falling toward the wall, having to push myself back up to the far side and then rolling back into the wall again. Eventually, I gave up and slept tightly wedged against the wall. It didn't help when I had to get up to go to the toilet during the night, as was the norm.

Some properties used only generators, so when they went off at night, I needed a torch for my nocturnal habits. It was a luxury when they had both generator for power and batteries for lights. Then I could at least turn on my light before venturing down the hallway to find the all-too-distant toilet. Fortunately, the house of the untamed bed had both.

One day I was driving down a farm road between properties when I noticed the adjoining paddock seemed to be on the move. I watched as a mob of kangaroos roused themselves and took off at a leisurely hop, across a grassy plain to another clump of trees to rest. I was astounded by the number, probably up to a hundred, in just one small area. You would never see them on the main road; they didn't need to be there. There was plenty of pick and water for them in the back paddocks, and that's where I came across mobs and mobs of red kangaroos. I wondered what those who claimed kangaroos were an endangered species would have made of that.

Then one morning, a mysterious family appeared at church. They seemed to know everyone, at least the children did, and then a tall, dark-haired, bearded fellow, with glasses, a happy smile, and a gentle voice and who looked a bit like Malcolm, got up and spoke in a friendly, folksy way. Then it twigged—Laurie embedded in my brain, Laurie on the piece of paper, Laurie in person was back. I was quietly pleased. After the service, I was introduced to Laurie, who apparently had heard that someone was waiting to meet him and be adopted by his family. What struck me most about Laurie was his candor, his generosity, his almost boyish enthusiasm, and the intelligence behind his laughing eyes, which focused on you from behind the circles of his glasses and then darted off as a pause stilled his mind while he hatched a plan. It was as though he had just thought it up, as if he first tested out on you, with a self-effacing grin and prefaced with a quizzical, "Hey ..." Yet his "What about ...?" was a suggestion said with such deference and jocularity, it neither offended nor prescribed but put you at ease as he waited for a response. We were like two schoolboys, planning an after-school rendezvous down at the creek, without telling our mothers. I immediately accepted his invitation to lunch, as now, with a twinkle in his eye, he said he'd better go and tell Elvira first. There was something old-fashioned about talking to Laurie. It had a sense of politeness and cordiality that put value on a person who, when made a friend, wasn't discarded easily. I met Laurie's wife, Elvira, who gave me a welcoming if partly amused smile that said, "I see Laurie's picked up another stray." And I immediately scored an invitation for lunch, which I gratefully accepted. Much better than having lunch back at the hostel. Then on to Lodebar, where I remembered that Elvira was Amada's sister, which I supposed made their children double cousins. Weird, like my double hat trick all those years ago, I mused.

Over the following weeks, the MacIntoshes became an important part of my life, providing friendship and stability and allowing me to enjoy rich times with their extended family of parents, sons, daughters, aunts, uncles, nieces and nephews, brothers and sisters, cousins and grandparents, all living under the same roof and with its own blend of Australian and Mexican culture. The unifying ingredients in this rich mix were love, respect, and humility. The relaxed lifestyle up there was typified by the laidback church services that just seemed to come together when the MacIntosh clan made their last-minute arrival. I sat in my seat on Sunday mornings at 9:26, like everyone else, just waiting for their 9:28 arrival and the commencement of the service.

The further west I went, the more my world was left behind. There were properties to visit on the way to Wanaaring and properties to visit on the other side of Wanaaring, which were closer to Tibooburra than to Bourke. The tyranny of distance was typified when I was making a second attempt to reach the border crossing at Hamilton Gate, a distance of nearly 200 miles from Bourke, only to come up short. I had already visited two properties that day and had been driving through back paddocks for an hour. When I left Yarrallee Station and finally hit the main road from Wanaaring, I was looking into a sinking red sun.

"How far is Hamilton Gate?" I had asked the farmer at Colane Station some hours earlier.

"Twelve gates," he said with a shake of the head. Now I knew what he meant. It wasn't the nearly forty miles through farm roads and back paddocks that was the problem—it was the twelve gates. Each had to be opened, driven through, and then closed. Time- consuming, especially when I miscalculated and the size of the gate and the distance from my parked truck didn't match, so I had to get back into the truck and drive forward a bit or back up a few feet more just to clear the gate. I couldn't hurry to the gate, either, which for a former fast runner was a bit frustrating, as well as a real waste of time.

Sitting in the truck on the main road, I found myself in a dilemma, for as much as I wanted to see the children, it was still another twenty minutes drive to Hamilton Gate. Then, after a short visit, it was nearly a hundred-mile drive back down the dusty road to Nocoleche Station, where I was staying. And that would have been in the dark on unfamiliar roads, with all sorts of nasties lurking about. So just twelve miles shy of Hamilton Gate, I reluctantly turned around and headed back to Wanaaring—and disappointed the family who had been waiting all day to see me. I was disappointed too and frustrated that I had come so far, only to find I could go no further. It was my only major regret, because I knew that the children who were the most isolated were still a few gates too far.

I stayed the weekend with the Peken family at Nocoleche, and then a large property about eleven miles south of Wanaaring. Katy was the Correspondence School student, bright and friendly, in a delightful family that highly valued education. Encyclopedia took pride of place on their bookshelves, and I soon realized that they had their children's education perfectly under control and wouldn't need any help from me in the foreseeable future.

I had heard horror stories about what wild pigs had done to livestock, so it was without any qualms that I went out pig shooting with the local policeman and teacher. I had seen their voracious appetite first- hand one night, when Don the policeman took me with him to get some food for his pigs he was cleaning up to slaughter for food. He shot a kangaroo and brought its carcass back to his pigs' enclosure. When he threw it in and the pigs smelled blood, they went at it in what I could only say was an orgy of unrestrained eating. They didn't even take a breath as they drove their snouts deeper and deeper into the kangaroo carcass. "Just wait until they reach the intestines," he said. Right on cue, the eating turned into a frenzy that didn't stop until they had consumed all they could, which was most of the kangaroo. "They'll finish the rest off overnight," Don said. "There'll be nothing left by morning."

The first time out, I used a .22, which seemed to have little impact on a big boar that had thundered past our vehicle as we drove down a track. As he disappeared off into the lignum swamp, a trail of blood suggested I'd made a bigger impact on him than I had previously thought. I did more damage, though, when I used a .303, first on the three little pigs who just happened to be passing by, and a boar munching on the carcass of a dead cow we had driven up behind. Even though I hit him where it hurts, he just walked off, so I followed him and it took four more rounds before he finally dropped. His large tusks became a trophy for my teacher friend's wall. After seeing what pigs were capable of doing the previous night, I felt happy there was one less pig to cause havoc among the local wildlife.

I arrived back in Bourke late on Friday, August 19, after my two-week sojourn and heard that Elvis Presley had died three days earlier. Although I wasn't an Elvis fan, the news had an unusual feel about it. It was significant to the outside world but was probably only of passing interest to the communities around Bourke. It underlined how isolated this part of the world was, as the news would have gone around the world many times without making much dent west of the Darling. Out there, life went on, and Elvis's demise was of fleeting importance, soon forgotten in the light of more pressing matters, such as droughts, overdrafts, dust storms, mouse plagues, and flooding rains.

The truck had taken quite a battering on the Bourke roads but had also inflicted its own sense of randomness on the local wildlife. I was heading east on a back road toward the Mitchell Highway when I discovered how death is a relative part of life in the bush. Coming over a grid late one afternoon, I surprised a doe feeding on some pick on the other side of the rise. I couldn't avoid her when she panicked and jumped under the wheels of the truck. It was distressing to see her so badly injured and suffering on the ground, with short shallow gasps, and I lamented not having a rifle with me. But the worst of it was seeing a tiny naked joey that had been in her pouch, lying just a little further up the road. Neither was going to survive, as I was in the backblocks about eighty miles from Bourke. Nor was there a suburban vet two streets away, so to leave them was to leave them to a slow, lingering death. It was better to be cruel to be kind, so I found a tree branch and put them out of their misery. And so just like that, two living creatures had their lives snuffed out, all because they were in the wrong place at the wrong time.

In the city, far from the harsh reality of the bush and where a person is brought up in a society where pets are often treated like family, my actions would have been seen as obscene. But when you are out there, you start to understand that life and death often travel together down the same path. I'd had reminders of the uneasy truce between those fellow travelers, such as the time I just made it off the crown of the

235

road into the table drain as a road train rumbled by, and when I finally stopped next to a tree rather than wrapping around, it near Yantabulla. Or the lonely deaths of farmers and workers through accidents and misadventure, or a farmer taking his rifle out into a back paddock and not returning after watching his sheep die after five years of drought, or a shearer's cook who got lost and ended up eaten by pigs.

That's why death wasn't hidden away; it was always there in your face. I had no desire to shoot kangaroos but pigs were a different matter, especially when I heard stories about the carnage they caused and what they did to sheep in lambing season.

I headed back "down inside," as the locals called all places south of Bourke, at the end of the term for a two-weeks holiday back home and a football match to watch. I left late Friday afternoon, planning to stay in Dubbo overnight before pushing on to Sydney the next morning. I drove past the railway station to see my school strapped to a freight car, waiting to be sent back to Sydney by the only means it would get there—a victim of the outback roads.

It was dark as I approached Nyngan. Fifteen miles out, there was a dead kangaroo on the road—so I hit it. As I drove on, the sweet smell of cooking flesh penetrated into the car. A bit further on, the car stopped and would go no further. It was dark and times were desperate, so I did a desperate thing—I prayed. "Thank you, Lord, for sparing me. Now please get me out of this mess," or words to that effect. Nighttime wasn't the right time to be driving on the Mitchell Highway, a wise man once said, but fortunately for me, the next car didn't obey that aphorism either. The driver stopped, looked, and drove off with the promise of sending a tow truck back to get me. Promise kept, tow truck sent, and a short time later, we pulled into the first garage on the right in Nyngan. There my car stayed for the next two weeks, while I caught the Broken Hill-to-Sydney coach for an uncomfortable ride back to Sydney.

The next morning, my father picked me up at the coach terminal at King's Cross. We only had a short time to get home, eat, freshen up, and choof off to Manly Oval to watch Ivan's team lose the grand final to Matraville. My old team, by far the best team in their competition, underperformed and was knocked out in the previous week's semifinal.

The players told me they would have won easily if I was still coaching them. They said the fellow who took over just said to them, "You know what you did with Ken; just keep doing the same things." I cringed when I heard that—not the right way to win a final. What I did with the players only worked when I was there, not when I wasn't there. By the time the finals had come around, apparently they hadn't worked out how to win the premiership. To rely on what I had done early in the season had left the team with no plan and running on empty.

After the match, I had more bad news when Ivan told me he was going back to New Zealand in a couple of weeks. He said he felt God was in the move, something I couldn't really argue with, despite my disappointment. Ivan had been a good and trusted friend for the past three years, and I knew I would miss him when I came back to Sydney, as I knew I would. But rather than feeling despondent, I felt happy for them and accepted it, because I was living for the present and trusting that the future would take care of itself. I wasn't sure where my future lay, but I did feel confident that for the present, it was back in Bourke, where I had friends and an important job to see through. I would be there for however long it took.

While in Bourke, I had heard that the wife of the minister at Dee Why Church had died suddenly. Because of all that had happened, I felt emotionally detached from the church but felt I should pass on my condolences to the family for their loss.

I was met at the front door of the manse by the family, and after extending my sympathies and, possibly to their relief, I left, feeling that I had at least made the effort.

Two weeks later, I flew to Dubbo and then hopped into a Cessna for the short leg to Bourke and resumed my outback travels. Then on the first weekend back, I was driven down to Nyngan by a friend from church to pick up my now-repaired car.

The Little Outback School had gone back to Sydney, undriveable, its shock absorbers destroyed by the Bourke roads. So without its cavernous capacity, there had to be a change of strategy. The truck would be replaced by a station wagon, and mini-schools would be held at local centers on Fridays for the children in the area I was visiting. I would carry enough equipment with me in the back of the station wagon for home visits, and someone would drive up from Bourke in another truck with the rest of the school material and meet me there. Then we would set up for a day of lessons, activities, and games. It seemed to be the next logical step in the program. At the very least, it would protect the replacement truck, as it would have limited exposure to the worst of the roads by only traveling out from Bourke to where we ran mini-schools. In the end, we were only able to fit in two mini-schools in the time available during the third term.

For the first mini-school, we planned to use the hall at Yantabulla on the way back from my next Hungerford run. But before that, I had to spend the night in Hungerford, a night I remember well. I had just come back from two "via Bourke" properties in Queensland, only arriving back in Hungerford at sunset. I was put up in the single-story hotel for the night and was, not surprisingly, the only guest there. Once the generators went off, it was pitch dark, deathly quiet, and I was all alone and at the mercy of any axe murderer who might have been lurking around. At some time during the night, the noises began. There was snuffling, ripping, and tearing sounds coming from behind the hotel, just behind a fragile-looking back door. It eventually stopped, and in the morning, I could see what it had been. The back "yard" looked like a just-ploughed paddock, as it had been dug up by wild pigs rooting around for food just a closed door away—an unnerving night, which I was happy to leave behind as I headed south early the next morning on my way to Yanatabulla and the mini- school.

I had made good time and had just come around a sweeping bend about twelve miles north of Yantabulla, when I felt the car starting to drift off the road. There was nothing I could do to stop it, so I braced myself and hoped for a soft landing. When the car finally stopped, it had ploughed a track through the scrub and was now resting next to a solitary tree. I was more annoyed than shaken, so after a few deep breaths, I drove back on to the middle of the road, where I inspected the car for damage. Apart from some scratches, which didn't seem out of place, everything seemed fine—until I inspected the tires. Two tires, front and back, were flat—the obvious cause of my losing control. Fortunately, I carried two spares for an occasion such as this. One blowout was understandable, two was unusual, but three would be diabolical. In a short time, I had jacked up the car and replaced the unusual and was just about to resume my journey, when I heard a hissing sound announcing the diabolical. I watched, fascinated, as the second back tire slowly deflated in front of me, just like it was hurrying to catch up to the other two. Unfortunately, this time I'd run out of spares (two be spares, but three be a shop), so I had to slowly drive the rest of the way to Yantabulla on one flat tire. I took it easy, and half an hour later trickled into the village in time to see the truck being unloaded and the mini-school being set up.

The day was very successful, with kids and mothers coming in from miles around. The mothers were able to have a social time together, as well as participating in the day's activities and the games. They were happy to hear that more mini-schools were planned for the future, while I was happy to see a new tire delivered later that day from Bourke.

Some weeks later, in mid-October, we had another mini-school, a six-day camp on Delta Station. It was attended by about twenty property kids, a good number of parents, and a few teachers who had come up for the occasion from the Correspondence School. My old friend Isobel had driven up from the Ivanhoe/Menindee area, where a similar scheme had started and where, like me, she had escaped from the Correspondence School to be part of it.

I felt the mini-school was a big success in getting everyone together for a social as well as educational experience. It was a tribute to the organization of the many who had been working behind the scenes to get the program moving. It also demonstrated the absolute commitment the parents and their association had to the ongoing development of educational experiences and resources for isolated children. There had been a lot of hard work and "hard politicking" to get things to where they now were. I was in the middle of something I didn't fully understand then but was happy to be able to play a part in it, small as it might be.

I had heard about the "Jolly Boys" from a young mother at Warroo Station, when I visited on my way to Hungerford. She told me they were a group of old gentlemen from the city who had been coming up to the area for years, camping out on the local properties, and fishing in the waterways and billabongs. Her words had such appeal for a traveler like me, a story of the outback that could easily have become a legend, if only a modern-day Henry Lawson or a Banjo Patterson had happened by and stopped to have a yarn with the locals at Hotel Hungerford. I could see him sitting there, pen in hand, jotting down on the backs of envelopes the stories he'd been told, some true, some stretched, but all about the Jolly Boys.

Some days later, I left Backwood Station, an oasis of citrus orchards on the Paroo River, after staying there overnight. I was on my way to Wanaaring, down the dusty road from Hungerford and the great beyond, when the understandable happened again. Fortunately, I was able to keep the station wagon steady and come to a stop in the safest place possible—the middle of the road. I inspected the tires and was pleased to see that only one tire was flat. I had the jack out and was ready to start, when an old battered car pulled up behind me. Out stepped a number of elderly gentlemen, who immediately got to work and changed the tire for me. As they laughed and chuckled their way through the exercise, it dawned on me who they were.

"I know who you are," I said. "You're the Jolly Boys." They found that title highly amusing.

"Is that what they call us?" one the men chuckled. Then they left as they had come, like a morning mist fading away in the heat of the day, and I continued on to Wanaaring with a warm feeling and the knowledge I'd crossed paths with almost legends of the outback.

One of the beauties of being on the open road around Bourke was the lack of traffic. That worked in my favor, considering my bladder's often pressing requirements. When I had to go, I had to go—now! So all I had to do was stop on a long stretch of road in the middle of nowhere, check there were no cars or road trains coming my way, and without a care in the world, relieve myself. Sometimes stopping at a gate before entering a property afforded me the same opportunity, although a few members of the local wildlife fraternity got a good hosing in the process. Still, I found driving long distances therapeutic; there was a certain contentment about it, where time stood down, and I could think and plan my next visit, knowing I had it all under control. I found the outback to be vast and friendly with open arms, but honest and unforgiving if you didn't give it its due respect and you tried to cut corners—much like life. And it was my road to travel—lonely but necessary and strangely invigorating.

As the temperature rose, my beach instincts kicked in. One Saturday morning, I was sunning myself in the quadrangle at the hostel. Up the other end of the quadrangle were a number of the female teachers and a local resident—a large brown snake. I heard shouting, saw girls darting, and saw a snake gliding my way—and at the rate of knots. As it came toward me, I could see it had one intention and that was escape, but unfortunately, I was standing in its way. I wasn't afraid of snakes but being highly immobile and with a large brown snake seemingly oblivious to my presence, I was less than understanding. I reasoned I had only one chance, so as he came close, I whacked him with my walking stick and broke his neck. From then on, my walking stick received hero status from the students I visited, when word got out.

Summer came early and by mid-October it was becoming hot. Just before eight o'clock one Monday morning, I set out from my flat, crossed the bridge at North Bourke, and headed north, bemused by the fact I was already dry. That's because minutes earlier, I had tipped half a bucket of water over myself and was saturated when I left Bourke, only to find that the dry heat, even at eight in the morning, had dried my clothes by the time I'd crossed the Darling. It was the beginning of the big heat, which was manageable because of the low humidity, even when it hit a hundred degrees, which it did often. It was only on my last trip west that the heat became unbearable, even though summer had just started. You knew it was hot when even the farmers stayed indoors, husbanding their energies until a "cooler" part of the day.

As had become my custom, I took as many loaves of bread as I could to pass on to the first few properties I visited. I was quite surprised to see how grateful they were for days-old bread, which in the city would have been thrown out. Just another reminder for me of how much is taken for granted by city dwellers, such as the freshness of bread. The ladies in the kitchen at the hostel were always kind and made sandwiches for me when I left, in case I was caught out on the road between properties at lunchtime. They also provided me with a gallon plastic container of frozen fruit juice to guzzle on the way. It remained cold all day, even when it began to thaw out. At night, it was put in the freezer at each property where I stayed, so that the next day I would set out with slightly less frozen fruit juice to drink. It usually lasted me a full week and was replenished by the ladies in the kitchen when I set out again the next Monday morning.

I had a unique experience in Bourke when I met a group of aboriginal tribal dancers from Mornington Island. They were in Bourke to perform their tribal dances for the local schools, as part of a national tour. I'd had limited contact with full-blood aborigines; they were mainly remote figures in books and films and even on postage stamps, so I found meeting them in the flesh a bit confronting. My first impressions were how humble and dignified they were. When one of the dancers introduced himself to me, I was surprised by his broad Australian accent and that it had none of the stereotypical aboriginal sound about it. I was further surprised by how confident and articulate he was as he talked about his culture and what they were doing in Bourke. In the brief time we chatted, my preconceptions changed and after they left, I was thinking what an impressive a bunch of fellows they were. Later, when talking to one of the high school teachers, I heard that the white kids were fascinated by their performance, whereas the aboriginal kids laughed at them and showed the dancers little respect. I found that very strange, as well as surprising.

Apart from a couple of dinners with teachers from the high school, my social life in Bourke revolved primarily around the church folk. I had become good friends with Laurie and Elvira and looked forward to invitations to Lodebar, where their families lived in an array of small dwellings that seemed to be connected by walkways, tarpaulin, and sticky tape.

Knowing them made my time in Bourke all the more enriching. As I drove into Bourke each Friday after a dry and dusty week on the road, I felt like I was coming home to an oasis, where I was accepted and could relax and be refreshed by their love and friendship. It was a good place to be, where the simple things in life had value and a taste that was uncommonly sweet. Then there were the wide open spaces with vast horizons and endless skies, which evoked a respectful view of life, when the grandeur of God was on display every night. I had to come a long way to see the simple honesty of life in the bush that was untainted by the false urgency of city living.

I also looked forward to visits to Darling Farms and Fort Bourke, where my American friends lived. I always enjoyed the Sunday lunches we shared, the magnificent food, and Esther Boone's carrot puddings. I particularly liked their son, Michael, a kind, gentle young man a year my junior. His Christian faith stood out in his words and deeds, and we soon discovered that he knew Ross, my college roommate, when they both did national service together. Michael had his pilot's license and took me up in a Cessna one day. We flew around the district and looked at the vast expanse of brown opening up before us. We went on and on to distant horizons and far places—places where I had been over the previous weeks. We often talked about life, and Mike expressed a desire to use his many skills for mission work in New Guinea. Years later, Mike and his wife and young family did just that and spent a number of fruitful years in New Guinea, until Mike was tragically killed in an accident there in 1992.

Although I had met a few single girls, starting a relationship with anyone was the furthest thing from my mind. I had responsibilities, and my total focus was on why I was there and what I was doing. As much as I felt comfortable in Bourke, deep down I knew that I was just there for a season, a "pilgrim" who was just passing through. But the main reason, I suspect, was that my heart was still wounded, and I wasn't ready to go down that path yet, nor was I interested in having a fling. If a girl had been interested in me, then she would have had to hit me on the head with a brick and tell me so, such was my disconnect from affairs of the heart.

1977 in the outback town of Bourke, New South Wales, Australia.
My "Little Outback School" is in the back of the truck.

CHAPTER 21

Leaving Bourke

It was hot when I began my last trip for the year to properties in an area west of the Warrego but close to the Wanaaring Road. It was so hot, even the farmers had downed tools and settled indoors to sit out the heat wave. It was hard going for the first three days, as I had picked up a bug that had been going around the district, and by the time I hit Harry Marshall's place, I was feeling pretty low. It worsened overnight, and I found myself laid up for two days, unable to spend school time with his kids. Harry didn't seem too pleased, but there was little I could do about it, and I had to head straight back to Bourke when I was well enough to drive. Although it was a disappointing end to the year, it was the right time to finish. The big heat was setting in, and the following week was the last week of term, and I would need it for some preliminary discussions about next year.

On Monday, I went to the high school to meet with Cliff. When I sat down, he looked a bit distracted, as though he had something on his mind. Without any preliminary remarks, he got straight to the point and told me I was finishing up at the end of the term and wouldn't be involved in the program next year. It took me by surprise, and when I realized what it meant, I was quite upset. It certainly wasn't one of my better moments, as the ramifications of the decision left me quite numb. For weeks, I'd been totally consumed by dusty roads, school families,

245

new friends, and the need that was still out there. But now I'd just been told that I wasn't going to be a part of it anymore. I had admired the resilience of the people out there and had felt so much a part of their world, a world where they didn't have the best things in life but tried to make the best out of what they did have. But all that had just come to an end, because it was obvious I had lost the support of key people and had put some noses out of joint.

As I thought about it later, I knew Roger and Mary were probably unhappy with me because of my less-than-frequent visits to the aboriginal reserve at Enngonia, visits that they had believed were a priority. But the reality was that because of my affinity with the isolated kids on the properties, I was more aware of their needs and became more so when I visited them and saw what they had to put up with. There was also another consideration. Although I'd taught in one-teacher schools, I had never had preschool children before, so I didn't feel as comfortable with that age as an infants teacher would have. Mary was single-minded and determined when it came to the children on the reserve, so when she said to me one time, "You know what to do with them, don't you?" I really wanted to say, "Not really. Could you give me some help?" but because I had been put off by the prickly tone in her voice, I was a bit defensive and said, "Yes, of course I do." I think in the back of my mind I wasn't really sure what her reaction would be if I'd said no.

Roger was generally an amiable fellow, but when I made a belated visit to the reserve later in the term, our relationship was quite strained. I didn't feel I could get back to the reserve again before the end of the year, so no matter how appreciative the kids on the properties might have been, I wasn't going to get any sympathy from Roger and Mary. If I had felt I could have been more open with Mary or been able to explain my position better, I'm sure we could have had a better understanding and worked together. I was working under Roger's submission, but if I spent as much time at the reserve as they would have liked me to, it would have been much harder to get out to the more isolated properties and probably would have been too physically draining as well. And that's something I would never have used as an excuse—my physical condition. It had to have no connection to what I was doing; otherwise,

I had no right being there and doing the job in the first place. Still, I did feel a bit let down, as Roger always referred back to the submission rather than showing any flexibility or willingness to talk it through. We all knew the submission was a compromise to get funding, and with forty to fifty properties to visit, the squeaking door was always out there, while there was not as much squeak at the reserve.

Although we all knew the program needed two teachers, I still had to try to please everyone. In the end, I didn't have enough pockets, so I didn't please some. I suspected I'd lost Roger's support, but I thought others on the committee would be more understanding, because I really felt the issue was much bigger than my spasmodic visits to the reserve. Stations such as Emaroo and Yarrallee (out past the twelve gates), as well as Waverly Gate scored only one visit, and they were whistle-stop visits at that, because I wasn't staying there at night, despite visiting them at the end of the day. Furthermore, Hamilton Gate and the family down the Tarcoon Road never had a visit, despite being on my run. I'd even had an inquiry from someone at Come-By-Chance, a place I declined to visit when I looked at the map. Paradoxically, it was no further east of Bourke than places I visited were west of Bourke, but significantly, it wasn't in the Bourke shire.

As for a reason as to why I was out, Cliff was vague and somewhat condescending in saying that "people" were worried about my safety, traveling out there on my own—not that anyone had asked for my opinion on the matter. He said nothing of a rumour going around that I didn't go to the "right" church, but told me, whether by accident or intent, they already had a couple of local teachers lined up to take over from me, a husband and wife team who lived in Bourke. I wasn't privy to what was discussed behind closed doors at their meetings and had no inkling of what was said. I felt I had a further six- to twelve-month contribution to make to the program, but that wasn't to be.

After that meeting with Cliff, no one else from the DCA spoke to me except Pat Edgely. She seemed to be genuinely upset by the decision and left me with the distinct impression that I had a lot of support from the families on the properties.

So I left Bourke with hardly a good-bye. I heard later that some of the parents were upset I wasn't coming back, so I felt my efforts were at least appreciated by some, as well as by my new church family, who were just as disappointed as I was that it was all over.

Before I left, the church family organized a farewell luncheon at Darling Farms, which proved to be a bittersweet moment for me. In a brief farewell remark, I told them how sad I was in leaving and that they had been a real family to me while I had been there. What I didn't say was that they had filled my spiritual and emotional needs and had made my time in Bourke so much more enriching and enjoyable. Like the wonderful families I visited and the western sunsets I drove into, I would miss them all—enormously.

These were the thoughts I didn't know how to express, but I did know I was thankful that God had led me up to Bourke and into the path of mature Christians, who had accepted me and made me feel a part of their families. When I left, I felt satisfied that I had done my best. Despite knowing that to some, my stay hadn't been entirely successful and there was more to be done, I had at least shown the human face of education to families in the bush. I hoped the legacy I left behind was good friends, goodwill, and a confidence that those in the bush hadn't been forgotten.

CHAPTER 22

Across the Ditch

I had been in constant touch with Ivan back in New Zealand and Jim and Pauline back in Sydney. They had talked and "decided" — albeit with not much resistance from me—that it would be good for me to cross the ditch to New Zealand for a holiday. So I did.

I came back from Bourke with the red dust of the outback still in my system. My mechanic took care of my Cortina's needs, whereas mine were never fully erased, so deep had it penetrated, despite the short time I had been there. That door had closed, so I left the outback behind me and flew over to New Zealand after Christmas with Jim and Pauline and their kids, landing at Auckland Airport, where we were met by Ivan and Pam. Jim and Pauline left me and headed off south to Tauranga, where Pauline's brother-in-law Des was the principal of the Faith Bible College. I would follow them in week or so, after spending time with Ivan and Pam on Arid (Rakitu) Island.

We flew over to Great Barrier Island and then caught the punt across to Arid Island, a small hilly outcrop a few miles away. We were met at the jetty by Pam's stepfather, Clive, who managed the island for the owner. He took us up to their house, perched halfway up the hill, and there we stayed until the New Year. We could easily have lived on smoked fish for weeks, because the local bluefish had a death wish and took everything offered to them, even when it was nothing. I briefly entertained thoughts that I was a "skilled" fisherman—until our last day out in the boat when I dropped in a line with no bait on the hook and quickly reeled in a fish. It was humbling to realize there was no skill involved in catching brain-dead fish. We caught just under two hundred fish over three days of fishing, so with stocks replenished, Clive prepared them and put them straight into the smokehouse. For days after, we gorged ourselves on smoked fish. Pam's mum was a marvelous host, as all she seemed to be doing was preparing meals for her voracious guests, who ate everything offered so that she had to do it all over again at the next mealtime, for the same result.

I spent New Year's Eve down on the beach with Ivan and Pam, until Pam decided to go back to the house. Ivan had a bottle of wine and desperately needed someone to help him finish it. I obliged, so after the good deed was done, we made our way back up the hill to the house. It was dark, and I was a bit more unsteady than usual, so I needed Ivan's help to make it over the rough bits. Despite his help, I spent a lot of time on the ground as we giggled and sniggered our way back up to the house.

I had another unsteady moment, on the back of a motor bike, as Ivan maneuvered it up the side of the hill along an impossibly narrow track, past sheep that could pass as mountain goats, to an impossibly small landing strip at the top. It was possible to take off but the sudden stop when landing—the side of the hill—was a worry to any pilot trying to land. Then we had to turn around and make our shaky way back down the track, back past the short-legged sheep, while Ivan tried hard not to drive off the mountain.

When it was time to head back to Auckland, our plan was to go back by launch, but bad weather had set it, making that impossible. The sea had become too dangerous to try to get a boat over to us, so it looked like we could be stranded there. The only way we could get off the island was by barge, which would take us over to Great Barrier Island, from where we would fly back to Auckland in two light planes. Unfortunately, the tide was low, and the barge couldn't get us close to the shore of Great Barrier Island.

"We have to walk from here," Ivan told me. "Do you think you can manage it?"

"I'll give it a go," I said optimistically.

It was quite an experience, wading through nearly waist-deep water with Ivan supporting me against the current, while carrying a large bag on his shoulder. Eventually, we all made it back to shore and then boarded the two small planes waiting to fly us back to Auckland. Ivan's plane took off first, and as he related later, he watched, horrified, as our pilot didn't bother taxiing down the runway and taking off into the wind but instead, to save time, he gunned it and headed downwind at top speed toward the fast-approaching foaming waters of the Pacific Ocean. He managed to get us airborne just in time, as we had reached the end of the runway. But then we had to endure an uncomfortable flight back to Auckland, where we flew into every pocket of turbulence he could find in our part of the sky. Ivan was livid and when we got safely back to the airport, he lodged a complaint about our pilot and his dangerous and irresponsible takeoff. If it had been my wife and daughter in the second plane, I would have done the same—lodged a complaint, I mean.

Soon after, we headed south to Tauranga, where we met up with Jim and Pauline at the Faith Bible College. I stayed there while Ivan and Pam continued on south to the Linton Army Base at Palmerston North, where Ivan's school residence was.

A week later, Jim borrowed Des's Audi, and Jim and I drove south to Palmerston North. We stopped at Rotorua and then drove past Lake Taupo down the desert road, past the three mountains—Ruapehu, Ngauruhoe, and Tongariro—and on to Linton Army Base, where we met up with Ivan and Pam. On the Sunday, we went to a big Pentecostal church in the old movie theater in the center of town. Later that night, we visited friends of theirs, Rex and Annette. Unfortunately, the visit coincided with my bladder giving me frantic signals it was full and needed relief, so when Rex and I were first introduced, I was over by a tree in his front yard, watering the grass. He was nonplussed, understandably so, by the sight of a complete stranger urinating in his front yard, but he handled it well. People who knew me understood that when I had to go, I really had to go, whether it offended normal people's sensibilities or not. Ivan and Pam were not the least put off by my hurried detour, especially when barging into a person's house I had just met and demanding to know where the toilet was could be circumvented if I could just find a dark and private spot beforehand.

Fortunately, Rex was easygoing and agreeably understanding, and we quickly established a good relationship, especially as Rex was a rugby tragic, was interested in my rugby background, and never tired of talking all things rugby.

A few days later, Jim and I drove back to Tauranga and stayed at the Bible college for another week, until it was time to head north to Auckland and fly back to Sydney.

A few hours later, we stepped off the plane, only to be hit by the searing heat of a Sydney heat wave. It was such a contrast to the mild summer we'd just come from in New Zealand. Jim just turned to me and said with a grin, "We're home."

CHAPTER 23

Another Year at the "Corro" School

When the 1978 school year began, I went back to the Correspondence School and back to the "classroom," When it came to organizing classes for the new year, I requested that two of my Bourke family, Rosita and Tonchi MacIntosh, be put in my class. With that arranged, I was asked to take on a girl who other teachers said was "difficult" to teach.

I had seen Samantha twice—once when she came into the Correspondence School with her mother to visit her teacher, and once in a television special some six years before. At that time, she was five and had been hailed as an art prodigy. Samantha was at the Correspondence School, like a number of students living in Sydney, because of a medical condition. However, there was more to it, as Sam was basically a square peg in the round hole of traditional education, and there was no educational institution more traditional than that of the Correspondence School.

Two other students who came into my class were twin boys from West Ryde. I had seen them on television as well, in an ABC special about the rare medical condition that had left them in wheelchairs. In the special, they motored around the hospital by sliding across the floor

253

on their bottoms and using their arms as "oars." My other students were some other "via Bourke" kids and other isolated kids, but no travelers, circus kids, lighthouse kids, or missionary kids overseas. I looked at each student's files and noted Sam's previous schools and the teachers' comments with interest. I was starting the year feeling refreshed after my time in New Zealand and confident after my Bourke adventure and was looking forward to new challenges and working with kids with special needs. And thankfully, my handicap didn't even seem to be a problem now.

Second week back, one of the mistresses told me that Samantha and her mother had come in to meet me. It sounded more like a warning, her tone being that of a harbinger of doom rather than a conveyer of information. When I previously had seen Samantha at the school, she had seemed quite passive when discussing her schoolwork with her teachers. However, when I met Samantha—or Sam, as she preferred to be called—and her mother, Gillian, the meeting had an exciting buzz about it. We hit it off straight away, and I came away with the same feeling that this was shaping up as an interesting if not exciting year. Their eyes seem to be saying, "At last, someone we can work with."

I was younger and less traditional than any of Sam's previous teachers and more flexible in my approach, which augured well for Sam, as they hoped I would be more amenable to her unique learning needs. As for me, it became a trip into the unknown with a girl of unlimited potential.

It didn't take long for us to develop an understanding. There were some things Sam just had to do, like maths, but with other things, we could be more flexible. My views on learning were still developing, but I knew some things worked with some kids and not with others. I would set Sam projects to do in her area of interest, and she would troop off to the museum or a library with her mother to research and gather information for the project. Her research and writing skills exploded over the year. The first project was on ancient Egypt, soon followed by projects on other ancient civilizations. By the end of the year, Sam's productions had progressed from a good sixth-class standard to the level expected of senior high school students.

One night a week, I would drive to Sam's place at Pyrmont to catch up with her schoolwork and afterward socialize with her family. I would mark her maths first, and then we would get on to the "serious" things she was doing. Sam had the curiosity of a world explorer and the intellectual energy to match. What's more, when she collected all the material, she knew how to best use it. She was highly motivated and worked best when given direction and then let go. Very early, I came to the conclusion it would have been short- sighted—foolish, even—not to have tapped into this potential, so I continued to encourage and nurture it, despite relinquishing much of the control over her education and placing it in her own capable hands.

For the ten months I was her teacher, I learned a lot. In what proved to be a most enriching, enjoyable period of my teaching life, I entered Sam's world of museums and libraries; lecture halls and theater, and of actors and directors of both theater and film. It was a world of erudition and style, of places I could visit in my own life journey along with Sam, as she went on hers.

A teacher's confidence comes from knowing how to teach, so stepping outside this comfort zone when confronted by an atypical learner can be threatening to a teacher, especially when pedagogy is hard rusted on, and inflexible methods are godlike and not loosely held. However, Samantha didn't fit this mold and could be quite threatening to teachers. She had her way of learning and showed more discipline in her approach than most do in the classroom. I was happy to be used by her, as we both went on a journey, as it were, of learning and exploring, which for Sam was like an endless adventure and for me was like a breath of fresh air.

The twins were a unique challenge. If Bourke had taught me anything, it was how much parents and students appreciated personal contact. I had the opportunity to carry that principle into my class, so I made an arrangement with the boys' mother to drive over to West Ryde and visit them at home. It was another salutary lesson for me to watch them zipping around the floor on their bottoms, to see their excitement and their zest for life. I don't know what my visit meant to them, but they did seem to appreciate it. We did keep in close contact, though, through the tapes I made for them. Some were the normal school tapes we used, along with written comments, where I'd talk about their schoolwork and add a personal word for them, but others I made in my new home. I read Ursula Le Guin's book, *The Tombs of Atuan*, in bite-sized chunks and sent the tapes to them with their normal schoolwork. This continued until the end of the year, but as I read each chapter, I wondered if it was the right type of story for the boys. However, their mother said they looked forward to the tapes and did enjoy the story.

My sister was living in her old room at home when I came back to Sydney. She was working as an illustrator at the Correspondence School after she had initially taken a job at Granville Boys High as an art teacher. But that was just for a short term, so the department found her a position at William Street. She started as an art teacher but moved to an illustrator's job. That worked well for me, for it meant I could resume my other career as a ferry master, ferrying Anne and my sister and any others who needed a lift from the northern beaches down the transit lane for a quick run to school.

I went back to the Cougars, back to my mates, back to coaching and eventually, back to coaching director. It felt different without Ivan, but there was a positive vibe among the players, and club spirit was high. I'd had misgivings about the club being promoted to the second division, and although we were probably a division too high, it turned out to be a satisfying year for the club. My relationship with the players had matured, and after my time away, I realized there was a strong bond of friendship there, so that coming back wasn't a retrograde step but was more like coming home to your family—but with all members being just that little bit older.

Throughout the season, the teams, including our nominal fourth team, played with the same gritty determination that had become part of the club culture in the brief years we had been a club. Although we lost more than we won, the players competed well in the higher standard competition and even had wins against the leading teams in both first and second grade. If things had gone our way, both teams would have made the semifinals but instead, we ended up as honorable also-rans. There were, however, side benefits for me from all the goodwill, as I was able to use the skills of the tradies in the club for electrical and plumbing needs when I bought a new house, as well as keeping my car running sweetly.

CHAPTER 24

Final Days

Back in Sydney, I picked up with Jim where we had left off before my sojourn to Bourke and resumed the round of meetings run by the FGBA. The cup of tea and scones afterward were always worth hanging around for, as I was able to catch up with the Christian folk I had gotten to know over the last few years. It was at one of the meetings that Jim introduced me to Alice, a girl about my age who was there with her South African parents. Alice was at the next meeting as well but this time on her own, so after the formalities were over, we met at the tea and scones table and talked some more. I found Alice was an intelligent, friendly, very attractive girl and was someone I felt very comfortable talking to. She wasn't the sort of girl you would trifle with either, and that suited me fine, because I didn't have any intentions of trifling with her, nor did I feel I had to impress her. Besides, I had my own distractions—unresolved issues of the heart and my old chestnut of not wanting to 'inflict' myself on anyone, a sentiment that I suspected might have been tugging at my self-confidence.

The FGBA used to conduct well-organized meetings with interesting speakers. One of the meetings arranged was at the University of New South Wales, where astronaut Neil Armstrong was to address a packed auditorium. Jim said that he heard that Armstrong was reported to have said that he "saw" God on the moon—or so we were led to believe. Armed with that belief, we all sat there, full of anticipation, waiting to hear about Armstrong's lunar encounter with the Almighty. The emcee introduced Neil Armstrong and then welcomed him to the dais, after restating Armstrong's reported comment. It was followed by stunned looks, head jiggling, and furtive whispering between Armstrong and the emcee, who then had to stand up and apologize to everyone and say that Neil Armstrong denied that he ever said that he "saw God" on the moon and that he, in fact, didn't see God on the moon. Those were the only words Armstrong spoke, albeit whispered, to the emcee, so the purpose of the meeting proved to be a non event, especially as he declined the opportunity to get up and tell everyone there what he did see on the moon. After the meeting Jim said to me, somewhat disappointedly, "He could have at least told us what it was like to walk on the moon."

One night, I was invited by a marketing firm to preview a television show at their Sydney offices. The invitation was for two, so for some company, I asked Alice to go with me. When we arrived, we were ushered into a small theater with about twenty others to watch scenes from the pilot episode of an English police drama called *The Professionals* and then answer some questions. It was all guns, cars, and whistles, and generally got the thumbs-up from the other people there. I found I could take it or leave it, depending on my mood or the company I was with, whereas it not surprisingly didn't impress Alice at all. We wrote lukewarm responses and then headed off into the night to find a coffee shop. From Alice's comments, I could see that she was a serious-minded person, probably more serious than I was, and was unimpressed by the flash and dash of this world, as were most of the mature Christians I knew.

Things hurried along a bit with Alice after that. She needed a lift home after the next meeting, so flexible Ken offered to drive her. We talked all the way to her parents' place and when we got there, it seemed appropriate to give her a respectful kiss on the cheek. That started something, because Alice responded by kissing me back quite passionately. It was then I realized that she liked me as more than just a friend, something I don't think I was prepared for. We went out together a few more times, but I was concerned that things were moving too quickly and out of my comfort zone.

It came to a head one night when Alice told me she was moving out of her parents' house and into a flat at Hornsby, and she asked me to visit her there. That changed the dynamics of our relationship and took the safety valve of her parents' house out of the equation. It also left me with a moral dilemma. As much as I liked Alice, "like" was what I felt for her. It would have been quite easy to just go with the flow and see how things turned out, but Alice was no flirty teenager. She was looking for a permanent relationship with someone and had every right to expect it. To spend time with her alone in her flat would have been an unwanted temptation as well, and to just sit back and see what happened, when I wasn't sure of my motives for being there, would have been unwise and disrespectful to her. So I stopped going to the meetings. When Jim told her I had some unresolved issues, Alice sent a message through him, saying that she realized things had moved too quickly for me, but she still wanted to be friends. I felt it had gone too far for us to be just friends. Over the past twelve months, I'd almost become reconciled to the fact that my relationship with Jenny was over. I could live with that if I was sure, but at this stage, I wasn't totally sure—until she came back to Australia. So with a lot of uncertainty clouding the issue, just being friends with Alice wouldn't have been fair to her. She was a lovely Christian girl who would have made a wonderful partner for the right person, but at that stage, I wasn't that person, so I felt the right thing to do was to end our relationship. Life was full of moral dilemmas, and this was another one for me to work through.

One of the benefits of working up at Bourke was a motel allowance of twenty-five dollars per day that I received for my to-ing and fro-ing into the outback (despite my futile attempts at giving it back when I realized there weren't any motels out there), as well as my normal wage, which I didn't spend, as my accommodation and meals were taken care of. So with all that hoarded money, as well as my penchant for saving, I decided to put it to good use and buy a house. Soon after coming back from New Zealand, I went out house hunting and eventually bought one around the corner from my parents' place. It was nothing flash; it had a weird lounge/dining area, three small bedrooms, a family room out the back, an internal laundry, and a tiny enclosed area, where I could stick a desk and do schoolwork, if I felt so inclined. The fellows in the football team provided me with some strange but useful knickknacks, and although I picked up pieces of mismatching furniture, I wasn't concerned—it was my house and that was all that mattered. When it was time to move in, I went down to the Time and Tide Hotel one Friday night, rounded up four of my players, and got them to help me cart my huge waterbed from my parents' place around the corner and squeeze it into my modest new bedroom. They helped set it up, fill it with water, make it, and turn the heater on, before heading back to the pub for a few more drinks, after assuring me they'd be perfectly all right for the match the next day.

As I was living on my own, I would go around and visit my parents, who had become immovable and never got away. My father's health had deteriorated over the last few years, beaten down by disappointment and my sister's woes, but more shatteringly for him, my brother's marriage breakdown and subsequent divorce. He had been reconciled to my problems, but each new disappointment was another stab in the heart that continued draining any remaining optimism out of him. He took tablets for his heart condition but didn't realize they were out of date, and they gave him no relief. Instead, his heart was further damaged, and he didn't know it. He spent most of his days sitting upstairs with the 'borrowed' cat in the room that was built for Geoffrey and Emily, reading the paper and admiring the view. Often, my mother would go upstairs with cups of tea and sit with him, so he wasn't alone. I'd drop by on my way home from school to read the paper and have a cup of tea with them. It was all pretty sad.

Rex and Annette crossed the ditch that year and rented a house at Killarney Heights. We reconnected, and soon Rex was keen to get involved with my rugby team and even pulled on the jersey when we were short. Unfortunately, he wasn't used to the hard grounds and in his first match, he dislocated his shoulder and immediately retired again—or so I thought.

A couple of months later, I had the doubtful privilege of hosting three teenage schoolboys who were over from New Zealand on a school rugby tour. They ate everything I cooked—which was plenty—even amazing me with their ability at putting it away. A piece of steak plus four or five chops, fellows? No problem. Anyone want seconds? No problem. I was off to the butcher's every few days, just so they could keep up their strength—poor lambs. On Saturday, Rex brought the rest of the team and their teachers over to my place to watch the rugby test between Australia and New Zealand. Much to the delight of the boys, the All Blacks won, and I had to listen to schoolboy experts surgically dissecting the game and pointing out the obvious weaknesses of the Australian team, not that they were obvious to me.

All this humiliation occurred because Rex knew people back home who were bringing a school rugby team over for a couple of games. They asked Rex to help organize a game for them, so Rex asked me. I knew the PE teacher at Cromer High from our church rugby days so I arranged a meeting with him, and a match was arranged for the following week. Simple. Unfortunately, it was during the school holidays, so only a few players from Cromer High turned up for the match, including the captain, who apologized for his absent team. The New Zealand visitors took it in stride, and despite the match being called off, they were desperate for a game, so they had a pretty full-on training run among themselves. Still, the three I looked after were well-behaved, polite young fellows who were obviously well brought up. A minor problem was that one of the boys, a well-conditioned seventeen-year-old, hadn't been told he needed to have a shower every day. His body odor was overpowering and filled the room. It had Rex and the teachers sniffing the air as they all crowded into my tiny lounge room to watch the test. None of the boys even noticed.

At the end of the year, I received a mixed bag of news. The first piece of news excited me. Ivan and his family were coming back to Australia—for good. The second piece of news caused a flutter in my stomach. I had heard from someone who had spoken to someone at Dee Why Baptists that Jenny was back home from Scotland. I quickly dismissed that news from my mind, reasoning that if I wanted to move on, then I didn't need to know what I didn't want to know.

As for Ivan, he had accepted the position of principal of Wahroonga Christian Academy, and he and his family would be back in Australia after Christmas. As they had nowhere to stay, they made me an offer I couldn't refuse. They would stay with me until they found a place of their own, and Pam would do all the cooking, washing, and ironing—which, to be kind, I struggled at—and they'd help with any expenses. They would rejoin their old church, Wahroonga Christian Fellowship. As I was no longer going to Jim and Pauline's church, I had decided to return to the church at Collaroy Plateau. There was too much pain and too many sad memories at Dee Why, so I did a full circle and went back to my old church and the people I had grown up with and where there were new things for me to do.

In the New Year I had to decide whether to go back to the comfortable surrounds of the Correspondence School and remain part of the system—and probably never leave, like some teachers— or go forward and leave my comfort zone for good. The Bourke experience had allowed me to stretch myself and rebuild my confidence, and it showed me I could be part of a bigger picture, where there were people I could help. But to stay any longer would keep my vision small and focused on my own limitations. I'd miss the possibilities God had shown me were out there if I was willing to give it a go. I spoke to Grahame Payne, the primary school principal, and asked him if there were any courses I could do. A few days later, he asked me into his office and told me Nepean CAE (College of Advanced Education) offered a post-graduate course in special education for qualified teachers. Once again, something had turned up that seemed to be just the right fit for me.

I had seen first-hand how distance could isolate children from mainstream education, while in the city, children were spoiled for choice and took it all for granted. Similarly, there were students known as atypical learners, who were also isolated from mainstream education, because teachers often didn't get to the heart of how they learn. Special Ed covered the students who were outside the scope of normal learners found under the general education banner. They were typically the bottom ten percent, as well as the talented and gifted found in the top few percent of the school population. But there were many who should have slotted into the general education regime but had learning disabilities and learning difficulties and were such an odd fit that they tended to slip down into the cracks, only to emerge later as behavioral problems or underperforming casualties of the system. It was those types of students that I would find myself working with for the next three decades.

What began as a one-year full-time course grew into three years of study. In the last two years, I did a graduate thesis on sequence training for students with learning disabilities. I was able to use students from my class at Cromehurst School as my subjects and thus open up a whole new world for me in special education.

It was the right time for me to leave the Correspondence School as well, because had I stayed, I might never have left. It had always been a place of readjusting to new directions in life, a means to an end and not an end in itself. I was no longer Ken, who could run fast, despite the specter of that person hovering somewhere in the background or ingrained deep in my psyche. At least my handicap wouldn't be a factor with the children I'd be teaching, it could possibly be to my advantage and allow me the freedom to be the teacher I wanted to be. Part of my relationship with children was linked to my perceptions of who I was. But that confident, active sportsman, at ease with his world, was gone and replaced by a more pragmatic, more limited person, who needed to rediscover his passion and his confidence as a classroom teacher. Hiding behind the anonymity of distance and the postal service meant I could be that teacher for a season, but any longer and it would be detrimental to my development as a teacher. I had realized that a few years earlier, when perky little Louise came in for a visit, and my self-confidence almost melted in front of her. I could now feel for the special-ed kids and not run on ahead of them but instead, walk with them as they tried to make sense of a world in which they were limping as much as I was. However, despite their handicaps, they had the advantage of not knowing any better, whereas I did.

So at age twenty-nine, I left the Correspondence School for good. For all its faults, it had been the right place for me to ease myself back into teaching. Yet going over to special ed, not the usual blokey area of education, had a further protective quality about it, as I didn't have to prove myself physically to myself or my students.

CHAPTER 25

Home Improvements

Ivan and Pam were back in Australia on December 30, 1978, and stayed at my house just until they were able to move to a house in Berowra, which would be closer to Ivan's new school. We spent a rich time together during those few weeks, but after they left, and with the beginning of a new school year looming, I was home alone again.

The following week, I was back at the Correspondence School, but I only stayed for a month, until the Special Ed course began. At a farewell morning tea, I could see that little had changed there. I passed my class on to another classroom casualty, goodwill reigned, farewell speeches were delivered, and the tea lady still ruled the floor.

But it was in the weeks before I left the Correspondence School that things really happened. During the last week of the holidays, I was surprised to receive a phone call from Jenny. Our conversation was fairly subdued, especially from my end, but I did invite her over to see the house when she showed interest. She did come over, and after taking her through the place, I demonstrated my mastery of the kitchen by making us dinner, with all the usual suspects on the menu.

We talked but not in great detail, as I wasn't open to hearing some things yet. But what came out was that after eighteen months away, she was a more traveled and life-experienced person and had had time to think about relationships and what was really important to her. Her relationship with the other fellow had faded away while she was overseas, and now she was back home, alone and single again. I was very cautious at first, as I felt the possibility of renewing our relationship was tentative at best, but my resistance soon melted when I realized my feelings for Jenny hadn't changed and were still as strong as ever. But where would that lead? I didn't really know, because much had happened in the nearly two years since we had been together, and the dynamics between us had changed over that period. I had to consider whether it was really me Jenny wanted, or whether there was no one else, and I was the last man standing. If that was the case, then it wouldn't have been fair on either of us, so I had to be prepared, once again, to let her go.

On the night of Saturday, February 24, a week before I started Special Ed, I went around to my parents' place and spent the evening with them. My father had been unwell and looked miserable, sitting there in his pyjamas, with his face badly swollen by an infection. We watched television together and talked about things we hadn't talked about for years. Although I often found his opinions pedantic and irritating, that night I felt I should spend time with him, so I did and felt all the better for it. He'd looked so sad when I arrived but had perked up during the evening and smiled at me when I left.

Next morning, my mother rang early to tell me he was in Mona Vale Hospital. He had woken at six, distressed and in pain, so she rang for an ambulance. I came around after breakfast, and a short time later, the hospital rang to tell us he was comfortable and responding well to the antibiotics, and we could visit him during visiting hours in the afternoon. Then, just after lunch, they rang again and asked us to come in straight away, as they needed to discuss his condition with us. Geoffrey had just started an afternoon shift at Darlinghurst and had been notified at the station, so he came straight to the hospital.

Soon after, I drove into the hospital car park with my mother and sister and went up to his floor, where we were ushered into a waiting room. We waited there for perhaps fifteen minutes, until a sister came into the room. The look on her face said something was wrong. It was two in the afternoon when she said simply, "Mr. Little died at midday."

Her words shocked us—not that he'd been in good health but because there had been no warning, nothing to prepare us for something so final as death, that thief who appears so suddenly, unannounced, and with so little emotion. My mother was distraught and found it incomprehensible that he would ever "allow" something like that to happen, because basically, he was indestructible. Maybe there'd been a mistake, and when we trooped into his room, we'd find him sitting up in bed in his pyjamas, embarrassed by all the fuss.

But it wasn't to be, because he had died and what was left was a painful emptiness. When death visits and steals a life from you, that's all it leaves behind—pain and emptiness.

The sister told us it was sudden. He had been eating lunch and chatting to the other patient in the room, when he suddenly stopped talking, gasped, and was gone. It happened just like that—quick and final. Geoffrey arrived, still in his police uniform, and took charge. He consoled my mother and then went with Jane to see our father. I wanted no part of it, so I stayed with my mother. I didn't want to see him as a lifeless shell, knowing that all the memories and hopes, the joys and disappointments; all that he had ever been was gone.

It was raining at the graveside ceremony at the Northern Suburbs Cemetery. My father had bought a double plot so he and my mother could be laid together, but it was my father who would be using it first. I was oblivious as to who had come, although I remembered seeing Stan from across the road looking so desperately sad, as well as others who had shared some part of his life. Geoffrey had arranged the funeral but now was overseas, at an appointment he had to keep. Jane was there, helping me support my mother, as were church friends, Jim and Pauline, and Ivan and Pam, and next to me was Jenny.

My relationship with my father had been one of ambivalence. Despite a life of many disappointments, he was always an idealist at heart, a man of a different age—the age of chivalry where he could ride off quietly and do noble things, maintain decency and order, and protect the weak and the vulnerable. Any affection between us was muted. There were never displays of emotion, just an encouraging word or a satisfied smile if I'd done well. Anything else would have been embarrassing to both of us. That's how I preferred it, for although I respected him and would miss him, affection had little to do with how I would remember him. But his ideals were my ideals, and maybe that was the measure of who he was, because his ideals didn't die with him. Instead, they lived on with me in my heart.

As for his relationship with God, only they knew. He never abandoned his beliefs, just the outward signs of it—the practice that he struggled to keep. He felt he was damned for not actively pursuing the Catholic faith, but I believe that God looked on him much more benignly than he thought. God knew his heart and when they met in that last moment, I am sure my good and honest father, with all doubts and disappointments cast aside, with all his faults, in death found the greater purpose of his life and was welcomed home.

The person hit the hardest was my mother, and for days after, she would hear a car come up the street and for a moment, her mind would be tricked, and she would say, "Roy's home," before realization snuffed out the thought, just as the words escaped from her mouth. She lived in a world of disbelief for the first few weeks, until her faith and church friends helped her come through the grieving period, a period that was both emotionally difficult and draining. Each afternoon, I came past and stayed for a while on my way home from the Special Ed course, while my sister provided constant support during the time she was staying there.

Over the next few months, my mother came to accept his passing and a life on her own. My father had put all his affairs in order to spare her that worry, but he had also done everything for her. Skills such as shopping and banking, she had to learn how to do all over again or even for the very first time. It's little wonder she developed agoraphobia and battled to overcome it over the next few years.

CHAPTER 26

Full Pockets

As I remember, it happened some time later, as I sat with Jenny in the lounge room of my house. We had been back together for a few months, but we both knew our relationship was at a crossroad. One way would take us out of each other's lives for good, while the other way would take us down the pathway I had been avoiding all my adult life, a pathway that I could no longer avoid. I had never allowed a relationship with a girl to go this far, but now, at that moment, I couldn't think of living my life without Jenny. So I said somewhat unromantically, "I think we should get married." Thankfully, Jenny agreed. It was all a bit low-key—just like two people agreeing to what flavor ice cream they would have. Although my emotions were quite controlled when I was growing up, I wondered if events over the past decade hadn't completely dulled them, as issues that affected other people just didn't seem to worry me. Or maybe I could see how unimportant those issues really were, because adversity tends to strip away the trivial, focuses on the important, and leaves you with a different perspective on life. Either way, when the decision was made, it felt like a load had been lifted from my shoulders. Finally, making a decision about the future put certainty into my life, and Jenny's too, as I wouldn't be living it alone; I'd be sharing it with her. Accepting who I was now rather than holding on to who I had been meant that I was no longer running away from commitment, and my wall of self protection had come down.

However, Jenny's recollection of that moment is different from mine. She felt it all happened in the car outside her parents' place, later that night, whereas I felt that was the time we prepared ourselves to go inside and tell them. Either way, it happened, and we both felt mightily relieved that a decision had finally been made, and we could plan for a future together.

After we set a date, there was much to do beforehand, so I called on my players for help. They were more than willing—and all at mates' rates. John was a builder, so he made some internal changes to the house. My tiny bedroom pinched some of the hallway and was enlarged into a decent-sized bedroom when the two tiny clothes cupboards were removed from either side of the bed. 'Bear' was an electrician, so he fixed up the lighting and electrical, as well as attaching two reading lamps to the wall above the bed, which had been turned around after some helpful grunt from some of my forwards. Then the following year, John built a large deck out the back around the above-ground pool I'd recently had installed. Then there was painting to do, furniture to rearrange and windows to clean, but before that, there was something more important to do. And that was get married.

On August 25, 1979, a warm sunny day, I stood next to Ivan, my best man. With family seated close by, I looked back at the crowd that had gathered in Max and Joan's spacious backyard and felt content that the people who meant so much to me and had been a big part of my life were there. On the back veranda, I could see a number of my football players, who had remained steadfast since those early days. On the grass were Bob and Jenelle; Jack Thompson, my creative writing mentor and Lake Albert teammate from college days with his wife, Shona; Judy Parker, my English lecturer and fellow godparent; roomie neighbor Ron; close and less close relatives; and friends from Dee Why Church, who had helped with the food and the preparation of the downstairs rumpus room, where we were holding the reception. As well, there were friends from the Plateau church, along with Jim and Pauline, Rex and Annette, long-time friend Grahame, and my mate Paul and his girlfriend, Liz.

271

Missing was roomie Ross, who was somewhere in Europe doing all things Ross and conquering the world. Samantha and her family were there, and so was the opportunity for Sam and Rosita to catch up with each other in person, rather than by post.

Standing with me on a tiered section and waiting for Jenny and her attendants to make their way from her bedroom into the carnival atmosphere of the backyard was Laurie, dressed in a long dark coat with matching beard and glasses and grinning with anticipation as he waited to marry us. Elvira and the children were close by with a Bourke native, an emu chick, warm and snug in a bag. Its later appearance created quite a stir and lent a nice outback touch to the day. It reinforced to my geographically ignorant mates the exotic nature of life in the slow lane, west of the Great Divide.

And so we were married in a backyard ceremony full of grace and good humor, where special friends had gathered, where good food was provided, and where kind words were spoken. Then later in the afternoon, when it was all over and it was time for us to leave, we changed our clothes, had pictures taken, farewelled friends, and headed north. I had asked that the car not be touched, so apart from some shaving cream on the windows and tinsel on the floor, all we had to do was turn off into Bantry Bay Road, wipe down the windows, clear out the tinsel, and head north to a number of destinations and a new life together.

1979 Full pockets when I married Jenny in a backyard wedding.
My father had passed away five months earlier at 68.
Next to me are two of my college lecturers Jack and Judy,
Jack›s wife Shona and with camera my best mate, Robert. (Bob)

Epilogue

So what happened next?

Jenny has reminded me that after our wedding, we spent the first two nights in a flash motel across the road from the Australian Reptile Park. She also has reminded me that I thought she would enjoy crossing the road with me and taking a look at the crocodiles and snakes and venomous spiders while on our honeymoon. The condescending smiles and nods from the women in my life when this is mentioned suggests to me I still had a lot to learn about women, a fact of which I am constantly reminded.

Fortunately, our relationship survived the snakes and lizards and a visit to Ian's Coffs Harbour banana plantation, on our way north, and we were able to safely return to our new home at Collaroy Plateau a couple of weeks later.

I returned to my Special Ed course and Jenny to work at the maternity unit at Ryde Hospital. Soon after, Jenny did further study in Mothercraft at the Tresillian Centre and worked there supporting mothers who were struggling with their new babies, until our son, Stephen, was born in 1981. Then daughter, Alison, arrived the day before Stephen's second birthday. Years later, our forthright daughter often reminded us that Stephen had two birthdays—his and sharing hers. The day after Stephen's birthday just happened to be our wedding anniversary, so I had no excuse for ever forgetting it— birthdays of offsprings one and two my constant reminder.

When I finished the Special Ed course, I was appointed to Cromehurst SSP (School for Specific Purposes) at Lindfield, on the full-time learning disability class at the Learning Center. In my first two years there, I did a research study on improving learning efficiency through sequence training. It was a bit like sending up weather balloons at Wagga; it looked impressive and wasn't terribly difficult to do, but it took time and commitment to do properly. There were obvious benefits, such as providing research material for someone else to take further; kicking along my academic qualifications and importantly, convincing me of the importance of improving the learning efficiency of not only special-needs students but students of all levels of ability.

One of the highlights of my six years at Cromehurst was our Christmas musicale, *Super Scoop*, with our learning disabilities kids as cast members. We used a large church hall up the road from the school, which, on a warm summer's night in '82, was packed with proud parents, friends of Cromehurst, and some local dignitaries. Writing the script and lyrics for the songs was pretty straightforward, but the music score was another matter. Fortunately, our music teacher was somewhat qualified. Margaret had been a soprano with the Australian Opera and did her teacher training at Narrabeen High when I was in the choir. She remembered me, not for my singing ability but for my stage manager's antics, and she came on board straight away and joined the madness by writing the score for the show. An interesting sidelight to all this came when I learned Margaret and Penny, the girl who had helped me when I did English ten years earlier, now shared the same surname. They were married to brothers.

Being Christmas, I thought we might as well do a pretty outrageous theme, such as "the meaning of life." The story was about a struggling newspaper that needed to sell a million papers to survive, so the reporters were sent out to get a super scoop about the meaning of life. The responses were disappointing until they came across Joe and his wife, Mary, who were in the throes of having a baby. They all helped to get them to hospital and in the process discovered the real meaning of life. I thought it was pretty cool that we were able to put in a strong Christian message, albeit in an age before today's political correctness. The kids, on the other hand, were magnificent and afterward, everyone there left as happy as a fat spider.

I had no qualms in moving around the school without my walking stick. The kids were very accepting and hardly noticed my lurches to the right or my occasional stumbles to the left. They were all very special and had unique personalities, exemplified by a visit to my room one day. I had recently cracked my heel in the school swimming pool when retrieving floatation vests, and had to use crutches for a few weeks until it healed. One of the boys from the OF part of the school (students with moderate to severe intellectual handicaps) noticed the crutches. He had once been excited by the visit of an amputee to the school, so it wasn't surprising when he turned up at my room one lunchtime and breathlessly informed me I had crutches. I agreed with him, and then he asked if he could use them. I said he could, so he proceeded to limp around and around the room, using the crutches until he came across a model skeleton I had standing upright in a closed cupboard. He took one look at the skeleton, handed back the crutches, and said, "Goodbye, Mr. Little." Then he rushed out the door. That was the last time he ever came near my room or my crutches again.

I had six good years at Cromehurst, working with a wonderful staff, before leaving the department and joining Northern Beaches Christian School. There, I started a Special Ed unit and taught different subjects for the next eleven years. As well I served a few years as the school's sportsmaster, careers adviser, and discipline master. My two children started at the school in kindergarten and went right through primary and high schools until the Higher School Certificate. Each day, we would leave home and drive ten miles to school. When Alison started kindergarten, Jenny came with us and did volunteer work in the school for the next nine years. We really were a family that worked together and stayed together.

About this time, my mother had heart trouble, so we sold our house and moved around to my old family home and built an upstairs living area. We didn't know how long she had, but at least she would be close to us and two of her grandchildren for however long it was.

My eleven years at the school were very enjoyable. Working in a place that was strongly Christian was invigorating; working with a great staff and working alongside and sharing my beliefs with my students was so releasing. That environment opened up an opportunity to sharpen my pencil and write a script for a school musicale and later plays for the children at my church.

We returned to my old church at Collaroy Plateau and saw it through a number of changes over the next twenty years. I served in the church in a number of capacities—first as a deacon, treasurer, and church secretary, and after we went through a major change in our church structure, an elder for eleven years. I continued working with children during those years in our children's church and after-school Kids Club and Friday Night Live program. I had just completed a two-year film script-writing course at the Australian College of Journalism, so naturally there was more drama to write and children to perform at Easter and Christmas times. At this time, I was halfway through a master's degree in ministry, but then we went through a church split, and I had to abandon my studies.

We are blessed by having two wonderful children. Son Stephen is very artistic, so after finishing high school, he studied graphic design and is presently finishing a second degree in fine arts. We were blessed when he married a wonderful Christian girl, Danielle, and have been further blessed by last year's birth of Eli, our captivating little grandson, who sees all, hears all, and remembers all and has the zest for discovery of an explorer. Their second son is due in April so we can only guess what he might be like.

Alison is a high achiever, so after finishing school, she took an honors degree in education, qualified for the doctoral program, and works nearby as a highly regarded schoolteacher. But before that, she had a "gap" three years with the Australian Children's Prayer Network as assistant to the national director. She travelled the world, leading their young team to various churches where they ran children's programs at church camps and other special meetings.

She still has the travel bug and recently went down to the Antarctic and now happily calls herself an Antarctic nerd.

My teaching career ended some years ago, so Jenny went back to work in aged care and then back into her chosen field as a midwife and a lactation consultant where she is highly regarded and loved by her colleagues and patients alike.

I have been tutoring students privately now for more than twelve years, more often the ones who have been past casualties of an education system that just didn't understand how they learned. In recent times, I had two novels published, based on the life of a young country teacher, so my life is full, albeit a bit slower at times than I would like it to be.

Recent years have seen a gradual decline in my mobility. No amount of gym work I did was ever going to repair the damage to my spinal cord, just help me work around it. Despite the fact the miracle never happened—and contrary to Marmaduke the magician's statement in *Super Scoop*—life is certainly no illusion, as I have been able to experience the reality of God in mine and His enduring faithfulness.

I found when I have swapped my walking stick for a wheelchair, it has allowed me to go places I wouldn't have been able to go to before. I have resisted using a wheelchair in the past but have seen good sense in Jenny's suggestion and have been able to enjoy doing things without worrying about distances or standing for too long and falling over. It shows that for every problem or inconvenience, there can be a way of working around it if you look hard enough for a solution.

My mother lived for another twenty-five years after we moved around the corner to look after her. She died in 2012 at ninety-eight, and although the last three years were not good years for her, she remained a faithful servant of God and a loving mother, grandmother, and great-grandmother to the end.

My brother retired from the police force, during which he received some international notoriety as the "Smiling Policeman." In his own time, he raised money for various charities in "fun runs" in places such as Manila and Jerusalem. He still works with the NSW Justice Department and enjoys life as a doting father and proud grandfather.

My sister moved up to Queensland's Sunshine Coast and has forged an interesting life for herself through her great resilience and ongoing desire to help people live healthier lives through natural medicine. All the while, she continues on with her never-ending spiritual journey.

There is nothing special about my life. Many have endured far worse than I have or led lives more interesting. I dealt with my problems in ways that worked for me but not always. You couldn't write a textbook and say this is what you need to do. It wasn't like that; it was just my way of working through pretty unique circumstances, often clueless, with my only reference book, the Bible, and a belief in never giving up.

Sometimes people don't understand why I do things or don't do things they can do without thinking. That's because they have never walked in my shoes, where even walking across a darkened room has consequences, and they have never had to set the boundaries that are limiting but protect me and allow me to work within my function zone. My strategies aren't for everyone—everyone has to find his own—but they worked for me, and in hindsight, they allowed me to do more than I probably ever thought I could do. However, the one constant through all this has been God.

So when I see Jesus one day, I won't even ask why. I'll probably just know, but it won't matter then, because I won't be looking back—just ahead to eternity.

So that's my story. Not as exciting as some, just different. Nor is it extraordinary in a way the world sees things as being extraordinary. I didn't achieve anything remotely great and had an undistinguished academic and sporting career, so that wasn't the reason for writing this. Friends who have made a lifetime contribution to advancing

God's kingdom through the Cornerstone Communities in Australia asked me to. Through that ministry, they have helped many people, so if any of my words help just one person, then it has been a story worth telling. I am always reminded that in God's plan for His creation, I am a small and insignificant person, and there are many others who have made and continue to make far bigger contributions to it than I ever have. But I am His child, and that makes me very important to Him, so important that He died on the cross for me. That is my identity, and I am happy to live with it.

1981 Taken at my first house with my mother
and brother Geoffrey for added ballast.

1986 Holidaying on the North Coast of New South Wales at
Urunga on the Bellinger River with my daughter Alison 3.

281

The Present 2022

2021 Going for a Roll with my youngest grandson.
Curl Curl on Sydney's Northern Beaches.
My wheelchair is now my permanent means of travel.

It has been eight years since I penned my last words in 'More Pockets, Please'. Much has happened during that time in my world in particular and the outside world in general. What can be said though is that today both worlds are caught up in strange and confusing times both of which bear comment.

Apart from a couple of short term 'favours' I finished tutoring in 2014 but found I still had a heart to teach. In the area where I live on Sydney's northern beaches, visitors and migrants from South America, Asia and Europe have come to Australia to enjoy the climate, lifestyle and for some, the political freedom and stability. Many have come with little English while others merely want to speak and understand English the way Australians speak it. Of this my church saw a need and started spoken English classes for those who had come into our area. I volunteered my services in 2015 and had been running a daytime class for about five years until covid hit in 2020 and we had to close down our activities. It's only now in 2022 we have been able to resume both evening and daytime classes. At present a number of Ukrainian refugees have come into the area. Some attend our evening class so I am anticipating resuming my daytime class and connecting with people who are suffering and traumatised from having their country invaded. We have had similar needs in the past from Chinese, Nepalese and Tibetans who all fled their countries when they came under persecution from authoritarian governments.

In recent years I have been able to catch up with some old school friends and former teammates. I was invited to a group which met up at North Narrabeen surf club once a week for a cup of coffee and a chat. I only knew three of them but soon realised there was a strong bond between all of them. The thing that drew them together was one common thread: they all served for the Australian armed forces in the Vietnam war. One was a naval petty officer who was a radar operator on the Australian destroyer Hobart, and later on the aircraft carrier Melbourne. He fought alongside Americans and saw things in combat that scarred him for life. The others were mainly gunners from the Australian 107 Field Battery whose mission was to give fire support to the troops when they were out in the jungle making contact with the Vietcong. Others were forward observer signallers (FOS) who were attached to the infantry and tasked with calling in fire support from the 107 if it was needed after contact had been made. Another of my old teammates had been assigned to the command centre where the fire support missions were co-ordinated. Initially I listened to their conversations and asked questions and learnt a lot about PTSD and agent orange which has since been linked to the cancers two of them are suffering from. One in particular has needed radical surgery on his head and face and a new 'wonder' drug called Keytruda to survive this far.

In 2018 I collaborated with a number of them and recorded their stories in a book called 'Cease Fire'. The title was dripping with irony because for many the firing never stopped until post traumatic stress disorder (PTSD) had been recognised twenty plus years after Vietnam and treatment was made available for the Vietnam veterans and a degree of 'normalcy' was returned to their lives. Unfortunately years were wasted and lives were lost as some were overwhelmed by the stress and depression which resulted from their experiences in Vietnam. We published the book under Kitbag Publications in 2020 but its launch and distribution were affected by covid lockdowns. Still it's out there and it allowed the fellows to tell their stories and close a difficult chapter in their lives. A group photo of the fellows mentioned is enclosed in the pages of this book.

As for me my back surrendered to the inevitable in 2020. The years of dragging my legs around with a walking stick had put enormous strain on my spine and led to a lumbar disc prolapsing in August, 2020. After nearly a year of hospitalisation and rehab I now find myself permanently in a wheelchair. Walking is limited to short shuffling steps around the place with a walking frame. Much of the independence and freedom I enjoyed before has been lost and I now have to adjust to a life of further limitations. It has meant mentally accepting that some things I could do just two years ago have been lost and are gone forever, such as driving, and new impositions have to be accepted in sleeping patterns, general daily life and social outings. I even use a 'grabber' for objects that land on the floor and I can't reach. It worked quite well too until I sat on it. Now it doesn't work quite as well.

Still I've had a good life. My wife is still working part time as a midwife but is looking forward to retiring in a year or two although she will always be on 'duty' even if it's just for our grandchildren and my requirements.

My son finished his second degree in fine arts and has become a successful visual arts teacher while his wife Dani works as a massage therapist. Their two boys are ten and eight with one being a high achiever in maths and the other a budding marine biologist with an interest and knowledge of sea creatures that's second to none. Our daughter is finishing her second masters degree in special ed for the gifted but has taken time off to have her second child, a girl who was born in early October. Her little son is also a smart healthy little bundle of energy approaching three. Alison had the good sense to marry another teacher and both their schools are just a mile from each other.

And so to the present. Major events have shaken the world on many fronts. The war in Ukraine and the continuing fall out from it, floods in Europe and Pakistan, droughts in Africa and elsewhere, heat waves and bushfires in both America and Europe. In Australia we suffered from a long drought and above average temperatures while bushfires raged up and down eastern Australia. Then when it came, heavy rain not only broke the drought but caused major flooding along Australia's east coast and inland rivers. And just now "Ian" a powerful hurricane has caused severe damage in Cuba, decimated parts of Florida and damaged places further north.

We are also experiencing sadness with the passing of the longest serving monarch in the world Queen Elizabeth II whose Christian faith bore her through many difficult times and who for many years stood as a symbol of constancy and stability.

In recent years in some countries there has been domestic unrest and political turmoil while in 2019 Covid hit sapping energy and hope, wealth and the health of people of many nations and precipitating domestic unrest and major economic turmoil. In fact one could be pessimistic as to where it's all heading.

However as difficult as things are at the moment I believe our real enemy is fear and feelings of helplessness. As in the past I believe they have no power over us because we can be assured and encouraged by the knowledge that God is in charge and all things are under His control. Nothing surprises God and His promise that He will walk with us through difficult times if we ask Him to, still stands. In that we can take comfort. Life's lessons can be hard and difficult to accept. With my physical condition deteriorating over the last few years I am learning that it's better to focus on the things I can do and adjust my plans accordingly, rather than be disappointed by the things I can't. So my daily challenge is to see that my glass is always half full and not half empty.

2015 Family Photo in the backyard.
Stephen with Harvey and Dani holding
Eli. Myself, Jenny and Alison.

2018 Our extended family on Jenny's side. Her parents Max and
Joan sitting in the front. Max passed away in 2021.
My mother passed away in 2012 at ninety-eight.

2019 Meeting up with the fellows for coffee and
chat at North Narrabeen Surf Club.
Before 'Cease Fire' was published and before covid-19 hit

An Easter Journey

Once I took a journey
From a jail that was life
And although my chains still bound me
I was led into the night,
To a row of crosses
Where I was horrified to find,
Disfigured by their sin and shame,
The faces of the blind.
When I looked again I saw,
That the faces all were mine.

It was, my jailer said to me,
The place where I belong
But he'd been told because of grace
To take me further on.

So he led me to a hill,
Where I saw against the sky,
One large cross, that was firmly fixed
Right before my eye.
And on it was the face of God,
Bearing all the pain,
Of all my sins, unconfessed,
Of all my acts of shame.

I couldn't bear to look at Him,
Or at His noble face.
And down on bended knee, I said
"Lord Jesus, You died there, in my place."

Then my chains fell off,
And I was sent away.
"You're free," my jailer said to me,
"Your face is no longer on the tree
It was removed at Calvary."
Away I stole past crosses,
Where countless eyes were blind.
And when I looked again, I saw
That none of them were mine.

I paused a moment, and then I cried,
"If it's for my life, that Jesus died,
And that's the price that God demands
Then that's a love I can't comprehend."

His Spirit whispered in my ear,
"Who are you to question me?
My foolishness is greater than,

The wisdom of the wisest man.
Conviction brought you to the cross,
Now your sin is in the grave,
And redemption is complete,
Because the Son of God was raised."

Then I saw God's perfect plan
Jesus lives, I understand.

Ken Little 1996 (Revised 2014)

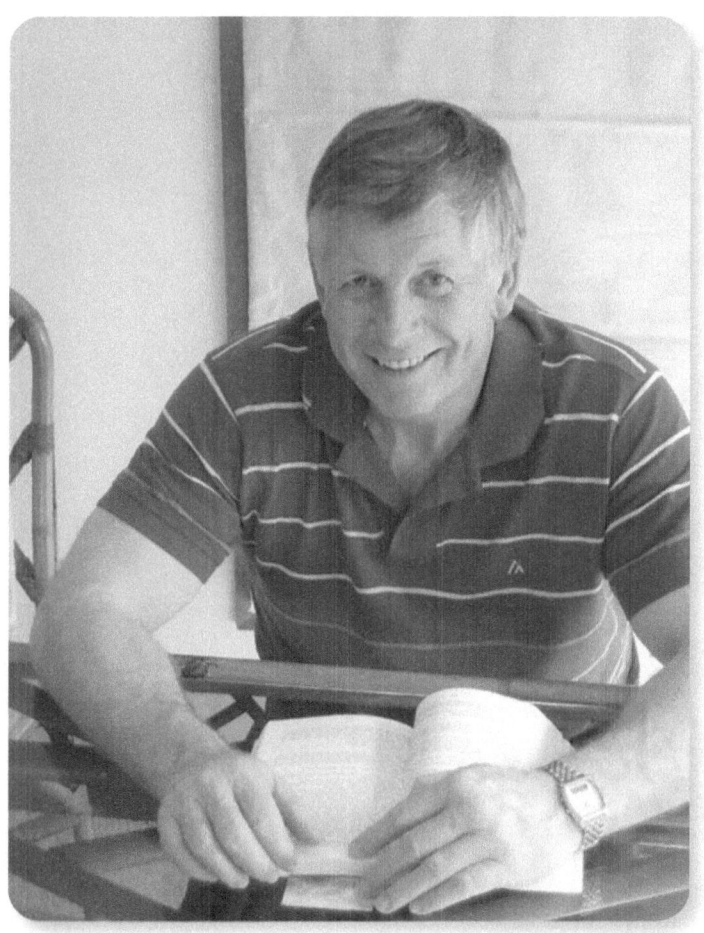

2007 At my second house on Collaroy Plateau, Sydney.
Going over my first book "Three Miles in the
Dry and Twelve in the Wet." It's about a clash of cultures
when a city boy goes out to the country to teach.

Glossary of Australian Terms

Clay.tons relationship	A relationship when you're not supposed to be having a relationship. A pretend relationship (that everyone knows about.)
Chuffed	Very pleased.
Chuck	To hurl or throw something – often lands where you can't find it.
Dobber	Someone who dobs you in - you know, tells on you.
Dork	It's a silly word that means as it sounds – a 'silly' person.
Dunny	A pretty crude word for 'toilet'.
Fox	What you do when someone 'chucks' a golf club away. You go and get it of course because he's paying you to. (See above, 'chuck'.)
'Over' something	Disappointed with, fed up with, as I was with my first trip to the snow.
Pencilled in	Considered part of something or put into something.
Poser	Someone who puts on the airs. (They usually get sorted out.)
Prac (practicum)	Practise teaching with real kids that break.

Q.M. Store	Where equipment is kept for school army cadets. In this case a store room in the school assembly hall on the girls' school side of the hall.
Shallow drop kick	Someone with not too much to offer. Hopeful visitor of my sister.
Shout	To buy food or drink for someone. (Then it's someone's turn to shout you something.)
Sook	As it sounds. Petulant, immature reaction to a disappointment like mine was when Celeste's 'buddy' wouldn't leave.
Spiffy	Nicely dressed. Unusual for young Australian males back then.
To 'spring' cadets	Catch them in the very act of hanging around the QM store past bell time for the sole purpose of checking out the girls.
Super Conch	Very responsible and conscientious person. A pain in the neck.
Very Chuffed	Very, very pleased. (See above, 'chuffed'.)
Wagga Wagga	Aboriginal word for place of many crows.
(pronounced Wogga Wogga)	Large country town of about 60 000, over 300 miles SW of Sydney in the rich farming district of the Riverina. Usually just called – Wagga - which means 'crows'. However in 2019 it was accepted that the Wiradjuri tribe word 'Wagga' actually means 'dance' so Wagga Wagga means 'dancing or celebrating'.

www.ingramcontent.com/pod-product-compliance
Lightning Source LLC
Chambersburg PA
CBHW021612120626
46545CB00001B/193